The Islamic Roots of Democratic Pluralism

The Islamic Roots of Democratic Pluralism

Abdulaziz Sachedina

CENTER FOR STRATEGIC
AND INTERNATIONAL STUDIES

OXFORD
UNIVERSITY PRESS

2001

OXFORD
UNIVERSITY PRESS

Oxford New York
Athens Auckland Bangkok Bogotá Bombay Buenos Aires
Calcutta Cape Town Dar es Salaam Delhi Florence Hong Kong
Istanbul Karachi Kuala Lumpur Madras Madrid Melbourne
Mexico City Nairobi Paris Shanghai Singapore Taipei Tokyo Toronto

and associated companies in
Berlin Ibadan

Published by Oxford University Press, Inc.,
198 Madison Avenue, New York, New York 10016

Library of Congress Cataloging-in-Publication Data
Sachedina, Abdulaziz Abdulhussein, 1942–
The Islamic roots of democratic pluralism / Abdulaziz Sachedina.
p. cm.
Includes bibliographical references and index.
ISBN 0-19-513991-7
1. Islam—20th century. 2. Religious pluralism—Islam. 3. Religious pluralism—
Islamic countries. 4. Islam and reason. 5. Rationalism. I. Title.
BP163.S285 2000
297.2'8—dc21 00-022598

The Center for Strategic and International Studies wishes to acknowledge the generous support of the Carnegie Corporation of New York, the Winston Foundation for World Peace, and the William and Flora Hewlitt Foundation for this study.

9 8 7 6 5 4 3 2

Printed in the United States of America
on acid-free paper

To those who uphold the equality and dignity of all humans

Foreword

Abdulaziz Sachedina's study comes at a time of major transitions in the post–Cold War environment. The collapse of the simple bipolar framework of the free world in a life or death struggle with Communism revealed the more profound reality around the world of religious and ethnic groups and nations with unfinished business. National groups became freer to focus on their memories of loss and the feelings of existential injustice that accompany these memories. The process was exacerbated by the breakdown of political institutions that had provided a modicum of predictability and security in daily life, the collapse of Yugoslavia being the most dramatic example.

The disintegration of the former Soviet Union also increased ethnic tensions, especially in the Caucasus, contributing to the destruction of Chechnya and the instability of the Russian Federation. In the 1980s, as an ominous prelude to these events, the United States and its allies, including several Muslim states, had become deeply involved in the military struggle against the Soviet occupation of Afghanistan. The last major confrontation of the Cold War, it was a defeat for the Soviets but had disastrous results for the Afghan people. One of the most serious consequences of this engagement was the emergence of a body of Arab, Pakistani, and Iranian Muslim veterans, who blooded in combat were ready to carry their fight to other targets perceived as betrayers of justice and collaborators with corrupt regimes. The Islamic revolution in Iran had already heightened the sense of religious resurgence against a domineering West, and the enduring struggle between Israel and the Palestinians provided an enduring example of Muslims fighting for rights against a Jewish state they saw sustained by the Christian world, with the United States in the lead.

The West and Russia also came to see real and anticipated Islamist violence and terrorism as a major threat to domestic and international security. Ideals of democratic pluralism and ecumenism competed with popular fears—fanned by a small but visible minority of politicians in Russia and Europe and more quietly shared by certain officials in the United States—of a broad Islamic conspiracy to create mayhem in their cities. In this environment, the image of Islam in the West, where knowledge of the faith and values of the more than one billion Muslim souls was almost non-existent, became simplified and often ominous. The violent and quite spectacular acts of terrorism carried out by a minority of Islamist actors against American and, indeed, other Muslim targets, like Algeria, nourished this dark stereotype.

This situation was very much in the minds of a group of researchers at the Center for Strategic and International Studies (CSIS), in Washington, D.C., gathered in the early 1990s by then–executive vice president Douglas Johnston, to study the role of religion not only in violent political conflict but also in the art and science of conflict resolution and peacemaking. The strong Western bias against studying religion in history, political science, and international relations was understood, created by a legacy of the Enlightenment in Europe that effectively blinded scholars, political analysts, journalists, and diplomats to the meaning of religion for the vast majority of humanity. This ignorance, paired with the knowledge that religion had been used by politicians and clergy to justify political violence from the Crusades, the expulsion of Jews and Muslims from Moorish Spain, the Catholic-Protestant wars in Europe, and the endemic genocidal violence by European Christians against Jews, had given religion a bad name among the Western intelligentsia.

Yet there was sufficient evidence to suggest that spiritual values of religious people from high clergy to simple lay persons could have significant appeal in establishing trust for themselves as mediators in ethnic and religious conflicts. The CSIS group gathered case histories of effective faith-based mediations in political conflicts in Europe, Africa, Latin America, and East Asia in *Religion, the Missing Dimension of Statecraft* (New York: Oxford University Press, 1994). The project also resulted in the establishment of the conflict resolution project at CSIS that quickly became a permanent commitment known as the preventive diplomacy program.

From the outset, the preventive diplomacy program has been preoccupied with the religious aspects of ethnic conflict and strategies for involving people of faith in conflict resolution. There has been, for example, an ongoing project of mobilizing Catholic, Protestant, Orthodox Christian, and Muslim clergy and religious lay people in Croatia, Bosnia, and Serbia who are committed to rebuilding interreligious community as the basis for genuine peace in their countries. The program staff is also planning projects for Muslim-Jewish-Christian engagement with a special focus on the Middle East peace process. A major project, "Reviving the Memory of Moorish Spain," will bring knowledge of the extraordinary levels of civilization Muslims and Jews, in particular, created in Andalusia from the eighth through the thirteenth centuries CE to Israelis and Palestinians who despair of ever establishing mutually respectful and cooperative relationships in the twenty-first century.

But the first ripe fruit of the program's efforts is Abdulaziz Sachedina's *The Islamic Roots of Democratic Pluralism*. For several years the author and I had discussed the necessity of dealing with the consequences of Western ignorance of the basic values of Islam that contributed to fear and destructive stereotyping. We believed that there was a "value gap" between Islam and the West, and the Jewish people of Israel and the Diaspora in particular. But we knew that, like every great world religion, Islam embraced certain universal human values that could be recognized and accepted as the basis of community by non-Muslims if they could be highlighted in a work of unimpeachable scholarship. After consulting with many Muslim and non-Muslim scholars and experts, I concluded that Professor Sachedina was the best person for the job. He was recognized as a meticulous scholar and a devoted Muslim. As an intense student of the Koran and a believer, he knew he could highlight those parts of the Koran, the only source of authority for all Muslims, that emphasized the dignity of the individual, freedom of conscience, and God's love for all his creatures, People of the Book, and even people without a book. He also highlighted the guidance in the Koran on reconciliation and forgiveness in the service of peacemaking. We believe that the teachings in the Koran that Professor Sachedina explains in this book are essential in reestablishing the basis for mutually respectful and democratic relationships among Muslims and between Muslims and the non-Muslim world. Democratic pluralism thrives on the ability of citizens to value each other and respect each other's dignity and human rights. In spiritual terms, democratic pluralism succeeds where citizens accept that the individual is created in the image of God and that all religions share membership in a loving relationship with God.

In sponsoring *The Islamic Roots of Democratic Pluralism,* CSIS hopes to contribute to the closing of the psychological gap between Islam and the West, thereby offering a measure of preventive diplomacy in the service of peace in the Middle East and everywhere Muslims and non-Muslims meet. We are not alone in this effort. Just as Pope John Paul II made a pilgrimage to the Holy Land in the spring of 2000, to atone for the sins of Christendom against the Jewish people, he had been preaching to Muslim audiences for the previous twenty years. In Davoa, Philippines, in 1981, he said, "Dear Muslims, my brothers. . . . Just like you, we Christians seek the basis and model of mercy in God himself, the God to whom your Book gives the very beautiful name of *al-Rahman* [Most Gracious], while the Bible calls him *al-Rahim*, the Merciful One." In Casablanca in 1985, the pope addressed 80,000 Muslim youths saying, "The witness to God, the father of all mankind, cannot be separated from the witness to the dignity of the human person . . . therefore we must respect, love and help every human being . . . and we must stimulate each other in good works on the path of God."

The reader will soon encounter similar expressions of belief in the Koran as Abdulaziz Sachedina explains it. Whether one is a believer in any faith, or a practical agnostic, it should be apparent that there is enormous value in attempts to reaffirm for people who are believers of different faiths that they share basic, human values on which they can build, or rebuild, mutually respectful, peaceful relationships. This is the author's gift to humankind.

Joseph V. Montville
Director, Preventive Diplomacy Program
Center for Strategic and International Studies
Washington, D.C.

Acknowledgments

Human beings are members in a body whole related,
from a single essence are they all created.

Shaykh Saʿdī (d. 1292)

No intellectual work is possible in a vacuum. Ideas are inspired, formulated, and systematically presented in an interaction with teachers, students, and friends. I can say without any hesitation that the present work would have been impossible to write without many fruitful discussions with colleagues, students, and community leaders on the subjects of tolerance and pluralism. I was waiting for the right time to undertake penning my personal aspirations for interfaith relations. I have advanced my views about the subject for a long time in Muslim communal functions and ceremonies. It took the crisis I faced with the Muslim religious establishment in 1998 to convince me that the time had come to state my firm belief in the Koranic notions of human dignity and the inalienable right to freedom of religion and conscience. Attempts were made to silence me through a religious edict (*fatwā*) and to stop Muslim audiences in North America from listening to my well-articulated plea for better intercommunal relationships through mutual tolerance, respect, and acceptance of the religious value in all world religions.

Joseph Montville, the director of the Preventive Diplomacy Program, Center for Strategic and International Studies, became instrumental in my search for a universal language of Islam. Mr. Montville himself is a personification of the spirit of interreligious and intrafaith ecumenism. His commitment to reach out to humanity and to engender good relationships between peoples of different faiths and ethnicities is exemplary. His two children were christened by

Sunnī and Shīʿī imams. For almost a decade now we have worked together as the preliminary research for this project began.

In search of religious sources for conflict resolution among the children of Abraham, I initiated the project of religious pluralism in Islam. It was in *Dār al-Iftāʾ* in Cairo in November 1991 that I first presented the Koranic resources for harmonious existence among the Abrahamic communities. In addition to my personal faith in coexistence among the children of Adam and Eve, our first parents, I took careful stock of Islamic resources to convince my fellow believers that Islam is committed to peaceful coexistence on earth. Joseph Montville and Douglas Johnston were convinced that such a study will serve the objectives of the Preventive Diplomacy Program at CSIS. They wholeheartedly supported my work. I hope that I have been able to reach out to fellow humans in conveying the God-given dignity in the Koran we all share as "equals in creation." The views expressed in the book are mine, and CSIS bears no direct or indirect responsibility for them.

Charlottesville, Virginia A. S.
December 9, 1999 / Ramadan 1, 1420

Contents

1 The Search for Democratic Pluralism in Islam *3*

2 The People Are One Community *22*

3 Compete with One Another in Good Works *63*

4 Forgiveness Toward Humankind *102*

5 Epilogue *132*

Notes *141*

Bibliography *163*

Index *169*

The Islamic Roots

of Democratic Pluralism

1

The Search for Democratic Pluralism in Islam

And if thy Lord had willed, whoever is in the earth would have believed, all of them, all together. Wouldst thou [O Muḥammad] then constrain the people, until they are believers?

(K. 10:99)

The Present State of Scholarship

At the dawn of the twenty-first century, the theory and practice of Islamic government are posing a formidable challenge to prevailing secularist modernist ideas. Western scholars are divided in their assessment of the threat that a government founded on an exclusivist religious system like Islam poses to liberal, secular, democratic values. The debate centers on contrasting assumptions about the role religion should or should not play in politics. The secular culture tends toward a negative characterization of anything religious as soon as it crosses the boundary from the private to the public sphere. The religious culture, on the contrary, holds that religious values are a valuable resource in combating social and political injustices.

Conventional political theory, which presupposes the desirability of the separation of the religious and the political, has been slow to acknowledge a paradigm shift that recognizes the reemerging centrality of religiosity in the public sphere. The persistence in the "disestablishment"[1] proposition that privatizes religion, banishing it from a secularized public arena, has become a major obstacle in understanding societies in which religious obligation is a key element in managing social problems and sustaining a sense of community. The secularist outlook, while preventing the dominance of one religion over others, can also marginalize communities of faith and thus push them toward militancy, aggression, and separatism.

The political role of religion has also been overlooked in the comparative analysis of cultural systems in which the presence or absence of an organized religious institution like the church (as is the case with Christianity and Islam) has allowed the emergence of a different kind of religious-intellectual discourse about the goal of governance in society. In a "political society"[2] in which there is no impassable barrier between church and state (as is the case in some Islamic regimes), public discourse, rather than pressing for the domination of the religious by the political or vice versa, emphasizes the role of governance in furthering relationships and responsibilities that conform to values rooted in the spiritual sense of life.

In the last three decades, religion has reemerged as an important source of the moral imperatives needed to maintain social cohesion. Religious commitment has not only helped to mobilize people's sense of outrage in resisting the state's autocratic power but has also played a constructive role in national reconciliation and nation building.

Nonetheless, religiously inspired and sustained nationalisms, with their attendant ethnic rivalries and conflicts, have raised serious questions about the adverse impact of religious ideology in the public sphere. The problem of religion as an instrument of political ends is as old as history. There is nothing modern about it. What magnifies it today is the unprecedented extent of dissemination of information about it. Whether in Ireland, Pakistan, or India, televised scenes of sectarian violence and graphic commentaries about the abuses of religious regimes highlight the problem of blurring lines between the spiritual and the secular in contemporary governance. Secularists point to the undeniable authoritarian dangers of religious leaders who found their claims to legitimacy in a supernatural realm beyond the reach of contestation or dialogue.

THE POTENTIAL PROBLEMS of religious governance intensify in proportion to the exclusivity of the religious doctrine. Exclusivist religious ideologies can become divisive forces that aggravate sectarian conflicts and thereby retard the emergence of a national identity in the public domain. Moreover, the public domain, which must seek consensus among different groups with conflicting political/religious convictions, becomes difficult to manage under a regime that privileges a particular tradition.

In the Muslim world, where religion permeates the national culture, Islamic tradition maintains an active interest in issues of national politics and social justice. But the limits of strictly religious values in determining the national policies of a modern Muslim nation-state have never been fully explained or generally accepted by Muslim communities.

In response to the rise of contemporary Islamic regimes that seek to construct political societies ordered by religiously based moral precepts, a number of Western scholars have tried to uncover and recover the essence of the political history of Islam to remind their readers about the "lost" meanings of now defunct concepts of a classical juridical tradition that divides the world between believers and nonbelievers. Among such defunct legal constructs in Islamic jurisprudence that continue to dominate the scholarly enterprise of neo-orientalism[3] are the *dār al-islām* (literally, "sphere of submission"; technically, "territories administered by the Muslim state") and the *dār al-ḥarb* (literally, "sphere of war"; technically, "territories to be subdued"). The two phrases, which appear in most of the works that deal with the rise of political Islam, highlight the normative foundation of Muslim religious convictions about forming a transcultural community of believers who must ultimately subdue and dominate nonbelievers. Such works are flashing red lights to the international community about the threat posed by the Muslim extremists, who, they argue, are reviving the historical *jihād* to destabilize the secular world order.[4]

Many of these scholarly works are alarmist, mistakenly positing a conceptual and political continuity between the traditional Islamic views about *jihād* and the increasingly dangerous geopolitical quandaries of the Middle East today. This is the oft-cited "clash of civilizations," with religiously inspired militancy massed against the liberal and democratic values of the West.

The other view about the ascendancy of religion (and Islam in particular) in the public sphere comes mainly from Muslims themselves. As regards the political tensions sparked by rising Muslim militancy, they offer, in most cases, an incoherent and contradictory record of conceptual changes in the political history of Muslim peoples. Their exposition lacks an analysis of the ethical-legal presuppositions that undergird church-state relations in Islamic polities. Although theoretically it is true that Islam does not make a distinction between the church and the state or between spiritual and temporal, in practice the Islamic tradition recognizes a de facto separation between the religious and temporal realms of human activity, including distinct sources of jurisdiction in the Muslim polity. The categorization of religiously ordained God-human and interhuman relationships in Islamic sacred law, the Sharīʿa, is an explicit expression of the distinct realms of religious and temporal on earth. Whereas God-human relations are founded on individual autonomy as regulated by divine jurisdiction, interhuman relations are within the jurisdiction of human institutions founded on political consensus with the purpose of furthering social justice and equity. This latter category of relations falls under the principle of "secularity"[5] in the Muslim state, which is empowered to regulate all matters pertaining to interpersonal justice. The same principle prohibits the Muslim state from regulating religious institutions unless the free exercise of religion is in danger. No human institutions can claim to represent God's interest on earth. Such is the foundation of governance and authority in Islam.

Much of traditional Islamic scholarship on the issue of God-human and interhuman relationships fails to account for the ethical-legal underpinnings of social organization and governance based on this essential distinction between divine jurisdiction of God qua God, and the human jurisdiction of the polity. The normative textual sources are treated as timeless and sacred rather than as anchored to a specific historical context.[6] As a result, they have failed to link organically the historically mutable and reformable political practices and institutions of interhuman politics to the stabilizing practices and institutions of divinely inspired religiosity. A rigorous and honest accounting of specific settings in Muslim social-political history, including the way political ideas have interacted with normative suggestions from the Koran and the Tradition (Sunna) could provide Muslim scholars an opportunity to engage in a critically needed conversation with the past in order to connect it with the present.[7]

Given the deepening global crisis arising from the misuse of religion by a vocal minority, it is important for Muslim thinkers to arrest the breakdown and corruption of political order by rediscovering and promoting a common moral concern for peace with justice, to map the boundaries of the possible in the political landscape of Muslim countries. No Muslim can afford to undermine the existing international order without first undertaking a critical assessment of the Islamic order. It is only when we are able to link political and conceptual change that we can gauge the ossification of old concepts and the extent to which they must be replaced in the interests of political and social renewal.[8] After all, in Islam, political and religious practices are distinct aspects of a historical dialectic whose aim is the establishment of a global community under God.

Religion in the Global Context

Religion's ascendancy in the world since the 1970s is different in form and substance from that in the first half of the twentieth century. In form, it is inclined toward the less rigid "general" (not generic) as opposed to the forms of "particular" confessional religions.[9] In substance, it seeks the realization of a universal global community with a common vision and destiny. This general, universal religion is visible in the peace movement, environmentalism, and debates on the ethics of biotechnology and human cloning.[10] There are increasing signs that in this general sense, the twenty-first century will witness a global religious resurgence in both public and private life, notwithstanding the marginalized role of traditional religious institutions in the everyday life of most of the populations. This general religious sensibility provides a universal creed derived from the interaction between the conventional, particularistic organized religions and the universal ethics of just human relationships.

The need for a general religion in modern society seems to be an inevitable consequence of the irrelevance of much of institutionalized religiosity. I am not using the phrase *general religion* in the sense of 'generic religion,' which has been criticized by some scholars as a religion that evades responsibility and that expresses an attitude "particularly characteristic of the academy, where religiosity without particular piety of an organized religion flourishes."[11] Rather, given the variety of religions and the growing awareness of diverse paths to the supernatural, the emerging religiosity of modern society does not see church and religion as identical.[12] This new religiosity is visible in those aspects of Muslim patriotism in which religious symbols inspire intense commitment. Love of one's country has tended to downplay the ever present idea of exclusionary religiosity. Cultural and linguistic unity has been afforded a larger role in developing citizenry. There is a growing majority in every religious community that is in search of a tolerant creed to further interhuman understanding beyond an exclusionary and consequently intolerant institutional religiosity.

Beyond the particularist domains of the church, mosque, and synagogue, the ecumenical sensibility of general religion has drawn the attention of people around the world, influencing their lives beyond the confines of their faith communities. It is, moreover, the noninstitutional nature of general religion, its resistance to classification as another particular faith, another confessional community, that has attracted a substantial majority of the world population. This attitude in no way compromises the particularity of confessional religion, which is both local and divisive. Religious consciousness goes beyond relative human response to the divine. It asserts the universal social dimensions of one's purely personal and private faith in order to project them in the world.

There is ample evidence to suggest substantial worldwide growth of a religious consciousness that points beyond particular religious traditions to embrace a pluralistic and tolerant attitude toward other faiths. This movement is evident even in those societies that have been historically plagued by violent racial and religious conflicts. Ordinary citizens' occasional willingness to defy the manipulative and divisive policies of their governments in order to come to grips with diversity and to work toward religious and cultural reconciliation suggests a critical role for religious consciousness in establishing fair and harmonious human relationships in the development of a truly global society.[13] But this religiosity, as pointed out earlier, must transcend the monologic exclusivity of institutionalized religion. It is not uncommon to come across a Muslim who professes a strong commitment to Islam's social-ethical dimension, but who never attends public prayers or observes prescribed rituals. Such common, though not generic, religiosity has been on the rise in many countries around the world since the late 1960s.

Scholars of religion in the last two decades have attempted to explain the phenomenon of religious affiliation and identification without taking the time to create appropriate intellectual constructs to gauge the intensity of the social and humanitarian commitments spawned by particular religious observances among a growing number of the silent majority in modern societies. The tendency is to attribute such modern piety to the secularization of particular religious traditions outside the church, as if working for peace or humanitarian causes has no basis in general religiosity. I contend, in fact, that the rise of religious militancy in various parts of the world is a growing reaction to the secularist denial of any religious inspiration for movements on behalf of peace and human rights. If the religious communities were afforded an independent voice in various nondemocratic polities of the Third World, they could muster the will and the resources to contribute to the communitarian tasks of nation building today.

Nonetheless, there still remains a question as to how religion, given the serious misgivings expressed by a number of prominent political and social analysts, can assume a decisive role in the vision of the emerging global society. There clearly exists a thriving religious subculture that expresses a profound sense of divine presence and purpose in human affairs and that gives voice to a general dissatisfaction with materialistic consumerism and individualistic secularism. The mass electronic media have been critical in the spread of this popular religiosity, so casually derided as insubstantial or even ridiculous in academic circles. The media, however, have also emerged not as disinterested bystanders but as secularist critics of the conflicts engendered by the abuse of institutionalized religions and the systematic patterns of intolerance and discrimination perpetrated and justified by claims of special religious and cultural entitlement. In the case of Muslims and Islam, the media have acted with a covert political and ideological agenda of representing the "absent other," thereby creating a powerfully negative image of religiosity that has become singularly difficult to eradicate.[14]

THERE IS LITTLE DOUBT that awareness of the abuses of organized religions led to a search for tolerant, nondiscriminatory solutions that would respect the differences between various religious traditions. This search is predicated on a belief in both public and private roles for religion. For many, the social dimension of their religious tradition defies any attempt at secularization through privatization. But there is also a realization that the social dimension controls the political realm and can thereby, in its most intolerant guises, give rise to dreadful episodes of religious bloodshed. The more the political role of particularistic religion is emphasized, the more intolerant its adherents become.

There are still deeper problems with political activism in the name of religion, however. We lack precise empirical tools for assessing the impact of what I call a vertical calling that relates a modern man and woman autonomously to a religiously inspired accountability. Religious commitment is inherently too intimate and personal for public display. Nonetheless, it is this personal commitment that seeks horizontal expression through a concrete social-moral vision that is central to the Abrahamic faiths: Judaism, Christianity, and Islam. It is the commitment to this activist vision that causes concern in the secularly oriented public order.

The decades following World War II have seen a steady rise of religiosity in the public arena that has confounded earlier predictions about the steady eclipse of religion by secularism. It is ironic that with the progressive elimination of all forms of religious intolerance and of discrimination in various parts of the world, it is religiously inspired leadership that negotiated a concrete, pluralistic solution to such violations in the twentieth century. The ability of religious leaders to get adversaries to the table of negotiated settlement has been phenomenal in places like Bosnia, Nigeria, and South Africa.

But it is also religion that has been successfully used to justify a particular status quo, leading to violations of basic human rights in a number of newly established democracies. It has, unfortunately, provided self-serving justification to political ideologues to resort to war, violence, and repression. The human capacity to fuel deadly conflicts with religious teachings cannot be underestimated. At the same time, there are individuals who devote their energies to promoting religiously inspired ideals of justice and peace. Recognition of the principle of tolerance has greatly contributed to the recognition of the dignity of all humans, irrespective of religious affiliation.

There is no doubt that each world religion treats the question of religious pluralism differently. Religious values and goals, and their political and historical settings, vary vastly. These variables have a direct impact on how the religious other is constructed and treated. The Islamic revival and its reentry into the public arena has diverted public attention from the positive role religion can play in keeping the government informed about the spiritual and moral needs of the people. Moreover, the public fervor of religious activists has caused much negative publicity in the Western media for politicized religiosity. One of the burning questions for secularist thought is the relationship between religion and politics. The misgivings about the role of religion in the public sphere are based on the traditional conviction that religion and politics should not be mixed and that religion—especially potentially influential institutional religion—should be neutral on social and political issues. But neutrality in social-political matters means depriving religion of its ethical foundation, its essential concern with moral questions relating to poverty, injustice, and peace.

Here we arrive at the key problem for contemporary religiosity: what is left of religious commitment and conscience if religion is debarred from dealing with issues relating to justice and peace? Neutrality in social and political matters could very well lead to the demise of the critical role that religion plays in shaping the moral conscience of the public order. Social responsibility, at least in Abrahamic traditions, has always been a major motivation for the cultivation of shared ethical concerns and objectives that are prerequisites to the very possibility of a just social order.

Because all religions have endured persecution and conflict, they have naturally shown special concern for infringements of basic rights to free religious expression. And, although political freedom and justice are, strictly speaking, outside the purview of religious institutions today, it is important to emphasize that interaction between the religious and political realms is necessary to guarantee religious freedom in a democracy. The right to worship freely or to propagate one's religion is intimately related to other inalienable human rights. It is not sufficient to advocate the basic religious freedoms without insisting upon the requisite legal and institutional structures. Hence, the quest for religious freedom entails accessibility to and influence on all walks of life. Freedom of conscience is realizable in a democratic system when individuals are also able to exercise their political rights. More importantly, individual freedom of conscience is the only way to further toleration.

Religious toleration is indeed a virtue that is intrinsically related to the right to believe in or renounce religion altogether. However, the mere toleration of diverse religions in a particular society does not mean that people of different religious affiliations are necessarily accepted or afforded their political rights.[15] In fact, empirical data compiled by the U.N. Commission on Human Rights in a number of countries in the Muslim world show that political discrimination often coincides with religious discrimination.

The role of the state as a guarantor of freedoms needs to be clarified. The state must ensure that free expression of religion does not infringe on the rights of others. It cannot support one religion and suppress others. The function of the state is to make sure that free exercise of religion is guaranteed equally to all religions. There is an inevitable connection between freedom of religion and the institutions and policies that can guarantee such freedom.[16]

There is, no doubt, a correlation between a society's degree of religious, cultural, or ethnic diversity and its vulnerability to conflicts, tensions, and even violent confrontations. One of the ways in which the state can deal with this diversity is to keep the groups separate and segregated through an absolutist ideology proclaiming the privileged position of a certain religious or racial group. An alternative would be to institutionalize diversity by publicly acknowledging and regulating it. In such a case, diversity can enrich the cultural heritage of that society. But in a number of situations, cultural diversity disguised as religious diversity has fostered extreme intolerance and violence, leading to the breakdown of nationhood. It is critical, then, to appreciate the ways in which religious diversity and pluralism can become not merely a grudgingly tolerated right but rather a cornerstone of democratic nation building, a fundamental principle of a political society. Religious pluralism is a fundamental resource that can be tapped by humankind to establish peace and justice in any contemporary society.

The Present Work

This work undertakes to map some of the most important political concepts in Islam that advance better human relationships, both within and between nations. It aims at uncovering normative aspects of Muslim religious formulations and specifying their application in diverse cultures to suggest their critical relevance to the pluralistic world order of the twenty-first century. I question the lack of serious analysis about the concept of religious pluralism among religiously oriented Muslim groups. Such analysis would enable them to take a principled stand against ahistorical references and legal-doctrinal analyses of both freedom of religion and political participation in Islam. This lack of interest in religious pluralism and its intrinsic connection with democratic governance has helped to prevent a healthy restoration of interpersonal and intercommunal relations in the Muslim world.

The goal here is not to glorify the Muslim past but to remember it, retrace its path, interpret it, reconstruct it, and make it relevant to the present. It is only by remembering the past objectively that we can gain a clearer and a more critical perspective on our present. It is not surprising that modern Muslim states attempt to control the past by rewriting history, or, failing that, by obliterating memory altogether. Muslims adrift in the present and cut off from their past become more manipulable and pliable subjects. I hope that intelligently retracing and retrieving the relevant past will enable Muslims to resist the politically stultifying confines of a parochial and increasingly dangerous, potentially violent, present.

The Scope and Method

Although the collapse of global Communism in the last decade marks the beginning of a new era in the role of religion in the emerging international order, from all the predictions about the inevitable, imaginary "clash of civilizations" and the supporting evidence largely gathered by social theorists and political scientists,[17] there does not seem to be a plausible chance for religion in general and Islam in particular to play any positive role in preventing a looming destructive ideological conflict. Such an apocalyptic prediction about human religiosity seems to arise from the advance of religious fundamentalism (in the pejorative sense of the term common in academia and the media) in the Muslim world in the second half of the twentieth century.[18] In the conventional view of the academy and the media, not only are Muslim fundamentalists engaged in destabilizing the regional security arrangements in the Middle East, but they are also zealously opposed to anything that smacks of Western liberal and democratic values.

This skewed viewpoint has been perpetuated by scholarship that treats Muslim fundamentalism as qualitatively distinct and irreducible to any common ground, representing an image of Islam in abstraction. Although it is important to consider Muslim beliefs, actions, and practices impersonally, that is, in abstraction from the subjects, it is important to underline the fact that opinions and actions do not float subjectless in the air; they can also be held with integrity, chosen freely, followed authentically. In judging whether Islam, as a religious-moral system, is inimical to liberal and democratic values, we need to turn our attention to the beliefs and actions in interpersonal relations, national as well as international, in Muslim society. The way Muslims relate to one another and to the outsider other can reveal the true nature of Islamic precepts pertaining to human intentionality and rationality in communal and intercommunal settings. Understanding such precepts in the sphere of interpersonal relations can provide opportunities to engage in dialogue with Muslims as fellow humans. Like many other religious communities today, Muslims are engrossed in resolving the contradictions they discover in the complex web of their beliefs, actions, and practices as they seek an ideal world order under divine guidance.

An essential prerequisite in commencing any dialogue, to be sure, is toleration, not acceptance, of what we consider to be the morally or religiously wrong position of the other. This tolerance begins when we no longer see a group as the other but as a concrete human community with very real and ancient values. This cognitive leap is a difficult one, especially when the cultural other happens also to be a religious other. Muslims themselves sometimes treat their fundamentalist cobelievers as an other without quite denying them membership in the Islamic community. Our analysis begins to assume a different epistemic position, however, when we deal with radically different cultures and religious communities. The only way to bridge this cognitive gap is to allow the sources and the people we are studying to speak for themselves.

Moreover, since religion is not typically central to the thinking of political scientists, we need to hear about religious phenomena in the public arena directly from their practitioners. As we shall demonstrate in this study, it is for religion that many are willing to fight and die in the Middle East; unless we begin to understand the nature of this primal religious loyalty, it will be impossible to prevent sectarian conflicts in the most politically and ideologically volatile region of the world.

This project, then, seeks to provide to both Muslim religious and political leaders and non-Muslim policy makers the information needed to evaluate the key universal aspects of Islamic tradition, the better to offer pluralistic possibilities to renascent Muslim communities. The project's guiding tenet is the value of preventive diplomacy in promoting democracy, communication, and pluralism as antidotes to the tragic violence that wracks the globe.

Although the twentieth century saw a number of apologetic works purporting to show that Islamic tradition is in full harmony with modern parliamentary government, these works have further mystified the actual import of Islamic institutions and their revival in modern times. The call for reviving such classical democratic institutions has been marred by tendentious evaluations of their practical implementation in the modern world in which a Muslim state is situated in a non-Muslim international order. The call to create a Sharīʿa-based state has overlooked the need to take a fresh look at a religious epistemology requiring extensive rethinking before it can guide decisions affecting the lives of Muslims in a modern nation-state.[19]

I firmly believe that if Muslims were made aware of the centrality of Koranic teachings about religious and cultural pluralism as a divinely ordained principle of peaceful coexistence among human societies, then they would spurn violence in challenging their repressive and grossly inefficient governments. The main objective of this study is to allow Muslims themselves to tell us their story without fear of our disapproval, condescension, or restraint.

This study presupposes a distinction between a core or universal aspect of the human personality and a periphery of particular beliefs and actions. It treats beliefs and practices not as isolated entities but as belonging to a personal cognitive system or a form of life. It is the cognitive system or the form of life that can reveal the personal background of motives, intentions, or other beliefs to which a specific action or belief is related. In analyzing the conceptual development of pluralism or the rights of religious minorities in Islam, for instance, I search for the intrinsic value of the concepts in the Koran and the Tradition, situating them in the context of the whole of the Islamic way of life. The concepts of pluralism and rights of non-Muslims in a Muslim polity relate to the practical dimension of community relationships rather than to the cognitive realm of belief about the religious other. But they afford a glimpse of the social philosophy of Islamic tradition.

This approach seeks to explain systematically the justification for a particular belief or action. By anchoring the justification in the Islamic way of life, ethical deliberations about specifically public virtues that further communal cohesiveness presuppose their adoption as social virtues by the community. In other words, I aim to expound Muslim beliefs and practices by showing how beliefs and practices related to a public order have been adopted or cohere with beliefs and practices in a whole system held by Muslims. For instance, in treating the Koranic position on the rights of non-Muslim minorities living under Muslim states, I try to show how the Koran treats other religions and their adherents and then seek to relate those positions to the actions of Muslim political actors in contemporary contexts.

Islamic revelation presents a theology that resonates with the modern pluralistic belief that other faiths are not merely inferior manifestations of religiosity, but variant forms of individual and communal responses to the presence of the transcendent in human life. All persons are created in the divine nature (*fiṭrat allāh*), with a disposition that leads to the knowledge of God, the Creator, to whom worship is due simply because of the creation. This universal knowledge of the Being in the creation holds equally for the believer or nonbeliever, the worshipper of One Being or of idols. More important, both a monotheist and an idolater can understand that God, by inspiring faith in divine mercifulness and forgiveness, can guide anyone He wills to save.

My analysis is founded upon the universal human religiosity that strives to discover the ethical standards needed to implement a just, harmonious order here on earth. Consequently, I believe that ethical reflection supersedes law and theology in this quest for a universal language of human dignity that would adequately mediate the diversity of true pluralism. Moreover, I am convinced that the other-regarding dimension of Islam provides ethical presuppositions capable of grounding a public rationale for a religious pluralism that is fully in accord with the Koran and the Tradition.

In searching for the roots of democratic pluralism in modern Islam, I cannot deny the influence of modern concepts in my formulation of questions about human dignity versus communal identity, religious community versus religious autonomy and the overarching reality of the modern nation-state. In fact, it is impossible to engage in any conversation about democracy without first recognizing that "[d]emocratic theory is the moral Esperanto of the present nation-state system, the language in which all Nations are truly United."[20] Notwithstanding the imprecision about the necessary and sufficient conditions for democracy, it becomes ever more crucial to understand the role of religion in a democratic system as an important source of public opinion on matters of state. Hence, when I deal with the human rights or political participation of the Muslims in their respective nation-states, I am in search of the religious teachings and examples in Islamic revelation—in the Koran, the Tradition, and the Sharīʿa—not simply to recycle the classical formulations but also to offer modern interpretations that show Islam's adaptations to modernity.

In this work I use the word *Islam* in three interrelated senses:

1. Islam as a religious system that provides a creed, a set of doctrines, a rite of prescriptive practices, and moral-spiritual attitudes
2. Islam as a historical phenomenon that provides its followers with a transnational religious and national cultural identity
3. Islam as a civilizational force that continues to shape the Muslim response to social-political realities and contingencies, allowing for necessary adjustments to membership in a diverse global community

All three of these senses of Islam are important to our exploration of the resources and attitudes that could provide the necessary keys to Islamic self-understanding of the social and political relations that bear on citizenship in a modern nation-state.

The Exegetical Materials on the Koran: Hindrance or Aid to Modern Understanding?

Since this book is concerned with the analytical examination of Koranic ideas about pluralism and individual autonomy, and since the Koran itself does not deal with these ideas directly or systematically, there is a legitimate concern in the minds of many scholars: Are the modern Muslims simply superimposing modernist notions on the premodern worldview of the Koran? To overcome this antinomy of the Koran as both timebound and timeless, I will pursue two lines of inquiry. First, I will examine Koranic exegetical material in order to discover the teachings of the ancient authorities on Islamic scripture on these issues of modern concern. Second, I will analyze these materials in the light of modern debates among Muslims from different schools of thought and explore their implications for religious pluralism, freedom of conscience and religion, and the legal status of religious minorities in Islamic revelation.

Does my first line of inquiry fly in the face of scholarly concerns about imposing modern categories of analysis on traditional Islamic literature? The classical commentaries on the Koran are important in understanding particular schools of theology or jurisprudence. The theological positions were, to be sure, post-Koranic extrapolations that attempted to grapple with issues like individual freedom of conscience or freedom to change one's religion. The distinctive outlook of each theological school conformed to its interpretation of the interplay of God's omnipotence and human free will under complex historical conditions. At the same time, the Koran by its nature does not propound detailed prescriptive or theological guidelines and so offers no explicit positions on the questions I have raised in this book. It is therefore important to trace the development of these ideas by examining the ways in which Muslim philologists-cum-theologians have interpreted ideas of intercommunal ethics. To explore the Koranic notion of religious pluralism, for instance, and to assess its congruity with the Koranic notion of salvation through revelation, one must seek spiritual and ethical guidance from the Koranic exegeses in the theological literature.

Since the Koran's appearance in the seventh century, there have been numerous commentaries that have ventured to make sense of this classical document. The historical method of interpretation, which requires that the text be interpreted in accordance with the rules of grammar and of the meaning of words, has had a long and creative history in the development of the Koranic exegesis. It is remarkable that even when most of the commentaries were guided by dogmatic prejudices, Muslim commentators paid close attention to the historical setting of the text's Koranic language.

The fact that every text speaks in the language of its time required the interpreters to deploy historical knowledge of the language and its speakers in explaining the relationship of the message to the vagaries of society and history. There was an implicit recognition that understanding the Koran required understanding the history in which Muḥammad emerged as the Prophet of God and launched his mission to establish the ideal public order. The assessments of the historical forces connected with the Koran gave rise to the divergent interpretations of the occasions of revelation (*asbāb al-nuzūl*), which, in turn were related to the distinct views held by the individual exegete engaged in formulating specific lines of inquiry into the meaning of the text. To be sure, the inherently subjective nature of any historical enterprise—stemming from an inevitable relation between an interpreter's presuppositions and the substantive assessment of the written documents—was the major factor in the continued interest among Muslim scholars to refresh their own insight by reaching back to an earlier commentator's preunderstanding of the revelatory text. Additionally, although the text of the Koran was fixed soon after the Prophet's death (perhaps even earlier, as maintained by some recent studies on the history of the text),[21] the absence of the only authoritative interpreter of the message, namely the Prophet himself, precludes any claim to a definitive understanding of the Koran on the part of the community. Furthermore, with the development of Muslim society and its ever expanding legal and moral requirements, the intellectual groundwork of Muslim legal scholarship was transformed by an ever expanding need to expound the historical setting of the revelation in order to discover practical rules for deducing judicial decisions.

The Koran, then, was approached as a living source of prescriptive guidance for the community. Muslim jurists sought solutions to concrete problems under given circumstances by applying the rules derived from the Koranic precedents. Through this necessity-driven melding of theory and practice—searching for historical precedents and extracting the doctrinal and juridical principles from cryptic Koranic passages that might be wrestled into a contemporary application—the Muslim interpreters of the text stood within the event of the revelation as responsible participants in its "life-orientational" directions.[22]

The Koranic cosmos was thoroughly human—profoundly anchored in human experience as humanity tried to make sense of the divine challenge to create an ethical order on earth. As long as the belief about establishing the ideal order on earth remained the major component of the living community's faith and of the active response to the divine challenge, there remained the need to clarify the Koranic impetus in order to promulgate it at each stage of the community's drive toward its ultimate destiny.

Hence, the history of the Muslim community's movement toward a just and equitable society provides creative and fertile ground for an evolving interpretation of the divine purposes indicated in the Koran. At the same time, the representation of the community and its ideals, both the past and the contemporary, has not yielded an authentic rendition of means that were and are still at its disposal to accomplish those ideals for humanity. Undeniably, scholarly pretext[23] plays a significant role in the explication of particular circumstances and denotations of the text. In this interpretive realm, an insightful investigator is able to discern the authorial pretexts of the earlier commentators that led to the distortion of the otherwise objectifiable context of Muslim existence. In addition, it is through the investigation of such distorted explications that a Muslim exegete is able to recontextualize the Koran and afford a fresh understanding of the divinely ordained Muslim *umma*.

These considerations suggest the need for a meticulous sifting of the Koranic exegetical materials, both classical and contemporary, in order to bring to light the various (and subtle) possibilities of interpretation. After all, the classical commentaries were produced by well-trained philologists and historians, who, although they were committed to this or that theological position, frequently discussed their opponents' expositions at length before offering an alternative of their own. By weighing their arguments, very much as we do those of more modern exegetes, I hope to come a little closer to a reliable interpretation of the key ethical terms and passages in the Koran.

My primary task, therefore, will be to analyze, on the basis of Islamic exegetical literature, ethicoreligious concepts relevant to contemporary concerns about religious pluralism and individual autonomy. I hope to elicit a clearly formulated account of the structure and content of these concepts in Islam. The investigation of this literature, which was produced by different schools of Islamic theology and ethics, will involve an analysis of the terms each group used to express its beliefs and its assumptions regarding the notion of conscientious commitment in Islam. I hope that this investigation will account for the conflict in today's Islamic world between the spirit of tolerant pluralism on the one hand and regimented exclusivity on the other.

The history of the interpretation of the Koran begins with the Prophet himself. Explication of the divine intention of the revelation was among the functions that the Koran assigned to the Prophet. The Prophet functioned as the projection of the divine message embodied in the Koran. He was the living commentary, the speaking (*al-nāṭiq*) Koran, intricately related to the silent (*al-ṣāmit*) text. Without the Prophet, the Koran was incomprehensible, just as without the Koran, the Prophet was no prophet at all.

Following the Prophet's death, a number of prominent disciples involved themselves in interpreting the prescriptive aspects of the Koran in order to provide rulings for specific situations in the community's social and political life. The result of this endeavor formed the groundwork for legal methodology in Islamic juridical studies. The key achievements of this work were the following:

1. Analysis of literary and linguistic aspects of the revelation
2. Determination of the historical context of the revelation
3. Clarification of meanings through intratextual reference
4. Explanation of passages by using the materials that were transmitted in the form of *ḥadīth*-reports attributed to the Prophet as the commentator and teacher of the Koran

It was the last of these, exegesis based on the traditions (*ḥadīth*), that found greatest acceptance in the community because it seemed to recapture the essential meaning of the text under discussion. Yet exegeses based on the *ḥadīth*-reports were the most vulnerable to factional disputation and doctrinal prejudice. The reason was that these *ḥadīth*-reports represented diverse political and theological trends. Only certain reports, related on the authority of certain narrators deemed reliable by a particular scholar and the group he represented, were accepted as authoritative documentation for the specific exegetical opinion on the Koran. Some of these commentaries also exhibited suspicion toward any opinion that was based on the apparent sense of the passage because such an approach was regarded as founded upon rational presumptions about the language and its ordinary usage in the Arab society. However, such meaning-based investigation was fundamental to the discussions of grammatical points, semantics, and the application of linguistic conventions. This mode of analysis proved to be indispensable for establishing the authoritativeness of the apparent sense of the Koranic passages in the works that dealt with legal principles and rules (*uṣūl al-fiqh*).

Out of the growing interest in theological issues related to free will and predestination, religious-moral obligations, and divine benevolence, there arose a creative, interpretive approach to the meanings of the Koranic text. Various Islamic schools of thought, like the Sunnī Muʿtazilite and Ashʿarite, and various Shīʿite factions, whose claim to validity for their doctrinal positions depended upon the citation of the Koran, introduced brilliant ways of interpreting ambiguous Koranic passages.

During the ninth and tenth centuries, Hellenistic and Indo-Persian cultures permeated Muslim societies through Arabic translations. Islamic civilization scaled new heights of creativity, spurred by heightened interest in philosophical and mystical exegesis of the Islamic revelation. Hence, Muslim exegetes have responded not only to their own doctrinal and philosophical interests and purposes in seeking out an additional interpretive dimension of the Koran. Their commentaries clearly reveal the cultural, methodological, and intellectual influences of the age in which they produced a creative understanding of divine revelation.

Thus, in addition to the major classical commentaries, I have frequently referred to two important contemporary commentaries in deciphering the social-political implications of a number of Koranic passages dealing with pluralism and related topics:

1. A Sunnī commentary by a leading member of the Muslim Brotherhood in Egypt, namely, Sayyid Quṭb, *Fī ẓilāl al-qurʾān*, thirty parts in six volumes (Beirut: Dār al-Shurūq, 1973)
2. A Shīʿī commentary by a renowned scholar, ʿAllāma Ṭabāṭabāʾī, *al-Mīzān fī tafsīr al-qurʾān*, in twenty volumes (Beirut: Muʾassasa al-Aʿlamī, 1972).

The exegetical literature examined for this study reveals many examples of these methodological considerations in the Koranic exegetical tradition in Islam. The commentaries by Sayyid Quṭb or by ʿAllāma Ṭabāṭabāʾī are not interested in merely reproducing the history of contextual hermeneutics; rather, they seek to undertake the more complicated task of establishing general rules of intratextual hermeneutics. Both Quṭb and Ṭabāṭabāʾī have followed the intratextual method of elucidating the Koran (*tafsīr al-qurʾān bi al-qurʾān*) in order to relate sometimes different parts of the Koran that strike the nonspecialist as atomistic compilations of disparate themes and to demonstrate coherence in the present structure of the text.

According to both these commentators, there are four major prerequisites to intratextual hermeneutics:

1. The commentator should not preformulate an opinion about the passage under consideration. If he/she does have an opinion, he/she should not impose it on the text but should seek its confirmation externally.
2. Lexicographical investigation must be thorough enough to acquire the most comprehensive sense of a term and its properties.
3. Intratextual investigation must be based not merely on comparison of verses on a similar topic. It should undertake to distinguish and determine the general from the specific, the absolute from the conditional, the literal from the apparent, and the explicit from the implicit.
4. Careful attention should be given to the method that was employed by the Prophet and the early leaders to interpret one verse by another verse, just as ʿAlī b. Abī Ṭālib has stated: "One part of the Book of God explains another, . . . and one part serves as a witness to the other."[24]

It is possible to discern three basic approaches to Koranic interpretation: (1) traditional (making much of the exegetical traditions of the early community to explicate the "occasions of revelation" of the text); (2) theological (expounding theological standpoints through the Koranic interpretation, that is, those held by the proponents of various theological schools); and (3) mystical (interpreting through extensive allegorization of the Koranic language in order to apprehend the inner meaning of the text). The works consulted for this study are largely theological and traditional, since they yield the most relevant materials.

Both the commentaries by Quṭb and Ṭabāṭabāʾī represent in general the Sunnī and Shīʿite theological exegeses. The discussion of the Koranic material in these and other theological commentaries was dominated by the proponents of the two major Sunnī schools of dialectical theology, the Muʿtazilite and the Ashʿarite, and one Shīʿite school, the Twelver. It was precisely in the works of these schools that the questions of ethical knowledge and the possibility of a common morality for humankind were treated in detail, according to conflicting ethical theories and doctrinal positions. Since the questions of individual autonomy and human moral agency are directly relevant to our discussion about pluralism, conscience, and salvation, it is worthwhile to describe at the outset the two respective theories.

The Muʿtazilite (and by theological extension, the Shīʿite) approach to Koranic interpretation is based on a metaphorical interpretation of the text to support certain dogmatic presuppositions and conclusions. The basic Muʿtazilite thesis is that human beings, as free agents, are responsible before a just God. Furthermore, good and evil are rational categories that can be known through reason, independent of revelation. God created man's intellect in such a way that it is capable of perceiving good and evil objectively. This is the corollary of the main thesis, for God's justice depends on the objective knowledge of good and evil as determined by reason, whether the Lawgiver pronounces the thing to be so or not. In other words, the Muʿtazilites asserted the efficacy of natural reason as a source of spiritual and ethical knowledge.[25]

The Muʿtazilite standpoint was bound to be challenged. The question of how extensive the Koranic allowance for independent reasoning in matters of value might be is a complex and difficult one. And thus, while, as we shall demonstrate, the Koran admits some capacity for ethical knowledge independent of supernatural guidance, it is not surprising that the Ashʿarites rejected the idea of natural reason as an autonomous source of ethical knowledge. They maintained that good and evil are as God decrees them to be, and that it is presumptuous to judge God on the basis of categories that God has provided for directing human life. For the Ashʿarite there is no way, within the bounds of ordinary logic, to explain the relation of God's power to human actions. It is more realistic simply to maintain that everything that happens is the result of His will, without explanation or justification. It is, however, important to distinguish between the actions of a responsible human being and the motions attributed to natural laws. Human responsibility is not the result of free choice; rather, God alone creates all actions directly. In some actions, a special quality of "voluntary acquisition" is superadded by God, making the individual a voluntary, responsible agent. Consequently, human responsibility is the result of the divine will known through revealed guidance. Values have no foundation but the will of God that imposes them. This attitude of the Ashʿarites to ethical knowledge became known as theistic subjectivism—ethical values are dependent upon the determination of the will of God expressed in the form of eternal, immutable revelation.[26]

It is impossible to go into further detail about exegetical materials in this introductory chapter. However, it is worth noting that in the modern exegesis of the Koran among the Sunnī Muslims, it is the Muʿtazilite thesis that has prevailed over the traditional and the Ashʿarite ones, especially in connection with the individual freedom to negotiate one's own spiritual destiny and the related doctrine of the freedom of conscience in Islam. Sayyid Quṭb and ʿAllāma Ṭabāṭabāʾī are among the prominent figures in maintaining the responsibility of free individuals before a just God.

2

The People Are One Community

The people were one community (umma); then God sent forth the Prophets, good tidings to bear and warning, and He sent down with them the Book with the truth, that He might decide the people touching their differences. (K. 2:213)

Religious Pluralism and Communal Identity

The term *pluralism* is one of the catchwords of a new world order whose diversity of cultures, belief systems, and values inspires both exhilaration at the endless shadings of human expression and dread of irreconcilable conflict. The invocation of pluralism has become as much a summons as a celebration, an urgent exhortation to the citizens of the world to come to terms with their dizzying diversity. The endless conflicts between Christians and Muslims, Hindus and Sikhs, Tamils and Buddhists, and the attendant atrocities committed against innocent civilians, have imparted a dire urgency to the moral imperative of recognizing the human dignity of the other, regardless of his or her religious, ethnic, and cultural affiliations.

This imperious ethical need to acknowledge the other is a byproduct of snowballing technological advances in transportation and communication. Until recently, nations existed in relative isolation from one another, and past encounters with diversity have not always been friendly. In fact, as many conflicts around the world indicate, clashes of diverse cultures can become a major source of dehumanizing the other. Each tradition, armed with its self-awarded patent on divine revelation, seeks supremacy rather than accommodation when confronted with an alien faith.

Recognition of religious pluralism within a community of the faithful promises to advance the principle of inclusiveness, which would counsel accommodation, not conflict, among competing claims to religious truth in religiously and culturally heterogenous societies. Such an inclusiveness should lead to a sense of multiple and unique possibilities for enriching the human quest for spiritual and moral well-being.

Is the promise of pluralistic religiosity, of an enhanced acknowledgment of spiritual difference, an unintended consequence of relentlessly advancing technological and economic interdependence, with its increasingly visible and ever nearer other? Or, is this hope of reconciliation a long-germinating part of the human heritage, preserved in classical religious discourse that had to come to terms with comparable and competing claims of exclusive salvation both in relation to other faiths and within the community of the faithful?

In dealing with pluralism in the Islamic tradition, I intend to demonstrate that the revelation of the youngest of the Abrahamic faiths actually found expression in a pluralistic world of religions that Islam acknowledged and evaluated critically but never rejected as false. In fact, the spiritual space of the Koran, as I shall demonstrate, was shared by other monotheistic religions. The major task confronting the early Muslim community was to secure an identity for its members within the God-centered worldview shared by other traditions. How could the community provide the necessary instruments of integration and legitimation without denying other religious groups their due share in God-centered religious identity? Could it build its ideal, a just public order, without creating an inclusive theology to deal with the broad range of problems arising from the encounters between Muslims and human beings of other faiths?

"The People Are One Community"

To find the answer to these questions, I turned to the Koran and discovered the oft-repeated avowal that humankind is one community and that God reserves the power to unite people to become one community.[1] In the citation that introduces this chapter (K. 2:213), three facts emerge: the unity of humankind under One God;[2] the particularity of religions brought by the prophets; and the role of revelation (the Book)[3] in resolving the differences that touch communities of faith. All three are fundamental to the Koranic conception of religious pluralism. On the one hand, it does not deny the specificity of various religions and the contradictions that might exist among them in matters touching on correct belief and practice; on the other, it emphasizes the need to recognize the oneness of humanity in creation and to work toward better understanding among peoples of faith.

The major argument for religious pluralism in the Koran is based on the relationship between private faith and its public projection in the Islamic polity. Whereas in matters of private faith, the position of the Koran is noninterventionist (i.e., human authority in any form must defer to the individual's internal convictions), in the public projection of that faith, the Koranic stance is based on the principle of coexistence, the willingness of a dominant community to recognize self-governing communities free to run their internal affairs and coexist with Muslims.

Islam, with its program of organizing its own public order, defined its goals in terms of a comprehensive religious and social-political system, requiring its adherents to devote themselves exclusively to the well-being of the community of believers, and to defend its social system. Such unremitting loyalty has been the reason for the survival of many a nascent religious movement. Yet, such loyalty has also been the source of intolerance toward those who do not share the movement's exclusive claims to truth and right conduct. The record of Islam, as a religion and a civilization, reveals major tension: on the one hand, there is the Koranic recognition of pluralistic responses to divine guidance and the freedom of human conscience to negotiate one's own spiritual space; on the other, there is the emerging new social-political order constructed upon unquestionable and exclusive loyalty to the tradition. The immediate concern of the community was to alleviate this tension by limiting its jurisdiction only to the public projection of human faith, that is, its commitment to build a just social order.

Islam as a Public Religion

Of all the Abrahamic religions based on the Old Testament ethos of shaping the public culture in accordance with the divine will, it is Islam that was from its inception the most conscious of its earthly agenda. In its conscious commitment to founding an ethical public order, Islam has been accurately described as a faith in the public realm.[4] In comparison to the performance of the religious-moral duties (*takālīf al-sharʿiyya*) that are laid down in minute detail in the Sharīʿa (the sacred law of the community), the official creed plays a secondary role in orienting the faithful in their social conduct. Even today, communal identity among Muslims is, therefore, defined less in terms of a person's adherence to a particular school of theology and more in terms of that person's loyalty to one of the officially recognized rites of the Sharīʿa.[5] Personal faith is a private matter and, hence, inaccessible to public scrutiny. By contrast, the performance of the duties, especially in congregation, makes one's private religious commitment objectively accessible to others in the community. The *uṣūl al-dīn* (the fundamental principles of religion) form the private facet of a person's religious expression and are thus subjective, whereas the *furūʿ al-dīn* (the religious practices derived from one's belief) form the public facet of a person's religious life, both individually and collectively, and are thus objective. In the full scope of the Islamic way of life, the private side of religion is scrutinized indirectly through its manifestation in the public order.

The Sharīʿa regulates religious practice with a view to maintaining the individual's well-being through his or her social well-being. Hence, its comprehensive system deals with the obligations that humans perform as part of their relationship to the Divine Being, *ʿibādāt* (all forms of service to God), and the duties they perform as part of their interpersonal responsibility, *muʿāmalāt* (transactions). Public order must be maintained in worship, in the marketplace, and in all other arenas of human interaction. The *umūr ḥisbiyya*—social transactions based on an ethical standard of conduct in the Sharīʿa—deal with enforcing the law by taking into account only what appears in the public sphere of human interaction. Though the injunctions of Sharīʿa cover even the most private acts, the judiciary in Islamic courts may rule only regarding what is brought to its attention without prying, unless the rights of an innocent party are being infringed.

Religious pluralism for the Sharīʿa was not simply a matter of accommodating competing claims to religious truth in the private domain of individual faith. It was and remains inherently a matter of public policy in which a Muslim government must acknowledge and protect the divinely ordained right of each person to determine his or her spiritual destiny without coercion. The recognition of freedom of conscience in matters of faith is the cornerstone of the Koranic notion of religious pluralism, both interreligious and intrareligious.[6]

It is important to keep in mind that without the Koranic endorsement of the essential guiding principle of a religiously pluralistic society, namely, the acknowledgment of salvific value in other religions, the story of Islam's treatment of its religious minorities throughout history would not have been any different than Europe's treatment of the non-Christian other. One needs only to consider the violent forms that anti-Semitism generated by Christian redemptive theology took in Europe. The state policies of different Muslim dynasties are reflected in the legal decisions passed down by Muslim jurists that allowed for maximum individual as well as group autonomy in adhering to a particular religious tradition.

Nevertheless, the political situation of Muslim societies has resulted in a good deal of convenient sidestepping of the Koranic teachings in order to gain control over conquered peoples. The active engagement of contemporary fundamentalist[7] leaders with the violent precedents from dark moments in Muslim history points to the tension between the Koranic principles of justice and the demands of maintaining the classical vision of an ever expanding *dār al-islām* (the territory over which Muslims ruled). The Muslim world is deeply divided over the shape of the public culture, the style of life that is visible in the civic forum. The key principle at stake in this controversy is respect for the other, the foundation of coexistence among peoples of diverse faith and cultures. It is for this reason that in my search for the Islamic roots of democratic pluralism, of respect for the other, I begin with religious pluralism in the Koran.

The Koran on Religious Pluralism

I am relying entirely on the Koran as the normative source for a theology of inclusiveness. There is no other text that occupies a position of such unquestionable and absolute authority for Muslims. Hence, it is the key to locating and understanding Islamic notions of religious pluralism.

Muslims believe that the Koran is constitutive of a universal imperative that all humans ought to fulfil. The knowledge of this imperative is given at birth to all humans in the form of a primordial nature (*fiṭra*) with the necessary cognition and volition to fulfil the goals of humanity and to recognize and serve God. It is the responsibility of every individual to discern what it means to be in witness to God and to serve humanity.

But the full ramifications of the Koranic worldview are not readily grasped in its apparent meanings. To begin with, the text of the Koran is neither a systematic exposition of this worldview nor a chronologically arranged revelation that is an orderly progression through declarative, indicative, and imperative statements concerning different moments in the life of the Prophet Muḥammad as he organized his community. In other words, by merely identifying the chapters as being Mekkan or Medinan, we are not in a position to trace, for instance, various Muslim encounters with other religions and their adherents. Moreover, the Koran's theology of religious tolerance cannot be ascribed to the earlier Mekkan period of the revelation when Muslims lived as a minority in the midst of a hostile majority of the unbelievers, as some modern Muslim apologists have tried to argue.[8] While it is true that the Mekkan conditions were unfavorable to the Muslims and conducive to theological inclusiveness based on the view that religions need to coexist ("To you your religion, and to me my religion!" K. 109:5), it was in Medina where the real issues of coexistence among the peoples of the Book (*ahl al-kitāb*)[9] first arose. The Koran responded creatively to those formative moments in the development of intercommunity relations between Islam and other religions of the Book.

Accordingly, my method—extracting relevant passages that deal with the vision of a universal humanity and of interfaith relations—treats the entire Koran as a unified text, not as divided into its Mekkan or Medinan periods of revelation. Although historically it might be useful to determine the chronology of the Koran, I believe that the purport of its contextual meanings in its entirety provides ample material for extrapolating a pluralistic and inclusive theology of religions.

I have relied on other traditional sources to supplement and complement the Koran, for example, the commentaries of the Koran and the Tradition (*sunna*),[10] also recognized by Muslims as normative. While I acknowledge the problem of establishing the reliability of these other sources, the *ḥadīth*-reports attributed to the Prophet, his family, and his companions reveal much about the political and social culture underlying Muslim ethics and provide a fleshing out—contextual, textual, intertextual,[11] historical, and linguistic—of the core teachings of the Koran, with necessary intellectual caution and restraint. The universal message of the Koran can reveal, without subordination to a limited historical and cultural context, that the revelation accepts religious pluralism as given and even necessary, requiring Muslims to continually negotiate, transform, and emphasize the fundamental unity of humankind in its origin and creation by the Divine Being.

With this goal in mind, I need not document the historical development and transformation of the idea of religious pluralism in Islam throughout history. The limited scope of this work is to discover the Koranic theology of the other that assures humanity of God's commitment to mercy and forgiveness as a prelude to the attainment of peace on earth. Contrary to a number of gloomy predictions about the way in which religious ideas have been used to promote hatred and destruction in human societies, this work intends to demonstrate that the essential message in the Koran about the unity of human beings through God's creation can become a positive source for harmony and cooperation. The affirmative principle of diversity is the cornerstone of the creation narrative in the Koran, reminding people, "Surely this community of yours is one community, and I am your Lord; so serve Me" (K. 21:92). Instead of regarding this diversity as a source of inevitable tensions, the Koran suggests that human variety is indispensable for a particular tradition to define its common beliefs, values, and traditions for its community life:

> O humankind, We have created you male and female, and appointed you races and tribes, that you may know one another. Surely the noblest among you in the sight of God is the most godfearing of you. God is All-knowing, All-Aware. (K. 49:14)

Pluralism within the Abrahamic Family

Islam is the youngest of the Abrahamic traditions. Its self-understanding since its inception in the seventh century has included a critical element of pluralism, namely, its relation to the other religions. Instead of denying the validity of other human experiences of transcendence, Islam recognizes and even confirms its salvific efficacy within the wider boundaries of monotheism:

> Surely they that believe, and those of Jewry, and the Christians, and those Sabaeans, whoso believes in God and the Last Day, and works righteousness—their wage awaits them with their Lord, and no fear shall be on them, neither shall they sorrow. (K. 2:62)

The Koran clearly sees itself as a critical link in the revelatory experience of humankind, a universal path intended for all. In particular, it shares the biblical ethos of Judaism and Christianity, with a remarkably inclusive attitude toward the peoples of the Book, with whom it is linked through the first man and woman on earth. The unique characteristic of Islam is its conviction that belief in the oneness of God unites the Muslim community with all humanity because God is the creator of all humans, irrespective of their religious traditions. The Koran declares that on the Day of Judgment all human beings will be judged, irrespective of sectarian affiliation, on their moral performance as citizens of the world community.

The idea that "the People are one community" is the foundation of a theological pluralism that presupposes the divinely ordained equivalence and equal rights of all human beings. Although the verb in the first sentence can be translated in the past tense ("The people *were* one community"), in Arabic the verb *kāna* (to be), divested of all temporal connotations, is often used as a copula, which links a subject with a predicate complement without any reference to time.[12] Hence, the people are still "one nation" on the basis of the humanness that they continue to share. The statement also indicates that while this unity is justified theologically within the activity of the divine, it is best sought in the ethical sphere, which sustains relationships between peoples of faith; it is with the help of this innate ethical ability, the primordial nature (*fiṭra*) put by God in all human beings, that humanity acquires the ability to deal with the other in fairness and equity. This moral ability allows for the development of a "global ethic"[13] that can provide the pluralistic basis for mediating interreligious relations among peoples of diverse spiritual commitment, enabling them to build a working consensus of values and goals.

The Idea of Exclusive Salvation and Religious Pluralism

The idea of salvation—whether applied to individuals or communities—hinges on a standard of worthy conduct, living according to the true faith.[14] Since all religions are concerned with salvation, recognition of other religions implies a recognition of their claim to conduce to salvation. Unfortunately, Islam's readiness to recognize the legitimacy of other religions' paths to salvation has become obscured by the theological controversy over "supersession":[15] whether the Koranic revelation supersedes or abrogates all other revelations. Closely related to the question of supersession is the position of the prophethood of Muḥammad in the salvific efficacy of other monotheistic traditions.

Religious systems have traditionally claimed absolute devotion and a monopoly of redemptive powers. Such exclusivist claims have been regarded as natural and necessary instruments for the self-identification of a group against other claims of absolute truth. Even within the Muslim community, it was by no means always conceded that the direction taken by other schools of thought—for instance, the Shīʿa or Sunnī—could lead to authentic salvation.[16] The salvific value of the other, if admitted at all, was considered limited, adequate to inch people closer to the distant goal of spiritual transformation but most likely to leave them stranded partway.

From the standpoint of social organization, this exclusive claim was an effective tool of legitimation and integration, furnishing its members with practical means of asserting their collective communal identity. In addition, the newly fostered communal identity provided an equally effective basis for aggression against and exploitation of those who did not share this sense of solidarity with the community of the believers. Rationalization of such aggression, characterized in religious terms as a "holy war," made it possible for the believers of a given system to forcibly impose their hegemony over the infidels in the name of some sacred authority.

To be sure, the religious legitimation of such hegemonic interests and methods was questionable, and therefore they had to be justified by means of and sought in the very Scriptures that seemed to challenge any claim to compulsory devotion and the prohibitive social and legal structures of religious absolutism. It was this need for intellectual legitimacy that fostered the exegetical molding of revelational sources in order to provide a convincing interpretive prop for absolutist ends. The exegesis of specific passages of the Scripture provided the restrictive definition of soteriological faith in which other religions were systematically deemed to be superseded and, consequently, devoid of salvific potential.

Some classical Muslim scholars of the Koran attempted to separate the salvation history of the community from that of other Abrahamic faiths by attesting to the supremacy of Islamic revelation over those of Christianity and Judaism.[17] In an attempt to demand unquestioning acceptance of the new faith, Muslim theologians had to devise terminological as well as methodological stratagems for deemphasizing the ecumenical passages of the Koran that extend salvific authenticity and adequacy to other monotheistic traditions.

One of the methods of blunting the force of a verse was to claim its abrogation (*naskh*) by another verse. In the works of Koranic exegesis, many verses are said to have been abrogated. The modern scholarship of some prominent

Muslim jurists has provided incontrovertible documentation that all 137 putatively abrogated verses are in fact still valid.[18] Muslim scholars do agree that numerous injunctions from the earlier laws were abrogated by the Sharīʿa. But there is no such agreement about whether any Koranic ordinances were abrogated by other Koranic verses, by an authentic prophetic tradition (*ḥadīth*), by the consensus (*ijmāʿ*) of Muslim scholars, or by reasoning (*ʿaql*). Muslim scholars agree that abrogation cannot be established through the citation of a rare or a weak tradition, because a report from only one source is in itself proof of falsehood or error on the part of the narrator.

The major problem facing modern scholars is whether to accept the judgment of past scholars about a given abrogated verse.[19] Evidently, in finding a contradiction between an earlier and a later verse, scholars have tended to award legitimacy to the newer one, thus abrogating the earlier verse. This attitude is rooted either in poor judgment or in a loose application of the word *naskh*. The application of the generic sense of *naskh* (transformation, substitution, or elimination) to situations that required application of its technical sense (supersession) has created enormous difficulties in assessing the pluralistic message of the Koran.

We will examine the verses that require Muslims to deal tolerantly and fairly with the people of the Book in chapter 3. Chapter 4 will address the question of warfare with unbelievers and the moral restrictions placed on the use of force in general by the Koran. Here, it suffices to underline the pluralism conveyed by the verse K. 2:213, a passage that has created inordinate difficulties for Muslim scholars uncomfortable with its moral universalism. This and other verses that command Muslims to build bridges of understanding and cooperation between the once united human community have been viewed as abrogated by those verses that require Muslims to fight the unbelievers.

There is no doubt that K. 2:213 implies a universal discourse embracing all of humanity under a single divine authority, thereby relativizing all competing religious claims to spiritual supremacy. This universal idiom was based on the principle of *tawḥīd*—affirmation of divine unity. Acknowledgment of *tawḥīd* signifies a transformation of the human focus on self to one on the Self, the ultimate reality, the source of all other selves. It affirms the centrality of God without human mediation and the spiritual destiny of humankind. *Tawḥīd*, moreover, uniquely places God as the source of revelation (the Book) as communicated through the prophets. The prophets represented one and the same revelation, embodying different aspects of the divine will at different times.

As Islam laid the foundation of its political order, however, Muslim leaders sought out particular integrative discourses that would furnish the believers with a unique identity and a practical means of asserting it through the creation of an exclusive order based on the declaration of faith, the *shahāda*. This development marked a clear shift away from the Koranic recognition of religious pluralism in the sense of a God-centered, human religiosity (within each instance of historical revelation of the divine reality). It also deemphasized the unity of humankind in the sphere of universal moral-spiritual discourse.

The establishment of the first Islamic society was an important chapter in the Muslims' self-identification as a community endowed with a tradition of specific salvific efficacy. Moreover, in the sectarian milieu of seventh-century Arabia, early Muslims encountered competing claims to authentic religiosity by other monotheists like the Christians and Jews. These encounters, which generated interreligious polemics in the context of an Islamic public order where Muslims enjoyed a privileged position, led to the notion of the privileged status of Islam as a unique and perfect version of the original Abrahamic monotheism. The universally accepted notion that emerged from these polemics was the doctrine that the Koranic revelation was the culmination of its predecessors, which had no more than transitory and limited application. Such a notion also led to the doctrine of supersession among some Muslim theologians, who argued that neither the Mosaic law nor the Christian Scripture—directed as each was to a limited audience of followers—had any claim to eternal validity.

The apparent contradiction between some passages of the Koran that recognized other authentic salvific sources and other passages that declared Islam the sole source of salvation had to be resolved in order to establish a stable system of peaceful coexistence with these religions. The Koranic pluralism is expressed by promising salvation to "whoso believes in God and the Last Day" among "those of Jewry, and the Christians, and those Sabaeans" (K. 2:62). Islamic absolutism is also asserted in no uncertain terms: "Whoso desires another religion than Islam, it shall not be accepted of him; in the next world he shall be among the losers" (K. 3:85).

There is no doubt that the Koran is silent on the question of the supersession of the previous Abrahamic revelations through the emergence of Muḥammad. There is no statement in the Koran, direct or indirect, to suggest that the Koran saw itself as the abrogator of previous Scriptures. In fact, as I shall discuss below, even when repudiating the distortions introduced in the divine message by the followers of Moses and Jesus, the Koran confirms the validity of these revelations and their central theme, namely, submission founded on sincere profession of belief in God. However, in the classical exegetical literature, the question of the chronology of divine revelation and its applicability to subsequent communities forms an important theological strand.

The principle of chronology provided the theologians with the notion of *naskh* (abrogation or supersession) with which to expound various stages of revelation throughout history. Essentially, the same revelation was uncovered piecemeal in time, later revelations completing and thereby abrogating the previous ones. It is important to bear in mind that the Koran introduces the idea of abrogation in connection with specific legal injunctions revealed in particular verses but apparently repealed, that is, abrogated or superseded by other verses. Accordingly, applying abrogation to Islam's attitude toward preceding Abrahamic traditions was, to say the least, debatable.

Even classical exegetes like Muḥammad b. Jarīr al-Ṭabarī (d. 923)—who supported the principle of chronology to argue for the exclusive salvific efficacy of Islam and its role as the abrogator of the previous monotheistic traditions—could not fail to notice the incongruity of extending the notion of abrogation to the divine promise of rewarding those who believe in God and the Last Day and who work righteousness (K. 2:62). In fact, Ṭabarī regards such abrogation as incompatible with the concept of divine justice.[20]

Those who accepted the notion of supersession of the pre-Koranic revelations depended on a tradition reported in many early commentaries on the verse K. 3:85, which states that no religion other than Islam would be acceptable to God. The tradition purports to establish that the later K. 3:85 actually repeals God's promise to those who act righteously outside Islam in K. 2:62. Another Sunnī commentator, Ismāʿīl b. ʿUmar ibn Kathīr (d. 1373), has no hesitation in maintaining that based on K. 3:85 nothing other than Islam was acceptable to God after Muḥammad was sent. Although he does not appeal to the concept of abrogation as evidence, his conclusions obviously point to the idea of supersession when he states that the followers of previous guidance and their submission to a rightly guided life guaranteed their way to salvation only before Islamic revelation emerged.[21]

It is clear that the notion of abrogation of the previous revelations did not command universal assent even among those exegetes who otherwise required, at least in theory, other monotheists to abide by the new Sharīʿa of Muḥammad. It is difficult to gauge the level of Christian influence over Muslim debates about the supersession of the previous revelation. It is not far-fetched to suggest that debates about Islam superseding Christianity and Judaism, despite the explicit absence of any reference to the issue in the Koran, must have entered Muslim circles through the ardent Christian debates about Christianity having superseded Judaism, especially since Christians claimed to be the legitimate heirs to the same Hebrew Bible that was the source of Jewish law. The Muslim community, with its independent source of ethical and religious prescriptions, the Arabic Koran, and its control over the power structure that defined its relationship with others, was in little need of establishing its supremacy over previous Abrahamic monotheistic traditions, with which it never severed its theological connection. The Koran relates its experience of "submission to God's will" (*islām*) to Abraham, the "unitarian" (*muwaḥḥid*), who "in truth was not a Jew, neither a Christian; but he was a *muslim* and one of pure faith; certainly he was never of the idolaters" (K. 3:67).[22]

This Koranic spirit of ecumenism within the Abrahamic traditions always retained the potential to assert itself at various times in history as the community negotiated its relationship to the political power that dominated its destiny. Depending upon the social and political circumstances of the Muslim community during the colonial and postcolonial eras, Muslim exegetes have reanimated the Koran's pluralistic spirit in varying degrees, depending on the theological affiliation of the exegete.

There were essentially two theological positions regarding the moral and spiritual guidance toward salvation that God provides to humanity. Those theologians who maintained divine will as all-encompassing and all-omnipotent considered it necessary for humanity to be exposed to revealed guidance through the prophets. Other theologians insisted on the freedom of the human will, believing the human intellect to be capable of attaining godly life. It is for the most part the latter group, identified among the Sunnites as the Muʿtazilites—a majority among the Shīʿites—who conceded the continued salvific efficacy of the other monotheistic faiths on the basis of the revealed and rational guidance to which the Christians and the Jews were exposed. They regarded the people of the Book as responsible for acting upon their revelation, whose substance has remained recognizable despite the neglect and alteration it has suffered. The former group, on the contrary, postulating a theory of chronological revelation, afforded efficacy to these religions as a source of divine guidance only before the time of Muḥammad. After the emergence of Islam, they had to accept Muḥammad as the Prophet in order to be saved.[23]

Most modern exegetes of the Koran have maintained the Muʿtazilite theological position regarding the human free will. They believe that human beings are endowed with sufficient cognition and volition to pursue their spiritual destiny through the revealed message of God. Thus, Muḥammad Rashīd Riḍā (d. 1935), reflecting the Muʿtazilite attitude of his teacher, the prominent Muslim modernist Muḥammad ʿAbduh (d. 1905), maintained that human responsibility to God is proportionate to the level of one's exposure through reason or revelation to God's purpose. The purpose of revelation is to clarify and elucidate matters that are known through the human intellect. The basic beliefs such as the existence of God and the Last Day are necessarily known through it. Prophets come to confirm what is already inspired to the human intellect. Accordingly, there is an essential unity in the beliefs of "the people of divine religions" (*ahl al-adyān al-ilāhiyya*) who have been exposed to divine guidance, as well as an innate disposition to believe in God and the Last Day and to do good works.[24] Moreover, God's promise applies to all who have this divine religion, regardless of formal religious affiliation, for God's justice does not allow favoring one group while ill-treating another. For all people who believe in a prophet and in the revelation particular to them, "their wages await them with their Lord, and no fear shall there be on them, neither shall they sorrow" (K. 2:62). Rashīd Riḍā does not view belief in the prophethood of Muḥammad as a requirement for Jews and Christians who desire to be saved; hence, he implicitly maintains the salvific validity of both Jewish and Christian revelation.[25]

Among the Shīʿite commentators, Muḥammad Ḥusayn al-Ṭabāṭabāʾī (d. 1982), following the well-established Shīʿite opinion from the classical age, rejected the notion of abrogation of the divine promise in K. 2:62. In fact, he does not support the supersession of pre-Koranic revelations even when he regards them as distorted and corrupted by their followers. Nevertheless, he regards the ordinances of the Koran as abrogating the laws extracted from the two earlier Scriptures. Evidently he confines abrogation to its juridical meaning, in which it signifies "repeal" of an earlier ordinance by a fresh ruling because of changed circumstances. In connection with passages like verse K. 2:62 that support the ecumenical thrust of the Koran, he rebuffs the opinion held by some Muslims that God promises salvation to particular groups because they bear certain names; on the contrary, anyone who holds true belief and acts righteously is entitled to God's reward and His protection from punishment, as promised in K. 6:88: "God has promised those of them who believe and do good, forgiveness and a great reward."[26]

Some Muslim theologians sought to restrict the pluralist thrust of the universal discourse of the Koran, which defined true belief in terms of two aspects of Abrahamic religions: belief in God and the Last Day, and righteous action based on revealed guidance. Acknowledgment of the prophethood of Muḥammad was part of the exclusive discourse of the Muslim community. It was this exclusivist discourse that led to the idea that Islam had superseded all other religions and had thus invalidated their salvific efficacy. Nevertheless, given the Koran's pluralistic vision of human religiosity, even within this emerging exclusivist theological consensus there were strong and authentic dissenting opinions that refused to limit salvation to Muslims only.

Modern commentators like the Sunnī Rashīd Riḍā and the Shīʿite ʿAllāma Ṭabāṭabāʾī represent the unmistakable Koranic spirit of a God-centered identity for humanity in which the external form of religion is relegated to the inward witness of the divine and thus defies any exclusive and restrictive identification. In fact, religious pluralism is seen by the Koran as fulfilling a divine purpose for humanity: the creation of an ethical public order, the innate predisposition for which (lodged in the ability to cognize the good and differentiate it from evil) God implanted in humans, even before He sent the prophets and the revelation (K. 9:18). This divine gift requires humans, regardless of their particular religious affiliations, to live harmoniously with one another and work toward justice and peace in the world. The Koran, as we shall see in the next chapter, admonishes humankind "to compete with one another in good works" (K. 5:48).

Tensions within the Theology of Religions

In the article entitled "The Ring: On Religious Pluralism,"[27] Avishai Margalit adopts an antipluralist argument in his examination of the ecumenical potential of Judaism, Christianity, and Islam. In responding to his negative and even superficial treatment of the Islamic sources in the context of the three monotheistic traditions, I find his antipluralist framework useful in articulating the pluralistic Koranic theology of the other. Given the historical reality of the dialectical relations among the three peoples of the Book under the political dominance of Muslims, I insist, on both normative and empirical grounds, on the pluralist possibilities for just relationships among the Abrahamic communities today.

Religious pluralism calls for active engagement with the religious other not merely to tolerate, but to understand. Toleration does not require active engagement with the other. It makes no inroads on mutual ignorance. In a world in which religious differences historically have been manipulated to burn bridges between communities, recognition and understanding of religious differences require us to enter into knowledgeable dialogue with one another, even in the face of major disagreements. A morally and spiritually earnest search for common undertakings within our particular religious traditions can lead the way for society as a whole. Religious pluralism can function as a working paradigm for a democratic, social pluralism in which people of diverse religious backgrounds are willing to form a community of global citizens.

The Koran presents religious pluralism as a divine mystery that must be accepted as a given to allow for smooth intercommunal relations in the public sphere. Moreover, it presents its theology of the other in the form of an ethical model in developing a workable paradigm for an ideal society.

In searching for the guidelines for religious pluralism, we must ask whether a faith community can accept the idea that other religions have intrinsic spiritual value. This is the most challenging aspect of one's religious commitment, because our readiness to allow for alternative responses to the presence of the Divine within our own community prepares us to allow for similar diversity in our social and political relationships with the other. It is not a matter of mere tolerance: it is a willingness to accept the other in the quest for the Divine. The essential point to consider is whether monotheists (*muwaḥḥidūn*)—Christians, Jews, and Muslims—are willing to recognize one another as spiritual equals, each entitled to his or her distinctive path to salvation. This religious recognition could become an essential building block of a democratic political order in which an ascendant group's commitment to pluralism not only will restrain them from persecuting the others but will even encourage a diversity of spiritual expression.

Religious pluralism, to recapitulate, means acknowledging the intrinsic redemptive value of competing religious traditions. It is natural, however, that beliefs and values essential to one faith will contravene those of others; herein lurks the potential for conflict and violence, if religious teachings are not articulated with the necessary acumen and practical wisdom in the political domain. Let us consider some of the antipluralist assumptions that are operative in faith communities.

"Only My Religion Is Genuine"

The common attitude among the religious groups is that there is only one true religion and that competing traditions are false and valueless. This antipluralist argument flies in the face of the reality of the diversity of human faiths. The antipluralist problem can be stated thus: a religion based on constitutive, redemptive, revealed truths cannot ascribe value to a religion that contradicts these truths. Thus, each religion sees itself as the only true religion and ascribes no value to the others. In other words, there is no room for religious pluralism.

What is the Koranic stance about this reality of religious plurality?

To begin with, the pluralism of human religions is underscored by the famous chapter of the Koran entitled "Unbelievers":

> Say: "O unbelievers, I serve not what you serve and you are not serving what I serve, nor am I serving what you have served, neither are you serving what I serve. To you your religion, and to me my religion!" (K. 109:1–5)

The preceding citation from the Koran is in the form of a propositional revelation, transmitted to humankind by means that transcend the ordinary course of nature. Although divine revelation, according to the Koran, can occur in various forms, revelation that is transmitted through language is necessarily propositional. A proposition is indicative of the purpose of the speaker in regard to a negative or positive attribution. Accordingly, its significance, like that of a declarative (*khabariyya*) statement that aims at confirming or denying the existence of a thing in accordance with its situation, consists of nothing but the utterances that are made up of the conceived signs. However, revelation also includes imperative (*'amr*) sentences that command obedience to divine commandments. Both indicative and imperative sentences in the revelation are propositional in the sense that they are asserted as an expression of God's will. God's will, according to the Koran, is the mover of human history. Nothing moves without God's will: "But will you shall not, unless God wills, the Lord of all Being" (K. 81:29). This multidimensional encounter with the living God in the Koran suggests that although the revelatory experience can be formulated in propositional language, open to belief or disbelief by human beings, what ultimately comes to be regarded as revelation by the community of the faithful is an individual experience of something believed in rather than stated as a creedal belief.

"Only My Religion Rests on Truths Received in Revelation"

What is the significance of revelation for a religion? Whether in the form of indicative or imperative formulations, revelation bears the truths that are constitutive of the religion. Constitutive revelations reveal the religious path, whereas instructive revelations bring those who have strayed back to the known straight path. In Judaism, the distinction between constitutive and instructive revelations is a sharp one, the former having been completed in the Torah given at Mount Sinai; anyone who claims to have received a constitutive revelation after the Torah is by definition a false prophet. Jesus as revelation or revelation given to Jesus constitute Christianity.[28]

In Islam, the constitutive revelation is not limited to Muḥammad. Other prophets have also been recipients of constitutive truths. Remarkably, the Koran proclaims that there is a constitutive element in religion that is given through revelation to all prophets:

> We have revealed to thee as We revealed to Noah, and the Prophets after him, and We revealed to Abraham, Ishmael, Isaac, Jacob, and the Tribes, Jesus and Job, Jonah and Aaron and Solomon, and We gave to David Psalms, and Messengers We have already told thee of before . . . Messengers bearing good tidings, and warning, so that humankind might have no argument against God, after the Messengers; God is All-mighty, All-wise. (K. 4:163)

In order that "humankind might have no argument against God," it is impossible that God should confer His revelatory truths upon one community while excluding others. God's truths must be available to everyone. If human beings are to apply constitutive principles in everyday life, then these axioms, although beyond the grasp of rational analysis, should be intuitively understandable. The revelatory truth, on the other hand, should serve only to delineate the conditions and methods of applying the constitutive principles. Thus, for example, the necessity of giving thanks to God, the Benefactor, is a matter of reason and serves as an axiom. The particular way of giving thanks—that is, the method and timing of prayers—is given by instructive revelation.

Again, the Koran underlines this understanding of the religious practice as given through revelation. According to this view, the truths of revelation in various religions do not stand in contradiction to one another:

> And to you [O Muhammad!] we have sent down the Book in truth as a confirmor of the Books [i.e., all revelations] that have come before it and as a protector over them. . . . For every one of you [Jews, Christians, Muslims], We have appointed a path and a way. If God had willed, He would have made you but one community; but that [He has not done in order that] He may try you in what has come to you. So compete with one another in good works; unto God shall you return all together; and He will tell you of that whereon you were at variance. (K. 5:48)

This recognition of different communities having their own laws is the Koran's recognition of the validity of the Jewish and Christian communities, even if the Muslim community remains the "ideal" or "best" community (*khayr ummatin*), the "median" community (*umma wasaṭa*).

"Only My Religion Possesses the Intrinsic Religious Value for Attaining Religious Perfection"

Such a belief denies the basis of pluralism. It asserts that intrinsic religious value—that is, the capacity to lead the believer to spiritual perfection, privately or publicly, in order to be saved—belongs uniquely to a single tradition. The question of the possibility of religious pluralism lies in the willingness of any religion to grant members of other religions an equal share in the world to come. Thus the acid test of pluralism is whether a religion is willing to recognize members of other religions as potential citizens in the world to come. Is such citizenship conferred *in spite* of or *because* of the person's membership in another religion?

The Koran addresses the question of the intrinsic value of other religions in the clearest terms by introducing the desired framework for human perfection in terms of "submission" (the literal sense of the word *islām*) to the living God. The famous verse which is today read as "*dīn*, in the eyes of God, is in truth *islām*" (K. 3:19) originally signified something closer to "to behave duly before God (*dīn*) is to surrender (*islām*) to Him."[29] This verse in no way suggests that other religions have no intrinsic value. If, according to the Koran, "those of the Jewry, and the Christians, and those Sabaens" who believe in God and the Last Day and live a godly life have a share in the world to come (K. 2:62), how can Muslims conclude that the sole path to the ultimate perfection, and hence, entitlement to salvation, is historical Islam with its beginnings in the seventh century? The righteous among the other monotheistic faiths will be included in the divinely ordained path of salvation *because of* and not *in spite of* their fealty to another religion that equally generates right conduct.

Elsewhere the Koran says, "Whoso desires another *dīn* than *islām*, it shall not be accepted of him; in the next world he shall be among the losers" (K. 3:85). This verse has been interpreted, in both historical and modern commentaries, as restricting salvation to Islam only. But this passage is not incongruous with Koranic pluralism. It simply asserts the Koranic vision of humanity surrendering to God. It certainly signifies the importance of "surrender" (*islām*); the translation should read as follows: "Whoso desires to behave in any other way than surrendering [to God], it shall not be accepted of him [by God], who will punish the individual by making him among the losers in the world to come."

That the word *islām* refers to the act of surrender rather than to the name of a specific religion in this verse is corroborated by the fact that two verses preceding K. 3:85 use forms of the verb *aslama* ("he submitted, surrendered") in the literal sense rather than in the technical sense as derivatives of the name Islam:

> What do they desire another *dīn* (way of conduct) than God's, and to Him has surrendered (*aslama*) whoso is in the heavens and the earth, willingly or unwillingly, and to Him they shall be returned?
>
> Say: 'We believe in God, and that which has been sent down to us, and sent down on Abraham and Ishmael, Isaac and Jacob, and the Tribes, and in that which was given to Moses and Jesus, and the Prophets, of their Lord; we make no distinction between any of them, and to Him we surrender (*muslimūn*).' (K. 3:83–84)

A number of Muslim commentators have used K. 3:85 to argue for the finality and supersession of Islam over all other religions, thereby pressing the case for intolerance. Ibn Kathīr, in support of such an exclusive interpretation, narrates the *ḥadīth*-report ascribed to the Prophet, who is reported to have said, "The [religious] deeds of any person, which are not in accordance with our way, are repudiated [by God]."[30]

Among modern commentators, Sayyid Quṭb, the leader of the Muslim Brotherhood in Egypt, captured the essence of the preferred interpretation among modern Muslims, which asserts unambiguously that the only religion worthy of human commitment is historical Islam, which is, according to him, "in all its comprehensiveness and inclusiveness of all the religions that came before it," the religion that must be accepted by all people. True Islam, he further asserts, is not only faith, worship, mystical feelings, and devotions. "All this would have no effect on the lives of human beings unless they are embodied in a social system in whose pure and bright framework humanity would live."[31]

But such antipluralistic conclusions flagrantly contradict the explicitly pluralistic passages of the Koran. To resolve these contradictions, Muslim scholars have resorted to the principle of abrogation in the Koran, claiming that certain tolerant injunctions toward the people of the Book and other nonbelievers were abrogated by the verses requiring Muslims to "slay them wherever you find them" (K. 4:89).

An Islamic Theology of Religions for the Twenty-First Century

I have tried to show the Islamic roots of democratic pluralism in the theology of the other in the Koran. To be sure, a theological assessment of the religious other and its place in the sphere of ethical public order is best sought through interreligious and intrareligious dialogue. Yet after all these centuries of striving, we still lack adequate intellectual tools for forging a theology of rapprochement between world religions. The prerequisite for interreligious discourse beyond the confines of the academy is stripping away the centuries of prejudice against the other that have accreted to the abhorrently exclusivist monotheistic religions. By offering the community of believers an interreligious hermeneutic based on the inherently pluralistic nature of the divine revelation, there is hope that we shall learn to understand and respect the other for what he or she is rather than for what he or she ought to be.

Such an inclusive discourse has to begin with a sincere and open-minded conversation or critical exchange—our engagement with one another. I do concede that rising ardor among some religionists about living a correct life based on a true religion—that is, their own tradition—has widened the gap between some religions. Such antipathies are easily fueled by a glut of superficial, lurid, and instantaneous media images of the cultural and religious other. The exclusivist tendencies propagated by religious extremists and ethnocentrists are gaining far wider currency "in the name of God."

But I want to go beyond the theology of interfaith relations to the theology of international relations for the twenty-first century.[32] I hope that we can unstiffen our prejudices and presuppositions and empower, enable, and equip one another, because we need to find a public space for religion without succumbing to the claims of exclusivity. As a Muslim scholar, I find that to talk about religion in general, and Islam in particular, is to talk about finding a proper space for human spirituality in the midst of growing suspicion about the goals of those who claim to offer a religious alternative to the present system of public order. How do we deal with the limits and constraints imposed by the claims of the sacred and yet still tap the universal possibilities for human agency that inhere in those claims?

Any serious dialogue between peoples of different religious traditions has to be anchored in their normative teachings, for it is, finally, revelatory guidance that governs the possibilities for an interreligious relationship between communities with different doctrinal traditions. As I have shown here, the tendency in the hermeneutic of these normative sources, which acknowledge the inherent reality of plurality in human response to divinity, is to limit salvation to those within their own creedal boundaries. This antipluralist valuation of those outside one's faith community steers the inter- or intrareligious relationship toward toleration at best or confrontation at worst, but seldom toward respect.

The treatment of the religious other in any tradition has far-reaching consequences for human relations. Although the overall record of Islam's relations with the other shows them to have been relatively just, its theological and juridical traditions have not always shown consistent fidelity to the Koranic attitude of parity regarding the spiritual destiny of non-Muslims. The selective and even political appropriation of the Koran in legitimizing a de facto hegemony over the other has led these works to overlook the human dimensions of theology. Muslim mystics like Ḥāfiẓ and Rūmī intervened to remind these scholars of the dos and don'ts in Islamic law and theology, to reawaken an awareness that "there are as many paths leading to God as there are human beings."

It is for this reason that my proposed theology calls for a new (although perhaps once conceived and now forgotten) vocabulary of inter- and intrareligious understanding. It is time to engage actively in deriving a new mode of religious thought from Islamic revelation, to foster the original pluralism of the Koran by taking into account the constantly changing realities of human life.

Hence, my proposed Islamic theology for human relations begins within the sacred boundaries of Islamic revelatory sources. The selective retrieval of these sources by various Muslim interest groups has demonstrated the importance of such sources in their vision of a public order dominated by Islam. More importantly, the political use and abuse of revelatory sources has led to the emerging reality of unfriendly relations between peoples of different religions living under Muslim domination.

The fundamental problem, as reflected in the classical formulation of Muslim political identity, is religious authoritarianism founded on an exclusive salvific claim, which runs contrary to the global spirit of democratization emerging through the acknowledgment of religious pluralism. At the very core of the emerging democratic pluralism is respect for the human rights of the religious and cultural other in Muslim societies. Since the beginning of this century, Muslim religious and social thinkers have wrestled with the issue of Islam's capacity to create a political society that would transcend the traditionally drawn boundaries between believers and nonbelievers and thus allow for human dignity to emerge as the sole criterion for social and political entitlement.

In formulating my response to the question, I reiterate the Koranic understanding of the connection between this world and the next. The Koran reminds us that we are all terrestrial beings. We must begin with the fact that we live on land and must labor to survive. A so-called materialist element is thus a necessary part of Islamic analysis about the role of religion in the new world order. In relating this material existence to faith in transcendence, we come face to face with our natural disposition, our *fiṭra*, that tells us that existence needs meaning. The struggle to endow material existence with meaning is the essential aspect of the religious faith of Islam.

From its emergence in the seventh century as a tradition in which a prophet is sent as a lawgiver and an organizer of the community to lead it to its meaningful existence, Islam has provided its followers with a vision. This vision has something to do with a possibility—a potential—in the public domain of human existence, the possibility of a worldwide community, an ideal polity that would shape a Muslim identity for citizens who actively submit to the will of God as members of a global community. It is primarily the possibility of appropriating the earth for creating a God-centered transnational and transcultural society that animates the Koranic vision of interpersonal and international relations.

Among world religions, Islam provides the sole coherent worldview of any political significance, and consequently it serves as the only vital external perspective on the modern project of a secular world order. It is, probably, the only thoroughgoing religious critique of the international public order with its secularist and liberal presuppositions.[33] Moreover, as a religious system that founded and determined the direction of one of the world's most influential and sustained civilizations, one with universal and rational presuppositions, Islam stands out as the only monotheistic tradition that can help to deepen the West's self-understanding in its liberal project of a public international order. Hence, to dismiss the Islamic conception of a moral and political public domain as antithetical to modern Western values of liberty and democracy is to ignore the opportunity to engage the Islamic understanding of the world of communities (*umam*, plural of *umma*) with like secular concerns.

I MUST RETRACE my steps to a God-centered public order in order to decode the Islamic endorsement of a plularistic human society. There is an optimistic assumption in the division of the world into the domains of faith and disbelief (*dār al-īmān* and *dār al-kufr*) in Islam.[34] It is founded upon extraordinary faith in the perfectibility of human beings. The only prerequisite for attaining that perfection is to "strive" (*jihād*) to "submit" (*islām*) to the inner intimations—the *fiṭra*—of natural religion.[35] By implanting in humanity a natural predisposition to acknowledge the lordship of the Creator, God has made humans capable of responding to their original state when they come into contact with revelatory guidance through the prophets. This is the primary language of the Koran through which God provides the essential divine-human and inter-human connection.

Chapter 3 will deal with the Koranic model of religious pluralism founded upon the original state (*fiṭra*). But in the context of my proposed theology for the twenty-first century, it is important to underscore the significance of the Koranic universal discourse that calls upon humanity to respond to its original nature based on the objective value of good and evil. It is this language that no human endowed with reason can fail to understand. More importantly, as a source of unification among the peoples of different religions, this language not only asserts the divine origin of moral cognition, but it also establishes the necessary connection and compatibility between moral and spiritual guidance. Hence, in its natural theology, Islam binds all of humanity to its natural predisposition not only to cognize the meaning of justice but also to will its realization. In this universal idiom of Islam, no human being, then, can claim ignorance of the ingrained sense of wrong and right; it follows that none can escape divine judgment of a failure to uphold justice on earth.

The Koranic theology of allowing the other to be other becomes a reality in the sphere of ethics, where the natural knowledge of good and evil makes injustice in any form inexcusable. No matter how religions might divide people, ethical discourse focuses on human relationships in building an ideal public order. I believe, therefore, that an Islamic theology of the twenty-first century must communicate beyond the language of a particular tradition. Human relationships at the horizontal level provide us with a framework for defining the religious or cultural other in terms of "us" and "them." Islamic self-identification as a process of self-understanding becomes accessible to the outsider through its conceptual description of the other.

Such a description of the other is situated in the realm of law, the realm of revelation-based religious and moral activity. Islamic law as an expression of the human endeavor to carry out the divine will on earth is actually identical to the belief that faith is an instrument of justice. When law and faith merge in an individual's life, they create a sense of security and integrity about the great responsibility of pursuing justice for its own sake. And when this sense of security and integrity is projected to the collective life of the community, it conduces to social harmony. Peace, then, is belief translated into action. It is not sufficient merely to believe in justice for peace to come about. Rather, peace is the outcome of justice maintained at each stage of interhuman relations. The separation of law and faith, on the other hand, results in the lack of commitment to justice that leads to chaos, violence, and even war. Hence, the Islamic prescription for avoiding carnage is to respond to God's revelation, which calls for sincere God-human and interhuman relations. In other words, submission to the will of God becomes a kind of conduit for the creation and maintenance of justice and equity on earth. Ultimately, the vision of international relations in Islam is firmly founded on the world community's sharing in a cross-cultural moral concern for egalitarianism, peace, and justice.

But the interaction between this faith and history has not fostered an interreligious vision of spiritual egalitarianism. In fact, part of the Muslim self-understanding has led to intolerance, even to the exclusion of the other from the divine-human relationship. Such an exclusivist theology can envision a global human community only under Islamic hegemony; Islamic tradition, so interpreted, becomes an instrument for the furthering of Muslim political and social power over other nations.

However, in a diverse international community, insistence on agreement on matters of belief as a precondition for lasting peace is highly problematic. The solution offered by secular liberal theory is that peace arises not from shared belief but from a system of government incorporating the principle of religious pluralism. International relations today are conducted without any reference to the substantive beliefs of the member nation-states. Whatever their irreconcilable differences in matters of faith, all states are legally bound to do their part in maintaining peaceful international relations. The resolution of conflicts does not require member states to uphold certain religious beliefs, nor does it mean that they do not or cannot share a vision of a future world community that is inspired by the belief in transcendence. The Abrahamic traditions in general, and Islam in particular, have much to contribute to a discourse about the desirability of a just community of nations.

It is here that Islam, with its vision for the future world community, needs to assess its resources realistically in order to offer such a framework for a viable international community. I have expressly used *community* rather than *order*, which I believe to be the consequence of such a global project.

As a Muslim educated both in the traditional *madrasa* (seminary) and the modern secular university, I face the unique opportunity and special responsibility of taking up the challenge of a self-critical assessment of current Muslim thought and practice—hence my proposal to mine the riches of the Koran to forge a theology of the other for the twenty-first century.

I will deal with two inadequacies in current Muslim thought that have implications for contemporary political and social theology. First, I will address the issue of the failure to assess honestly the impact of history on the development of the normative Muslim tradition. Second, I will discuss the lack of empirical observation in assessing the normative Muslim tradition as a source of social ethics.

The Muslim understanding of its normative tradition must reckon with the interplay of history and faith as a groundwork for interpersonal and intrapersonal ethical reflection. Only in this way can it possibly fulfill its responsibilities. Human relationships, the subject matter of ethical reflection, are characterized by Islam as modes of responsibility that require us to answer various demands made upon us. Muslim thinkers, as I see it, have a twofold responsibility in social ethics in the context of the pluralistic contemporary society.

The first responsibility is to the Islamic tradition itself. As Muslims continue to search for solutions to the problems of daily life in a world where universal human values have fragmented under the impact of power politics, they are obliged to come to grips with the ordinary discourse of the Koran, which is intensely human and serves as a social context for the revelation. It is important to understand the historical unfolding of the Koran as a whole before trying to interpret isolated passages that deal with the concrete events faced by the early generation of Muslims.[36] If this revelation was meant as a permanent guide for humanity, then it must be adaptable to changing conditions of life and the attendant shifts in values. Islamic fundamentalism[37] in its extreme contemporary forms, even Sunnī-Shīʿī conservatism, is merely an attempt to cling to the safety of the past, not a meaningful project for facing the future.

The time has come for a fresh start from the points in normative tradition where the system of Islamic law makes extensive use of judgments of equity (*istiḥsān*) and public interest (*maṣlaḥa*) for the common good and where ethical theology encourages human reasoned judgments of right and wrong. The task is formidable. It requires Muslim thinkers who can prod believers to go beyond the normative community to foster a cross-cultural discourse in which the Islamic tradition, along with Christianity and Judaism, provides a credible voice of guidance, not governance.

The second responsibility is to the Muslim peoples. There can be no Islam without Muslims. Responsibility to one is responsibility to the other. As a member of the community, a Muslim thinker shares not only a historical connection with it; he or she also carries the greater responsibility of sharing his or her knowledge about Islam. In fact, one's training in the religious sciences renders one a link in the transmission of the revelation, which has become routinized through centuries of hermeneutical involution. As a scholarly link between the beliefs and practices of the past and those of the present, one is obliged to actively engage the primary expository sources of revelation, utilizing traditional as well as new investigative procedures for uncovering the relevance of Islam for this generation.

Unfortunately, this critical task has suffered an irreparable setback in the hands of the traditionalist religious establishment in the Muslim world. Traditionalists warn that aping the epistemology and investigative procedures of Western academia might lead to the kind of faithlessness that dominates, for instance, similar studies of Judaism and Christianity. The question arises, Does not application of modern methods of investigating religious truth neutralize the normative claims of Islamic tradition?

It is important for Muslims to recognize that in designating the Koran as essentially immutable and continuously transmitted (*mutawātir*), the normative tradition presupposes the intact and authentic transmission of religious data. The agents of transmission being human, this process is an active one, compounded of imaginative interpretation, implementation, and even supplementation, which are all legitimate and creative human modalities of the acceptance of the Koran as the word of God. The Koran remains in the hands of humans who have to decide how to make it relevant to their moral-spiritual existence at a given time and place in history. In the past, Muslims differed on many issues and could not resolve their differences by simple reference to the passages of the Koran without taking into account the extensive literature that grew out of intellectual engagement with the revelation. And today there is no guarantee that a shared belief in the immutability and completeness of the Koran would eliminate differences without earnest interpretive endeavors that incorporate the wisdom of our cumulative experience of earthly life. I do not underestimate the ability of some people to abuse the powerful text of the Koran to justify their ends. And, yet, for fear of just such abuse, I cannot deny the Koran its original purpose as a revelation from God for the guidance of humanity at all times.

The responsibility to the Muslim community with whom the thinker lives and works cannot be reduced to analyzing the interrelatedness of human conditions and offering the solutions sought from the normative sources. The political and social reality of the Muslim world provides the critical empirical data needed to assess the relevance of normative tradition to actual life situations.

The purpose of revelation is to serve humankind. Accordingly, the Koranic valuation of human beings is not limited to honoring humankind as the vicegerent of God. It is about believing in the abilities and potential of humankind, the value of time, the authority of the human mind in pursuing the truth, and the future of humankind. Critical evaluation of inequalities between men and women, of the degradation of human resources, and of the disregard for human experience provides the Muslim thinker with an opportunity to restate human values in an Islamic context and to restore the balance with other considerations such as national interests, priorities, and traditions.[38]

A search for answers to the questions raised throughout this chapter has to begin with an understanding of how faith relates itself to history and how the normative tradition interacts with human conditions. The early paradigm cases in the Islamic juridical corpus that deal with Muslim-other relations were arrived at through a heightened sense of realism in assessing the relative social and political milieu and its ramifications for Muslim power. The laws were stated in general terms with a view to revising or correcting ethical-legal judgments in the face of specific contingencies. Muslim jurists demonstrated a strong appreciation of diversity and practicality and an awareness of the need to interpret the normative documentation in reaching decisions about the treatment of religious minorities in Muslim society. They also understood the need to modify the generality and rigor of the legal contents of the Koran and the tradition to cope with the novel circumstances created by the vast territorial gains of the first two centuries of the political history of Islam. Christian-Muslim relations provide an unusually clear picture of the evolution of the virtue of this approach. To understand how Muslim jurists formulated judicial decisions affecting interreligious relations, we turn to the work of the jurist-historian Ṭabarī: *Kitāb ikhtilāf al-fuqahā᾿* (Differences of opinion among the jurists),[39] especially the section dealing with *Kitāb al-jihād wa kitāb al-jizya wa aḥkām al-muḥāribīn* (on *jihād* and tribute and the rulings regarding enemies). The book is pluralistic in its opinions about the treatment of the peoples of the Book. The author provides his readers with a rare insight into the workings of faith-history and faith-power relationships among the major legal scholars of the classical period (ninth and tenth centuries). The subsequent rulings and the reasoning behind them convey the religious justifications for hostilities against all the peoples of the world living in the sphere of war (*dār al-ḥarb*), that is, people who had yet not accepted Islam. More importantly, these rulings are not merely the jurists' statements of acts required by the Sharīʿa, but they also reveal the jurists' religious commitments, desires, hopes, and fears in dealing with non-Muslims.

The section opens with a citation of the following two verses of the Koran, which serve as a preamble to the discussion of *jihād* by various jurists:

> For We have written in the Psalms, after the Remembrance, "The earth shall be the inheritance of My righteous servants." Surely this is a Message delivered unto a people who serve. We have not sent thee, save as a mercy unto all beings. (K. 21:105–107)

> We have sent thee not, except to mankind entire, good tidings to bear, and warning; but most men do not know it. (K. 34:27)

Although there is no explicit mention of *jihād* against nonbelievers in the passages, they serve as the theological justification for territorial expansion of Muslim political power. These rulings, cited on the authority of major early jurists, judge issues of warfare against unbelievers and the people of the Book, who should submit to Muslim political dominance. Muslim jurists, as Ṭabarī informs us, did not make it a precondition for the non-Muslims among the monotheists to convert to Islam to avoid outright warfare. There was a tacit endorsement of the Koran's recognition of the salvific efficacy of the other religions of the Book, although unbelievers other than monotheists had to accept Islam to avoid bloodshed.

But this tolerant attitude toward other monotheists, including the people of the Book, was maintained only so long as they did not pose a threat to the Muslim community. When Muslim and Christian armies faced each other, the justification for engaging in warfare against the people of the Book had to be sought by means of the principle of abrogation of pluralistic rulings in the Koran. According to the jurists, the tolerant verses are abrogated by the Sword Verse (K. 9:29) that ordains warfare against the people of the Book.

There is unanimous agreement among scholars, says Ṭabarī, that those who paid tribute (*jizya*), as required by the Sword Verse, were the nonbelievers among the two peoples of the Book, namely, the followers of the *Tawrāt* and *Injīl*—Jews and Christians. Moreover, it was also permissible to collect tribute from a person before he submitted to Muslim authority while he was unable to protect himself. Tribute could also be collected from his companions among Arab idol worshippers, who were in the sphere of war (*dār al-ḥarb*) and who, through this member of the people of the Book, had asked to remain in their ancestral religion. Nevertheless, even under those conditions, Islamic laws were applicable to them. The Imam, as the political leader of the community, had the right to agree to collect tribute from a member of the people of the Book and allow him to remain in his religion, that is, Judaism or Christianity. The paradigm case for the derivation of this ruling, as Ṭabarī points out, is the practice of the Prophet, who himself used to collect tribute from the Zoroastrians.[40]

However, there was a different opinion concerning acceptability of tribute from non-Arab idol worshippers short of their conversion to Islam. According to Mālik, it was proper to accept tribute from Arabs if they belonged to the people of the Book. Moreover, it was permissible to accept tribute from non-Arabs, whether or not they belonged to the people of the Book, and even if they were idol worshippers.

In contrast, Shāfiʿī ruled that if someone's parents did not belong to the people of the Book (that is, any book that was revealed before the Koran was revealed), but that person was opposed to the religion of the idolaters as practiced before the Koran was revealed, he was not to be regarded as an idol worshipper.[41] In such cases it was up to the Imam to accept the offered tribute of the humbled one, whether he was an Arab or not.

However, if there was anyone, Arab or non-Arab, who was introduced to Islam when he was not one of the peoples of the Book, and he made an offer to the Imam to pay the tribute in return for permission to remain in his religion, then it was not permissible for the Imam to accept that offer. Rather, the Imam was obliged to fight him until he surrendered, just as he was required to fight idol worshippers (*ahl al-awthān*) until they surrendered.

If the Muslims fought those about whose religious affiliation they had no information, and who claimed to belong to the people of the Book, Muslims had to ask them when they and their ancestors accepted that religion. If they said it was before the Koran was revealed to the Prophet, the Muslims were required to accept their statement and allow them to remain in their ancestral religion. But if Muslims suspected that what they were saying was not true and could establish proper evidence to that effect, then Muslims had to spurn the tribute and challenge them to surrender or to fight.

The contextual analysis of these randomly selected rulings regulating Muslim-other relations under Muslim political dominance helps us to determine the effective causes (*ʿilal*) behind these jurists' opinions. Any rash application of these ordinances today without first discovering the purpose of the Lawgiver and ascertaining the objective situational or circumstantial aspects (*mawḍūʿāt*) of the rulings could lead to a faulty assessment of the changed circumstances of Muslim power. Moreover, in order to propose a fresh interpretation of the Koranic theology of interreligious relations, Muslims would have to face squarely the implications of a public international order in which Muslim countries share equal membership with non-Muslim nation-states. In other words, past juridical decisions have become irrelevant in the modern system of international relations, and they are thus unable to shed light on the pressing task of recognizing religious pluralism as a cornerstone of interhuman relations.

Religious Pluralism as a Divinely Ordained System

There is little doubt that the rulings regulating interreligious relations in the classical juridical texts cannot be mechanically applied to today's far different circumstances. The major problem facing jurists today is a confrontation between the hegemonic values of the past and the emerging reality of political conditions that challenge the applicability of those values. Although scholarly analysis reveals the extent to which so-called definitive precedents were actually conditioned by time and place, Muslim fundamentalists today reject any hint that the juridical decisions hinged on culturally or historically contingent circumstances. In other words, they refuse to acknowledge that while the Koran is a fixed text, the interpretive applications of its revelations can vary with the changing realities of history.

Islamic traditionalists maintain that Islamic law, as it was formulated by the jurists in the first three centuries of Muslim power, was in strict conformity with the divine will expressed in the Koran and the Tradition; their belief in a transhistorical, immutable law of God is blind to the interplay of culture, history, and faith. The human need for a truly ideal government can hardly be fulfilled if particular political practices of the past cannot be modified to bring them in line with the mores of the present.

This reinterpretive task is an internal one, requiring conscientious, intelligent Muslims themselves to undertake the decodification of the juridical corpus. It is Muslims themselves who must muster the moral and spiritual resources needed to uncover the relevant aspects of their tradition through a creative reappropriation of juridical sources now monopolized by the exclusivists. Without such an academic agenda, Islam, despite its vein of rich, pluralistic principles, cannot offer an alternative that would abide with otherness.

The Koran's pluralistic theology of the other does view interfaith relations as a divinely ordained system of human coexistence. Its narrative of sacred history is genuinely inclusive, starting with the first human couple, who inaugurate the human journey toward the creation of an ideal society on earth: "Humankind, be aware of your duties to Your Lord, who created you from a single soul, and from it created its mate, and from the pair of them scattered abroad many men and women" (K. 4:1). But that universal narrative that emphasized the common destiny of humanity was severed from its universal roots by the restrictive Islamic conception of a political order based on the membership of only those who accepted the divine revelation to Muḥammad. As this exclusivist community gained control of its public order and directed its political and military might in order to secure its dominance beyond the sphere of faith (*dār al-īmān*) to create the sphere of submission (*dār al-islām*, territories administered by the Muslim state), the jurists formulated the rulings legitimizing Muslim dominance, if not necessarily the ascendancy of the Islamic faith, over the world.

Undoubtedly, this tension between the pluralist and exclusivist strains of Islam can be resolved only through the reexamination of the specific contexts of the rulings, the ways in which they were conditioned by the beliefs, desires, hopes, and fears of that classical age, so that we might compare them with our contemporary issues and reapply them with a refreshed historical perspective.

The Crisis of the Fundamentalist Approach to Religious Pluralism

As someone with a firsthand acquaintance with religious fundamentalism and its impact upon interfaith relations in various parts of the Muslim world, I am not presuming to pass wholesale dismissive judgment on the supposed excesses of fundamentalist jurisprudence, an exercise usually undertaken by journalists and academics who lack any direct contact with the leadership of the movements and their supporters in the areas under consideration. My task, rather, is a constructive one: to interpret and elicit from tradition a religiously justified theology of the other, remaining mindful of the intensity with which religious identity is negotiated in the reality of today's Muslim world. In so doing, I have attempted to seek clarification of key elements of the prevailing frames of reference in Islamic fundamentalism, religious or otherwise, keeping in mind for now that it is only the fundamentalist form of Islam that claims to offer an alternative to secular ideologies.

The core of Islamic fundamentalism is a religious idealism that promises its adherents that once the Islamic norm prevails, it will dramatically sweep away the manifold social, political, and moral problems afflicting the Muslim peoples. Pristine Islamic revelation, stoking the righteous zeal of dedication in the faithful, becomes the key to create an ideal ethical order on earth.

Although I have elsewhere indicated the difficulties connected with adopting the term *fundamentalism* for Muslim religious nationalism, I have retained it in this study simply because it accomplishes the task of conveying to American readers the temperament of religious ascendancy among Muslims. In fact, the term means something very different as applied to the Muslim community than it means in relation to conservative American Protestants, who openly declare their intention of turning back to the "fundamentals" of their religion. It is difficult to find an equivalent for *fundamentalism* in any Islamic language that conveys a similar Muslim concern in modern times. Thus, Arabic newspapers, when translating articles from the Western media, have from time to time employed the term *uṣūliyyūn* as a literal translation of the term *fundamentalists*. The inadequacy of the word *uṣūliyyūn* became evident when it was discovered that the term has a long history in Islamic theological and juridical writings and carries a positive connotation in Islamic intellectual tradition. Hence, the terms *mutashaddidūn*, meaning 'bigots,' or *mutaṭarrifūn*, meaning 'radicals' or 'extremists,' were substituted for *uṣūliyyun* to communicate the pejorative thrust of the Western usage of the term.

Similarly, Persian has coined the term *bonyadgarā* (*bonyād* = 'fundament,' *garā* = 'inclined to') to relate the meaning of *fundamentalist*, because the term *uṣūlī* in the Iranian Shīʿī intellectual history has a distinct connotation that is quite the opposite of the literalism of Christian fundamentalists. However, *bonyadgarā* is a recent introduction in the Iranian sociopolitical lexicon and consequently is inadequate to convey the pejorative sense of the Western usage of the term. Moreover, the overt use of a more familiar term like *murtajiʿīn* to describe the 'reactionary,' 'backward-looking' attitude among religious-minded people in the Iranian cultural context is both inaccurate as an equivalent of *fundamentalists* and provocative in the Islamic Republic, where a hostile attitude to the religious establishment in general is expressed by giving it the appellation of *ṭabaqa-yi murtajiʿ*, that is, 'the reactionary class.'

At any rate, the difficulty of finding a precise equivalent in the Islamic languages should not deter us from applying the term *fundamentalist* to Muslims, because attitudes similar to those found among other religious groups called fundamentalist are characteristic of many activist Muslims as well. Certainly, if religious fundamentalism is used to describe "disparate movements of religiously inspired reaction to aspects of global processes of modernization and secularization in the twentieth century,"[42] then it is also possible to speak about a form of Islamic fundamentalism. Compared to other loaded terms like *conservative* and *traditionalist*, which have also been used to describe these religious movements, I find the use of *fundamentalist* a far more intelligible designation for "all religiously motivated individuals [in the modern age], drawn together into ideologically structured groups, for the purpose of promoting a vision of divine restoration."[43]

Accordingly, we must turn our attention to the "historical development in Islam with the hegemony of the West during the past century and a half which has given rise to the religious fundamentalism among Muslims in the modern age."[44] Muslim fundamentalism stems from the acute awareness of a disparity between the divine promise of success for the believers of Islam and the historical development of the world controlled by the nonbelievers.[45] To counter the spiritual crisis engendered by this awareness, Islamic fundamentalism has adopted a twofold strategy: first, introducing social and political reforms to prevent a further internal deterioration of Islamic religious life; and second, resisting alien cultural and intellectual influences in Muslim societies.

The first track, internal reform, typically features the repeated call to return to the original teachings of Islam in the Koran and the Prophet's exemplary life preserved in the Tradition. The response to the corruption and heedlessness among contemporary Muslims firmly asserts that the earthly power and success of the first generation of Muslims were due to their strict adherence to the pure faith, the fundamentals of Islam. Consequently, if the Muslims want to regain their early preeminence, they must revert to that ancient purity of practice in all areas of life, including governance. This puritanical religious fundamentalism has a considerable following among numerous sectors of the Muslim Brotherhood all over the Islamic world.

The second strategy of resistance has been far more challenging, for it has meant reverting to Islamic fundamentals in the face of sociopolitical systems and legal codes that have been imported or externally imposed over the past century and a half. However, this embrace of Islamic fundamentals is based on the acceptance of the notion of development of an Islamic society in a linear progression. As such, there is a selective retrieval of only the relevant teachings that would promote the building of an Islamic system adaptable to modern circumstances. In other words, this is an activist fundamentalism involving a creative interpretation of religious ideas and symbols to render them applicable to contemporary Muslim history.

The rise of fundamentalism during the Gulf Crisis of 1990–91 revealed an internal crisis in the entire Islamic world in response to the attempt by Saddam Hussein, a secular leader, to tap the enormous power that religion exercises over the minds of Muslims. He elicited fervent approval on the streets of the Muslim world; as far away as China and Madagascar, special prayers were held in the mosques for Saddam's supposedly Islamic victory over the "Crusaders" of the twentieth century. Clearly, Saddam's Ba'thist ideology is both socialist and secular, and he was known for his oppressive measures against religious groups, including the Muslim Brotherhood in Iraq. Nonetheless, Saddam cannily transformed himself into a Muslim hero in many Arab-Muslim circles by pandering to their long-simmering outrage over Western and U.S. policies perceived as anti-Islamic, especially the Palestinian problem, and to the unease that the umma felt because of the presence of non-Muslim soldiers in the Arabian peninsula. Fundamentalists recognized the potential for transforming this profound sense of injustice into enhanced political power. In so doing, they made tactical compromises with those in power, including the secularists, sometimes at the expense of their vision of presenting Islam as the only alternative to imported secular ideologies.

As the conflict of 1990–91 unfolded, many feared disastrous consequences for the entire region. I turned my attention to the universal discourse of Islam, which at different times in history has engendered a commitment to uphold justice and maintain peace in a pluralistic Muslim society. However, as the crisis dragged on, it became evident that in view of the human obstinacy and pettiness so aptly described in the Koran (K. 70:19–21), the universal message of Islam to "submit to God" in order to live in peace and security was almost forgotten.

The word *Islam* has, throughout history, been a vehicle for men of heavenly purpose as well as for men of earthly power, its meanings skewed to suit now one agenda and now another, irrespective of the enduring truths and standards set forth in Islamic theology. Beneath the surface of the debates about Islam and the Islamic underpinnings of a just public order, political struggles rage in cynical indifference to the Islamic tradition of just conflict resolution as set out in the Koran and in the Tradition.

In response to the crisis created by the Gulf War, many religious scholars, instead of looking for the relevance and applicability of those Islamic sources that promote tolerance in a traditionally pluralistic "culture of argument," one based on personal interpretation (*ijtihād*) of the Islamic legal sources, dusted off juridical decisions in the sections on *Kitāb al-jihād* (classical rulings on warfare), which were intended to deal with the treatment of the people of the Book when Muslim powers were at war with Christendom.

Even with the challenges confronting Muslim societies obliged to adjust to the vicissitudes of the modern nation-state, the Islamic religious leadership never undertook the intellectual challenge of elaborating the relevance and applicability of their adopted slogan, "Islam is the solution" (*al-islam huwa al- ḥall*).

Several movements in the recent history of Islam have claimed to be the best representatives of the Islamic solution. One example is Ḥizb al-Taḥrīr, which came into existence in Jerusalem in 1952 under the leadership of Shaykh Taqiyuddin al-Nabahānī. In its manifesto, "Ḥizb al-Taḥrīr's Method of Implementing Change" (*Manhaj ḥizb al-taḥrīr fī al-taghyīr*), he outlines three stages of implementing Islam in the modern nation-state. The first stage is identified as the "phase of informing people," during which the recruitment of believers to the objectives of the party takes place by educating them about these Islamic goals. The second stage prepares the members to interact with the nation and promote the adoption of the party's principles to set up an Islamic order as the entire nation's cause. In the final stage, the party would assume power and would implement Islam comprehensively in all spheres of national life. The manifesto goes to great lengths to define the universal goals of the sphere of Islam (*dār al-islām*) against the background of the classical formulation of this juristic concept. However, there is no systematic theoretical or conceptual exposition of the means of applying the classical Islamic legal heritage to the context of a modern, pluralistic nation-state situated in a diverse international order.

It is ironic that many Muslim scholars have fallen prey to the standards of cultural relativism in dealing with their Islamic heritage and have neglected to investigate the universal ethical presuppositions of the legal doctrines that could provide rational, ethical rules to govern modern societies, both Muslim and non-Muslim. Fundamentalist religious discourse, as a consequence, has turned into a unidimensional analysis of issues from the position of control rather than of power sharing. It assumes the existence of the other in the manner of the de facto Muslim governments whose legitimacy depended upon maintaining the status quo of the traditionalist ulema.

In dealing with conflicts like the Gulf War or that over the Palestinian question, it is important to emphasize the fact that at times, sincere religious convictions based on the attitude of the believer (believe that) rather than the truth of the thing believed (believe in) have led to the intensification of the conflicts. In some Muslim states, it is not uncommon for government officials to find religious justifications for policies that curb the universal rights of individuals, both Muslims and non-Muslims. Undoubtedly, such policies need to be examined in the light of Islamic jurisprudence, so that rationally deduced principles drawn from the divine revelation in the Koran can be connected to the core values and principles of contemporary Islam. It is only through investigations that seek the true reasons for these conflicts, the ways in which they serve the interests of powerful, that Islamic scholars contribute to their peaceful resolution. Islamic revelation conditions the resolution of conflicts on removing all the underlying infringements of the moral and religious rights of the people. The Koran's approach to conflict resolution stresses the need to restore violated justice:

> If two parties of believers fight one another, then make peace between them (*fa-ṣliḥū baynahum*) [by removing all the causes of conflict]; then, if one party of believers transgresses against another, [selfishly violating their rights,] then fight the transgressors until they obey once more God's commandment. Then, when the transgressors have submitted [their will once more to His], make peace between them with fairness and justice (*bi-l-ʿadl*), and act equitably (*w-aqsiṭū*) [so that the rights of neither party are violated]. Lo! God loves the equitable. (K. 49:9)

It is important to emphasize that in this passage the word for 'making peace' is the verbal form *aṣlaḥa*, that is, 'putting in order, restoring, making amends.' The Koran emphasizes that no lasting peace can be established without eliminating the causes of conflict, the violations of justice and equity. Considering the universal and absolute nature of the moral categories of "justice" and "equity" in this passage, it can be inferred that the Koranic prescription for conflict resolution is not limited to believers only. Rather, it conveys a universal significance and application by demanding that the peace between the conflicting parties be restored by their acting justly and equitably toward each other. "For surely, God loves the equitable."

The Koranic concern for an ethical public order based on justice is not merely the divine prescription for resolving conflicts in the family of Islam; its relevance to the wider context of the modern international order bears scrutiny as well.

This broader, internationalist application of Koranic prescription is the function of Muslim jurists (the ulema, the *faqīh*) who, by means of the conceptual and theoretical devices developed in Islamic legal theory, can undertake to make specific, contextual Koranic prescriptions for the advancement of peaceful coexistence among the nations. A serious elaboration and expansion of the legal foundation of Islamic jurisprudence can provide a practical religious approach to resolving international tensions.

The contemporary religious establishment in the Muslim world has, however, failed to recognize the impact of complex ethnic, economic, political, and social relationships in intercommunity conflicts. Such a recognition could direct a rigorous elaboration of Islamic ethical and legal principles in the interests of better governance. The Islamic tradition can shape legal models within the framework of international norms without subserving the political agendas of a specific government. While seeking to retrieve the universal norms of justice and equity from traditional revelation, Islamic legal thought must at the same time be flexible enough to explore a cautious and selective cultural relativism in the politically and historically mutable environment of international relations.

In order for the Muslim community to organize its affairs in the modern world by means of the tradition that promoted rational progress in the premodern age, its scholars must rehabilitate the rational methodology for deducing broader principles and their application. The irony is that the leadership of the fundamentalist movements never undertook the intellectual challenge of defining and elaborating the relevance and applicability of the system underlying their elected slogan, "Islam is the solution." According to the leading ideologue of the Muslim fundamentalists, Yūsuf al-Qaraḍāwī, the slogan signifies that "Islam is both the orienting maxim and the guide for the community in all areas of life, material as well as intellectual. 'Islamic solution' means that the entirety of life is molded into a fundamentally Islamic form and character." As such, each movement claims to be the best representative of the Islamic solution.

Each Islamic movement, however small, while disagreeing on the means of providing the solution, agrees that the solution includes setting up an Islamic state, implementing of the Sharīʿa, and liberating Arab/Muslim territories from unjust occupation. Yet the slogan adopted by the Muslim Brotherhood and other Islamic movements is in the service of the more pedestrian and pragmatic undertaking of campaigning for seats in parliament in Jordan. And, as might have been expected in the circumstances of 1990, the candidates were greeted with characteristic zeal and enthusiasm. But there was very little effort made to face squarely the difficult task of formulating the comprehensive ideology of a modern Islamic nation-state. "Islam is the solution" has evolved into an empty slogan used to exploit the political passions engendered by the Gulf War in order to harness popular support for political gain.

THE ABSENCE OF this intellectual undertaking is evident in the scholarly essays published during the Gulf Crisis by the leaders of the Muslim Brotherhood in the Sunnī-Arab world, including Muḥammad al-Ghazālī, Ḥasan al-Turābī, Rashīd al-Ghannūshī, and others, under the title *al-Ṣaḥwat al-islāmiyya: Ru'yat naqdiyya min al-dākhil* (The Islamic awakening: A critical examination from within). These essays point to what Alasdair MacIntyre has characterized as the "epistemological crisis" in a tradition that was at one time able to provide rational solutions to the problems faced by its adherents. Contemporary Islamic ideology is going through an epistemological crisis that must be addressed from within by Muslim intellectuals. One of the most unfortunate signs of the contemporary malaise of the Islamic world is that intellectual authorities have all but disappeared from the scene, leaving the field of legal interpretation to Muslim jurists whose chief qualities are their narrow-mindedness, lack of depth, and one-dimensionality.

Let us consider the "epistemological thesis" implicit in the Muslim fundamentalist slogan. The major proposition of the thesis is that Islam, unlike other monotheistic religions, is not concerned merely with humanity's spiritual salvation, but is also concerned with how it should live in the here and now and how—and to what end—it should organize its social, political, economical, and cultural life. In fact, throughout history, Islam has addressed itself to these concerns. After all, Islam from the outset faced challenges that obliged it to combine spiritual with nonspiritual concerns. The problem arises when these historical necessities are used to justify contemporary political policies. It is at that point that religious leaders need to establish a connection between Islam and worldly concerns that is more than historical. In other words, they need to establish rationally that the true nature of Islam embraces a comprehensive system of ideas and principles touching on all matters that are of importance for a human being's spiritual and mundane existence.

However, as most of the Sunnī fundamentalist leaders would argue, human beings are not in a position to know the right way to organize their worldly affairs without divine guidance from Islamic revelation: the Koran and the Tradition. In other words, Islamic fundamentalists believe that a godless secularization, oblivious to God's commands in matters of daily living, cannot succeed in creating the ideal world order.

Thus, the antisecular stance of the Muslim fundamentalists is a matter of epistemology as well as of religion; according to Yūsuf al-Qaraḍāwī and other fundamentalist ideologues, if Muslims fail to organize their worldly affairs in accordance with Islamic principles based on the revealed knowledge of the Prophet, they will not be appropriately positioned, epistemically, to give correct answers to questions pertaining to how they ought to organize their worldly affairs. They argue that in practice it is not possible for human beings to know how to organize their worldly affairs unaided by the divine revelation.

In view of this fundamentalist thesis, human reason is an insufficient foundation on which to build practical knowledge about the just organization of the Islamic public order. At the same time, Muslim fundamentalists have not proffered an objective evaluation of how rational decisions were achieved in applying Islamic norms during the glory days of Islam's past. Consequently, in the absence of religiously founded practical knowledge about realizing normative ends through worldly means, the Islamic tradition is faced with an epistemological crisis. By its own standards, the Islamic tradition has ceased to progress. Both the methods of inquiry and the forms of argument have disclosed inadequacies that have shaken confidence in the tradition's capacity to furnish solutions to the concrete problems faced by individuals and groups in contemporary social and political contexts.

The severity of this epistemological crisis in Islam is evident in the literature that attempted to address it in the early 1980s. With the victory of the Iranian revolution, Muslim fundamentalists everywhere witnessed the unfolding of the modern Islamic state (even in its Shīʿite, particularistic form), with its commitment to implement the Islamic legal and moral norms in its sociopolitical and economic organization; in this period, Ḥasan al-Turābī, a leading legal scholar trained in both the modern Western and Islamic legal traditions, wrote *Tajdīd usūl al-fiqh al-islāmī* (The revitalization of Islamic legal theory). In this extremely important booklet, Turābī's message to his fellow Muslim legal scholars was that if Islamic revelation hoped to once again become relevant in directing the community in all its mundane and spiritual affairs, it had to restore the primacy of the juridical method of deducing new rulings by developing an expansive application of analogical deduction (*al-qiyās al-wāsiʿ*), independent reasoning (*al-ijtihād*), and other such rational devices formulated in classical juristic theory. Even more to the point is his appeal to expand the usage of a rationally inferred principle of juristic practice known as *istiṣḥāb*. *Istiṣḥāb* is the process of seeking a link between an earlier and a later set of circumstances. In applied jurisprudence, this method has enabled jurists to establish the validity of existing practice by linking it to the idea of continuity with the past. In other words, the emergence of a new religious-legal system need not seek to destroy the already established conventions and customs of a given region; rather, its function is restoring justice by seeking the link between that which is desirable in the present and that which is worth retaining from the past.

Turābī's arguments are built on the absolute and universal nature of moral values like justice, equity, fairness, and so on, as established in the pure conscience of humanity. Significantly, Turābī takes up the question of the extent to which the modern Muslim jurist can rely on the legal theory of the classical age, with its limited scope and strategy, to deduce laws that are relevant to the politics and economy of a modern Muslim polity. In the final analysis, according to Turābī, the main problem that has hindered progress in accomplishing the goals of the Islamic movement in the last few decades is the lack of further development of classical legal methodology in the context of modernization.

In another work, *al-Ḥarakat al-islāmiyya wa al-taḥdīth* (The Islamic movement and modernization), also published in 1980, Turābī and his coauthor, Rashīd al-Ghannūshī, attempt to show the compatibility of Islam with modernization, arguing that what is true of Islam as a matter of historical fact is also true of it as a matter of logic. Consequently, Muslim scholars should realize that there are no obstacles to deriving conclusions from rational and religious premises—religious knowledge does not defy reason. As any student of modern Islam can attest, such an epistemological thesis was propounded earlier in the century by Muslim reformers like Muḥammad ʿAbduh and Rashīd Riḍā, who never undertook to weigh the epistemological priority of reason versus revelation; they understood the difficulty of maintaining a substantive-normative function for reason in view of religion's primacy as a source of practical knowledge.

A decade has passed, and very little has been produced in the area of juristic methodology to face the concrete realities of modernity. Mere Islamization of existing secular political and socioeconomic institutions, as some Muslim intellectuals have realized, cannot alleviate the epistemological crisis. Ḥasan al-Turābī and other fundamentalist leaders have acknowledged that their search for Islamic solutions has increasingly disclosed the inability of the juridical tradition to provide forward movement in the creation of Islamic public order. But so far, no one has risen to the challenge of providing a systematic and coherent solution to the problem of the modern Islamic nation-state.

Such a momentous undertaking depends upon honest and critical examination of the current applicability of the inherited framework, theoretical and conceptual, of the Islamic juristic method. Without such an unsparing evaluation, it is impossible to create new methodological devices in Islamic legal theory, a field that is intrinsically connected to the theological fundaments of Islam. It is ironic that in the modern faculties of Sharīʿa in the Sunnī world, there is very little interest, among students or teachers, in the Islamic theological tradition as preserved in the works of *kalām*. In other words, they ignore the inherent connection between the divine purposes discussed in the theological works and the implementation of those purposes in applied jurisprudence, thereby hindering the development of what I have termed new theoretical and conceptual structures in the field of legal theory.

Did the Gulf War in 1990–91, like the Islamic revolution of Iran in 1978–79, render more urgent the need for such a new theoretical and conceptual foundation? Were the ideologues of the various forms of Islamic fundamentalism, thoroughly grounded in traditional Islamic learning but bereft of the tools needed to clear a path through the thickets of epistemology, in a position to deliver to the public what they have been promising all these years?

These are some of the major questions that have arisen in the last few decades. It is worth stating that political anti-Westernism has been one of the stumbling blocks that prevents the Muslim fundamentalists from recognizing the varied and fruitful relationships that have prevailed between Islamic religious and philosophical thought and other intellectual traditions, like Greek philosophy, relationships that contributed to the development of Islam's rational theology in the Classical Age. The fact is that Muslim fundamentalist ideologues regard religious knowledge, for them the exclusive fount of practical knowledge as certified by Islamic revelationary sources like the Koran and the Tradition, as entirely nonrational knowledge, consisting only of divinely ordained, immutable Islamic principles (Yūsuf al-Qaraḍāwī, *al-Ḥall al-islāmī farīḍa wa darūra*) of social and political organization, applicable irrespective of time and place. Presupposing that unaided human reason does not have any substantive-normative function and is incapable of determining its own good on its own, the fundamentalists hear only divine commands and turn a deaf ear to both the quiet pleadings of rational discourse and the unruly cries of diverse and often stubbornly perverse historical circumstances. Normative reason, even if compatible with God's commands, is deemed deficient and unreliable. If only revealed religious knowledge affords human beings direct contact with God's ordinances, reason is entirely superfluous in matters of religious practice.

So far, we have dealt with the Sunnī handling of the epistemological crisis; Shīʿite religious fundamentalism has followed its own theological and legal paths in resolving the epistemological crisis in Islamic tradition since the 1980s. Significantly, although Sunnī religious discourse from the pulpits on Fridays resorts to Shīʿī religious symbols of resistance and martyrdom, of the suffering and passion of the family of the Prophet, in dealing with the political crisis encountered by the community, there is usually no mention of the intellectual tradition of Shīʿite Islam in legal theory and the task undertaken by some leading Shīʿī scholars to "strike a balance between the divine promise of the earthly success and their contemporary situation."[46] Without the efforts of the Shīʿī scholarly elite in classical juristic theory and practice to impart the necessary guidance to believers by taking into account various contemporary sociopolitical factors that were important for the establishment of a modern Islamic nation-state, the scholars would not have been able to direct the creation of an Islamic public order. The Islamic alternative had to be taken more seriously if the multifarious problems faced by postrevolutionary Iran were to be solved with the confidence of the people. To its credit, the Shīʿite interpretation of the Islamic tradition gives a prominent place to the faculty of reasoning in discerning and applying the purposes of God.

The priority of reason in the Shīʿite fundamentalist epistemological outlook has never been denied; in Shīʿite rational theology, reason is regarded as prior to both sources of revelation, the Koran and the Tradition. More to the point, it is reason, through its interpretive project, that acknowledges the comprehensiveness of the revelation and discovers all the principles needed to create a viable public order. Nevertheless, Shīʿism has not been free of controversy over who is authorized to undertake this decisive responsibility of making the tradition relevant and applicable. This lively debate, which centers on the role of the traditional sources in discovering solutions for modern times, pits traditionalist scholars against modern scholars in Tehran. Yet, there is absolutely no reference to these debates or to any other scholarly discourse in the Sunnī Arab world. To the extent that the Ayatollah Khomeini is mentioned with admiration by the Muslim fundamentalists in the Arabic-Sunnī world, it is mainly due to his anti-Westernism, anti-Americanism, and antisecularism. His creative and sometimes daringly innovative conceptual structures like the "Governance of the Jurist" (*wilāyat al-faqīh*) or "the Absolute Nature of Juristic Authority" (*wilāyat al-muṭlaqa*), with their implications for the development of applied jurisprudence in an Islamic nation-state, are mostly unknown, even among the prominent teachers of comparative legal theory, *uṣūl al-fiqh al-muqārin*, in the faculties of Islamic law and among the Muslim fundamentalist ideologues.

Islamic fundamentalism has entered one of the most critical stages in its competition with modern secular ideologies. Its method of conducting its public education in Islamic ideals to win public support has backfired. The pragmatic agenda of the fundamentalist leadership has been laid bare in the ideological and doctrinal compromises that have been made to convert politicians to the fundamentalist version of Islam and in the failure to take a firm stance on issues connected with the territorial integrity of sovereign Muslim nations like Kuwait. In many ways, the 1980s provided Islamic fundamentalism with the rare opportunity of creating the necessary tools to further the development of institutions with an authentic, unmistakable Islamic identity rather than merely trying to pass off a cosmetically Islamized counterfeit. In the harsh light of constant failure to provide a concrete Islamic solution, the outcome of the political crisis of Islamic fundamentalism will depend on its leaders' willingness and ability to undertake an earnest effort, at once theoretical and practical, to integrate the substantive-normative function of reason and revelation in restoring the earthly success of Islam.

3

Compete with One Another in Good Works

For every one of you [Jews, Christians, Muslims], We have appointed a path and a way. If God had willed, He would have made you but one community; but that [He has not done in order that] He may try you in what has come to you. So compete with one another in good works. (K. 5:48)

Ethical Foundations of Freedom of Religion

In the previous chapter we traced the course of the idea of religious pluralism from its Koranic origins to its historical appropriation in the Muslim community at different times in its encounter with the non-Muslim other. As the followers of a universal religion and in possession of God's final revelation, Muslims have at times regarded it as their religious duty and their privilege to offer the rest of humankind an opportunity to accept Islam, if necessary, by *jihād* "in the path of God." This belief, as discussed in the context of Koranic pluralism, has led some Muslim jurists to maintain an antipluralist stance, legally as well as theologically, citing the following verse as the main justification for a perpetual state of war until the complete conversion of the "domain of disbelief" to Islam: "We have sent thee (o Muḥammad) not, except to *humankind entire*, good tidings to bear, and warnings; but most human beings do not know it" (K. 34:27) (emphasis added). In Islamic jurisprudence, then, theoretical foundations of pluralism in the Koran have been periodically challenged by the hegemonic notion of war for faith that inspired the Muslim conquests.

The regions of the world that came under Muslim domination were diverse in composition and pluralistic in character. Even among themselves, Muslims tolerated significant differences in practice and belief. This tolerance was extended, though less fully, to other approved monotheistic religions mentioned in the Koran. Initially, non-Muslims in conquered territories were numerically superior to Muslims. This fact dictated a flexible policy toward them.[1] Hence, the first decades of Islam provide numerous examples of religious tolerance under the first caliphs. The prescriptive precedents were furnished in 630 in the agreement concluded by the Prophet with the Christians of Najrān, which guaranteed the preservation of Christian institutions,[2] and in the instructions about the rule of conduct given by the Prophet to Muʿādh b. Jabal, who was about to march to the Yemen: "No Jew is to be troubled in the practice of Judaism."[3] The same considerate rule of conduct dominated the peace treaties granted to the Christians of the Byzantine Empire as it continued to submit to Muslim commanders.[4]

Although there were social and economic incentives for non-Muslims to convert to Islam, many chose to practice their own religion. Psychological pressures notwithstanding, various settled Jewish and Christian groups that did not convert to Islam were given the status of protected minority, the *dhimmī*.[5] This tolerance was not extended to the pagan Arabs, who, as Muḥammad's own people, were expected to convert. Even the Christian Arab tribes were under intense pressure to become part of the Arab Muslim conquering class. The Fertile Crescent, which included the whole peninsula, was expected to house only Muslims. In this connection it is important to keep in mind that the majority of the references to "unbelievers" (*kuffār*) in the Koran, which are usually generalized by the fundamentalists to include any and all unbelievers today, are expressly directed at pagan Arabs and their hostility to the Prophet's mission before finally succumbing to Islam's growing prestige.[6] Such a generalized extrapolation of the historically circumscribed term *unbelievers* can defeat the very purpose for which the Koran was revealed, namely, to guide humanity toward faith in God through persuasion rather than coercion.

Contrary to the situation of the Arab unbelievers, *ahl al-dhimma* in the Koran and early history were the protected minorities, both Jewish and Christian, who had chosen to remain in their religions and were thus recipients of Muslim protection as long as they submitted to the political domination of Muslim rule by paying a poll tax (*jizya*). The poor and dependents were exempt from paying this special tax, and it was progressive—it increased in proportion to one's wealth—but not progressive enough to avoid creating substantial hardship in some cases.

The tolerance afforded non-Muslims did not translate into sharing spiritual equality, as one might have expected in the way the Koran projected the true submission (*islām*). After all, the true *islām*, even as a personal commitment, is seen by the Koran in the moral quality of a person's life rather than in external appurtenances. *Ahl al-dhimma* were ranked by religious allegiance rather than righteous action and hence were deemed inferior to even the most corrupt and misguided Muslim. Several discriminatory provisions (such as the prohibition against building new churches or repairing old ones), although projected in the early period under the caliphs, came into play in later times, as the rulings in Islamic jurisprudence indicate.

The discriminatory regulations in exchange for protection are usually traced back to a document known as the Pact (*ʿahd*) of ʿUmar.[7] The contents of this document suggest that its attribution to ʿUmar b. al-Khaṭṭāb, who ruled from 634 to 644, is doubtful.[8] The discriminatory stipulations—a non-Muslim's word was not to be accepted against a Muslim in the qadi's court; the murder of a non-Muslim was not to be treated as quite so heinous a crime as the murder of a Muslim—not only run completely counter to the spirit of justice in the Koran, but they also contravene the practice of the early community. The tendency among later jurists, in the eighth and ninth centuries, was to seek justification for the eighth-century rulings by ascribing the documentary evidence in support of these rulings to the early community, whose prestige in such matters was a source of authentication for the later jurists' extrapolations. Thus, for instance, the prohibition against building new churches or repairing old ones, which was instituted under some Umayyad and ʿAbbasid caliphs, did not prevail in the early decades, because it is well documented that non-Muslims erected such places of worship following the conquest.[9] When Muslims took Jerusalem in 638, the caliph ʿUmar b. al-Khaṭṭāb, on his visit to that city from Damascus, sent the inhabitants of the city the following written message:

> In the name of God, the Merciful, the Compassionate. This is a written document from ʿUmar b. al-Khaṭṭāb to the inhabitants of the Sacred House (*bayt al-maqdis*). You are guaranteed (*āminūn*) your life, your goods, and your churches, which will be neither occupied nor destroyed, as long as you do not initiate anything [to endanger] the general security (*ḥadath*^an^ *ʿāmm*^an^).[10]

It is difficult to see how the same caliph could have instituted the discriminatory laws against the protected people, as later sources report.

Notwithstanding this freedom of worship, non-Muslims were frequently subjected to regulations about flaunting personal wealth; they were forbidden to wear clothes that were fashionable among Muslims and were even required to wear a special token of their inferior or different status. They were not permitted to ride a horse, which was a public proof of one's affluence. The most unfortunate aspect of these regulations is that they were reinforced in the jurisprudence as a divinely sanctioned system of discriminatory provisions. The eminent Sunnī legal scholar Imam al-Shāfiʿī has included many of these regulations in minute detail in a section entitled "The Pact to be Accorded to Non-Muslim Subjects" (part of his monumental juridical work *Kitāb al-umm*) to underscore the sacred nature of his judicial decisions.[11]

It is a historical fact that the Prophet condemned oppression of the *ahl al-dhimma* as a sinful deviation, declaring in no uncertain terms, "On the Day of Judgment I myself will act as the accuser of any person who oppresses a person under the protection (*dhimma*) of Islam, and lays excessive [financial or other social] burdens on him."[12] In the most highly rated compilations of *ḥadīth* among the Sunnī Muslims, the *Ṣaḥīḥ* of al-Bukhārī, there is a chapter heading that reads, "One should fight for the protection of the *ahl al-dhimma* and they should not be enslaved." Under this heading Bukhārī narrates the following instructions on the authority of ʿUmar b. al-Khaṭṭāb, when the latter was stabbed and died of the wound inflicted upon him by a Persian slave:

> I strongly recommend him (the next caliph) to take care of those non-Muslims who are under God's and His Prophet's protection (*dhimmat allāh wa dhimmat rasūlih*) in that he should remain faithful to them according to the covenant with them, and fight on their behalf and not burden them [by imposing high taxes] beyond their capacity.[13]

After reading these instructions, left by the caliph as the head of Muslim state to honor the sacred covenant offered by God and his emissary to the people of the Book, it is hard to believe that the Pact of ʿUmar ascribed to the second caliph could be authentic in its representation of the situation of the non-Muslims in the early days of Islam. The Pact of ʿUmar compares well in substance with al-Shāfiʿī's section on the pact that can be accorded to non-Muslims.

To clarify, the Pact of ʿUmar is the document that the Christians of Syria offered to ʿUmar when the latter accorded peace to them. The document reads as follows:

> In the name of God, the Merciful, the Compassionate. This is a letter to the servant of God ʿUmar [b. al-Khaṭṭāb], Commander of the Faithful, from Christians of such-and-such city. When you came against us, we asked you for safe-conduct (*amān*) for ourselves, our descendants, our property, and the people of our community, and we undertook the following obligations toward you:
>
> We shall not build, in our cities or in their neighborhood, new monasteries, churches, convents, or monks' cells, nor shall we repair, by day or by night, such of them as fall in ruins [that] are situated in the quarters of the Muslims. . . .
>
> We shall not teach the Koran to our children.

We shall not manifest our religion publicly or convert anyone to it. We shall not prevent any of our kin from entering Islam if they wish it.

We shall show respect toward the Muslims, and we shall rise from our seats when they wish to sit.

We shall not seek to resemble the Muslims by imitating any of their garments. . . . We shall not speak as they do, nor shall we adopt their patronymics (*kunya*). . . .

We shall not display our crosses or our books in the roads or markets of the Muslims. We shall use clappers in our churches very softly.[14]

Shāfiʿī uses the Pact of ʿUmar in preparing a document that a Muslim ruler can use for the poll tax of non-Muslims. He writes:

> If the Imam (i.e., the ruler) wishes to write a document for the *jizya* of non-Muslims, he should write:
>
> In the name of God, the Merciful, the Compassionate.
>
> This is a document written by the servant of God . . . to the Christian . . . people of the city of so-and-so.
>
> I accord to you and to the Christians of the city . . . that which is accorded to the *dhimmi*s, in conformity with what you have given to me and the conditions I have laid down concerning what is due to you and to them . . . on behalf of myself and of all the Muslims, safe conduct (*amān*), for as long as you and they maintain all that we have required of you, namely:
>
> You will be subject to the authority of Islam and to no contrary authority. You will not refuse to carry out any obligation which we think fit to impose upon you by virtue of this authority.
>
> If anyone of you speaks improperly of Muḥammad, may God bless and save him, the Book of God, or His religion, he forfeits the protection (*dhimma*) of God, of the Commander of the Faithful, and of all the Muslims; he has contravened the conditions upon which he was given his safe-conduct. . . .
>
> You may not display crosses in Muslim cities, nor proclaim polytheism, nor build churches or meeting places for your prayers, nor strike clappers, nor proclaim your polytheistic beliefs on the subject of Jesus, son of Mary, or any other to a Muslim.
>
> You shall wear the girdle (*zunnar*) over all your garments, your cloaks and the rest, so that the girdles are not hidden. You shall differentiate yourselves by your saddles and your mounts, and you shall distinguish your and their headgear by a mark which you shall place on your headgear. You shall not occupy the middle of the road or the seats in the market, obstructing Muslims.[15]

As pointed out in the previous chapter, contextual analysis of the restrictive and discriminatory stipulations of Islamic jurisprudence under Muslim political dominance can help to determine the effective causes (*ʿilal*) that governed the juristic research in the traditions to infer these decisions. Some of these traditions led to decisions that resulted in outright persecution of those who professed other religions. There are potential hazards in a literal application of these ordinances in a contemporary nation-state in the name of implementation of the Sharīʿa (*taṭbīq al-sharīʿat al-islāmiyya*)[16] without first discovering the purpose of the Lawgiver and ascertaining the historical and political circumstances of the judicial decisions that were formulated by Shāfiʿī and others. Reinterpretation of the classical formulations in the theology of interfaith relations today would have to take into account the pluralistic nature of public international order in which Muslim and non-Muslim countries share equal membership. Most of the past juridical decisions treating non-Muslim minorities have become irrelevant in the context of contemporary religious pluralism, a cornerstone of interhuman relations.

To recapitulate, the self-understanding of early Muslims led to a relatively tolerant attitude toward the people of the Book in Islam. From the standpoint of Muslim theology, there is no doctrine in the Koran to suggest that Islam saw itself as the final dispensation in the line of prophetic revelations and hence viewed all the pre-Koranic monotheistic traditions as superseded by its emergence. Quite to the contrary, on the basis of the common belief in one God, a tradition going back to the Prophet confirms the legitimacy of the earlier religions and relates his mission to the missions of all the prophets by declaring: "We the prophets are brothers and our religion is one and the same" (*wāḥid*).[17] The spiritual ancestor of Islam is still Abraham, the progenitor of both the Jews and the Christians. Abraham was the first *muslim* (one who submitted) and a *ḥanīf* (a pure monotheist):

> People of the Book! Why do you dispute concerning Abraham? The Torah was not sent down, neither the Gospel, but after him. What, have you no reason? Ha, you are the ones who dispute on what you know; why then dispute you touching a matter of which you know not anything? God knows, and you know not. No; Abraham in truth was not a Jew, neither a Christian; but he was a *muslim* and one of pure faith (*ḥanīf*); certainly he was never of the idolaters. (K. 3:65–67)

The function of the Prophet Muḥammad was to restore the pure monotheism of Abraham, which, according to the Koran, had been distorted by Abraham's earlier heirs, Jews and Christians. Consequently, Islam, which Muḥammad presented to humankind, just as Moses and Jesus had done earlier, had priority over both those communities. By virtue of this priority, the

Koran invites the people of the Book to consider the shared religious commitment to "serve none but God":

> Say (o Muḥammad): "People of the Book! Come now to a word common between us and you, that we serve none but God, and that we associate not aught with Him, and do not some of us take others as Lords, apart from God." And if they turn their backs, say: "Bear witness that we are *muslims*." (K. 3:64)

By virtue of explicit recognition of a common ground shared between Muslims and the people of the Book, Islam has never harbored a widespread belief that Jews and Christians are to be denied salvation if they do not first convert to Islam.[18] Unlike the early Christians, the early Muslims felt no need to establish their sociopolitical and religious identity at the expense of another community.[19]

Moreover, Muslims, unlike the Jews, did not regard their own community as uniquely selected to receive divine guidance in a world otherwise bereft of it. Muslims thought of their community as one among many divinely guided communities, all at their beginning equally blessed. Furthermore, as acknowledged in K. 5:48, cited at the beginning of this chapter, the Muslims, like various other religious communities, are also an autonomous social organism with their own law for their own members. After the establishment of Muslim political power, the difference between the Muslims and other communities widened. Islam—and those that follow—was first to rule over and then supersede all others. Islam was to bring true and uncorrupted guidance to all humankind, creating a worldwide society in which the true revelation would be the everyday norm of all the nations. It must not guide merely an autonomous community; it must guide the practical policies of a cosmopolitan world.

This universal aspiration of the Islamic political mission on the one hand created the necessary cohesion in the development of the worldwide community under the sacred law of Islam, the Sharīʿa; on the other, it gave rise to the antipluralist theology of supersession, as analyzed in the previous chapter. To be sure, Koranic pluralism was founded on the ethical principle of doing good works. Its conception of universal moral order was grounded in the recognition of a nature common to all humans. It viewed this common nature as endowed with ethical cognition and the capacity to reason morally in order to do good. In spite of its reference to abstract universal human nature, Koranic ethics was founded on concrete and historical facts. It was this relative dimension of the revelation brought to human beings by Muḥammad, the Prophet of God, in a particular place at a particular time, that was going to lead to problems in searching for the common moral language in the Koran that can allow for a universal ethical paradigm to emerge as a principle of human interaction in society.

Without first recognizing the Koranic notion of freedom of conscience as part of the noble nature (the *fiṭra*) with which God has endowed each human being, it is fruitless to speak about an Islamic paradigm for human organization in which "competing with one another in good works" serves as an ethical principle of pluralistic coexistence.

The Islamic Paradigm of Common Morality

The call to "compete with one another in good works" in the Koran is clearly founded on a universally recognizable moral good (*al-khayr*, *al-maʿrūf*). What is not clear, however, is whether the Koran acknowledges a variable cultural or historical understanding of what constitutes that good. Since K. 5:48 is addressed to all religious communities,[20] it is consistent to maintain that the good in the passage is applicable across religious traditions. But such an interpretation has not been universally accepted by scholars of Islamic ethics.[21] In fact, in Muslim theological ethics, determination of the objective and absolute nature of moral values has been subject to some of the same problems that have been encountered in modern secular debates about general ethical principles of coexistence in society. I will discuss this problem in Muslim theological ethics in the larger context of the modern debates on the subject to highlight the Koran's emphasis on the universal nature of ethical values, their variable cultural or historical contexts notwithstanding. The analysis of this subject should allow us to assert that the Koran, if interpreted with the requisite rigor and integrity, could furnish a paradigm for common morality as a fundamental principle of interhuman "sociation."[22]

The search for principles of coexistence in a plurality of cultural and ethnic traditions has led to two conflicting views about the human need for some ethical framework. On the one hand, a number of secular and religious thinkers speak about the unavailability of universal standards of truth and morality that can be applied across cultural and religious traditions. On the other hand, some thinkers are convinced that there are universal, objective criteria that intuitively inform some essential principle of just and equitable interpersonal relationships.[23]

Muslim theologians are also divided on the issue of the availability of universal morality, clashing on whether it is totally conditioned by the social and cultural conventions or derived from a universal standard of rationality grounded in human nature (*fiṭra*). Islamic revelation provides a complex moral language that speaks about human beings, who, on the one hand, share some universal values and interests as equals in dignity and conscience, but who, on the other, are bound in particular brotherhood as members of distinct communities and nations. However, even within the restricted language of morality that characterizes the religious communities, the Koran seems to be speaking about a common morality that lays down a set of rules or directives—categorically obligatory for all in thought, word, and deed—as a projection of the human faith in God.[24]

Those who have advocated and defended a divinely approved pluralism in Islam have also maintained a universal morality that touches human beings as members of the human family. The Koranic view about the inherent dignity of the human person, in the following verse, provides incontrovertible support for this universalist position:

> We have honored (*karramnā*) the Children of Adam [with *karam*, that is, 'noble nature'] and carried them on land and sea, and provided them with good things, and preferred them greatly over many of those We created. (K. 17:70)[25]

As shown by Sayyid Quṭb, the passage clearly relates the *karam* to the very first qualities in virtue of which someone becomes human: autonomous in orientation (*ḥurriyat al-ittijāh*) and individually responsible (*fardiyyat al-tabīʿa*). ʿAllāma Ṭabāṭabāʾī regards *takrīm* also as a special endowment and honoring of human beings that no one else among God's creatures possess. That the special honoring of humanity as the carrier of the "noble nature" is connected with universal ethical cognition is evident in the following verses: "By the soul, and That which shaped it and inspired it [with conscience of] what is wrong for it and [what is] right for it. Prosperous is he who purifies it, and failed has he who seduces it" (K. 91:7–10).[26]

As part of their noble nature, all humans are endowed with an innate scale with which they can weigh rightness and wrongness. The Koranic paradigm of ethical knowledge is based on the belief that the Creator God does not leave human beings without an inherent guidance in the nature (*fiṭra*) he imparts to humanity:

> So set thy purpose for religion (*dīn*), a human by nature upright—God's original [nature] upon which He created humankind. There is no altering [the laws of] God's creation. That is the right religion (*dīn al-ḥaqq*); but most humans know it not—[that they should] turn to Him [only]. (K. 30:30–31)[27]

The crucial thesis about a "human by nature upright (*ḥanīfa*)" or created in "original nature" (*fiṭrat allāh* = 'God's nature') is that it cannot regard morality as something arbitrary. Moral epistemology is deduced from general principles (*uṣūl al-awwaliyya*) "inspired by God" that do not require any justification independent of the naturally given process of reasoning. As developed in Islamic legal theory (*uṣūl al-fiqh*), justification in religious-moral action consists of a dialectic between judgments (*fatāwā*) in specific cases (*farʿiyyāt*) and the generalizations (*aḥkām ʿāmma*) derived from effective causes (*ʿilal*) in new cases in the light of which the generalizations themselves are modified.[28] Hence, to derive a specific ethical judgment—for example, that an act of distribution of surplus wealth among the needy is obligatory—is to confirm that it satisfies a certain description of the religious-moral concept of justice according to one's belief in social responsibility. Social responsibility as part of the generalizable command to be just could then be applied to other acts.

The convergence between the divine command that human beings must treat each other justly and the rational cognition of justice being good underscores the importance of formulating specific judgments first and then searching for principles that can be generalized and then applied to new cases. The Koran uses the word *al-maʿrūf* (the known paradigms)[29] for these generalized principles, which must be inferred from the concrete ethical practice of everyday life. There is a correlation between known moral convictions and God's purposes as mentioned in the revelation. General moral beliefs that are guided by the revelation seek their application in specific situations, thereby furthering the authenticity as well as the relevance of the religious belief system.

The Koran leads humankind with "upright nature" to achieve a "reflective equilibrium"[30] between the known (the convictions determined through the process of reflection) and the unknown (*al-maṭlūb*)[31] moral judgments by placing the known in history and culture at the same time. In Muslim ethics, human beings are endowed with will power (*irāda*) and the capacity (*istiṭaʿa*) to grasp intuitively the consequences and the general principles arising from a particular act. Both good and evil values are thought of as attributes—that is to say, byproducts of one's ethical ground as grasped intuitively through reflection. It is for this reason that the Koran anchors moral convictions in the reflective process that involves pondering about the consequences of human action and their generalizability in other similar situations:[32]

> How many a city We have destroyed in its evildoing, and now it is fallen down upon its turrets! How many a ruined well, a tall place! What, have they not journeyed in the land so that they have hearts to understand with or ears to hear with? It is not the eyes that are blind, but blind are the hearts within the breasts. (K. 22:45–46)

The passage, while acknowledging the capacity of a sound heart to understand the consequences of evildoing, appeals to the human capacity for learning from past destructiveness in order to avoid it in the future. There is something concrete about human conditions that cannot be denied by any reasonable persons (with "hearts to understand"). But moral reasoning could become blurred if not fortified by belief in the transcendence, in obedience to the ultimate authority to whom "shall you return, all together" (K. 5:48).

Accordingly, the concept of a known moral language in Islam does not fail to acknowledge the concrete historical and social conditioning of moral concepts. But it insists that different cultures must seek to elicit the universal ideal out of the diversity of concrete human conditions—a common foundation upon which to construct an ethical language that can be shared cross-culturally in the project of creating a just society:

> O humankind, We have created you male and female, and appointed you races and tribes, that you may *know* (*taʿārafū*) one another. Surely, the noblest among you in the sight of God is the most morally [and spiritually] aware (*atqā*) among you. God is All-knowing, All-aware. (K. 49:13)

Both the known (*al-maʿrūf*) and the unknown (*al-maṭlūb*) moral principles in the Koran point to concrete ways of life constructed in different cultural idioms ("races and tribes") that must be understood in order to elicit the universals and to apply them in context. The *taqwā* that ennobles human existence and leads it to carry out duties to God and other humans functions as a torch of the divinely created *fiṭra*, innate human nature, enabling it to discover the universals that can build bridges of understanding across cultures.

Can Religion Become a Source of Democratic Pluralism?

The exclusion of religion as a source of democratic pluralism has been a common tendency in many societies that foster secular values and a clear demarcation between public and private spheres of human activity. Religion is to be tolerated and even abstractly supported without affording it a clear voice in the public arena. And although there is no secular conspiracy to suppress religious expression, religion is clearly seen as a threat to secular democracies when it challenges the secular values that increasingly promote self-gratification as the primary human imperative. Of course, the efforts by religious interest groups to impose severe, single-minded, and seemingly punitive alternatives to these claimed materialist indulgences have smacked of an authoritarianism that has evoked some of the less admirable chapters in religious history.[33]

All world religions, at one time or other, have succumbed to secular pressure and have subordinated their core spiritual-moral message to the political ambitions of their particular communities. Such marriages of convenience between exclusive faith communities and political power has actually led to the disestablishment of the universal ethical and legal foundations of various religious traditions. Abrahamic religions, as discussed in chapter 2, include among their theological doctrines of divine justice and human moral agency concepts of individual and collective responsibility to further a divinely ordained ethical order on earth. Judaism, Christianity, and Islam identify and articulate precepts of responsible individual living under accountable political authority—an indispensable ingredient of a democratic state. Human beings, endowed with *fiṭra* (innate disposition) and fortified with the upright *dīn* (system of belief and actions) that constructs individual responsibility through communal bonds, are morally and spiritually required to fulfill God's purpose, the establishment of justice and equity on earth.

However, historically, all three traditions when in control of political power have stumbled in fulfilling their ideals when dealing with the religious other. In the year 850, al-Mutawakkil, the ʿAbbasid caliph, ordered the destruction of newly built Christian churches and the nailing of wooden images of the devil to the doors of Christians' houses to distinguish them from the houses of Muslims. He forbade the display of crosses on Palm Sunday and prohibited Jewish rites in the street.[34] These policies against the *ahl al-dhimma* (the protected minorities) contravened the Koran. Although al-Mutawakkil's behavior contrasts sharply with the highly tolerant decree of Fāṭimid caliph al-Ẓāhir, who came to power in 1021, in general the treatment of the non-Muslim minorities depended on the political situation of the region and its relationship to the non-Muslim powers.

Moving from the past to the present, in February of 1994 (during the month of Ramadan), twenty-nine Muslims gathered by the tomb of Abraham and Sarah for early morning prayer in the mosque in Hebron were murdered by a fanatical religious Jewish settler who hoped thereby to sabotage the peace accord between Jews and Palestinians; this slaughter came as a somber reminder of the dangers posed to democracy by religiously inspired, exclusivist militancy in any group in the region. This is a theological problem that must be resolved through nonfundamentalist research in the Scriptures of the children of Abraham. The fundamentalist scholarship on the Jewish, Christian, and Muslim Scriptures has refused to grant an individual freedom of conscience in negotiating his spiritual destiny. The doctrine of individual responsibility to God, instead of conferring validity on the reality of the autonomous "noble *fiṭra*" of individuals capable of appropriating the divine message of accommodation and toleration, has given rise to a community of individualized moral agents pursuing the social program of excluding the other at God's behest. The political society is then driven to adopt the idea of intertwined private and public domains without requiring individual rational consent to legitimize the theology of the systematic exclusion of the other.

Thus arises the concentration of comprehensive religious-secular power in the hands of an exclusivist leadership whose views of private morality are divorced from a communalistic vision of society, with the attendant mistreatment of those within and outside the community who reject that community's religious exclusivist claims. Monotheistic communities have from time to time denied their individual members the right to dissent from or to reject the communalistic interpretation of their respective traditions because of the fear that such internal dissension (usually labeled apostasy) is potentially fatal to the collective identity of the faith community and its social cohesiveness.

There is a strong desire among people of various religions to prevent any form of oppression of one group of people by another. The conflicting and even incommensurable theological positions on freedom of religion in different world communities has led to the oppressive use of force to ensure adherence to a single comprehensive religious doctrine. The ensuing intolerance has manifested itself in intrafaith relationships as well. Whereas Muslims treated other religious communities with relative tolerance, they often treated their own dissenters with extreme cruelty. Thus, for instance, under various powerful Muslim dynasties, the Shīʿite or Sunnī minority suffered more oppression than did the Jews and the Christians. In the sixteenth century, when the Shīʿī Safavid kings came to power in Iran, they fought the Sunnī Ottoman rulers, each side claiming to represent the true Islam. The endless wars and civil strife that engulfed innocent peoples on both sides revealed the tragic reality that intrafaith conflicts within the umma of Islam had become so acute that they could be resolved neither by the use of force nor by any reformulation of traditionally exclusivist claims to the religious truth.

But if this was the condition of the Muslim umma in the sixteenth century, when it depended upon its traditionally formulated antagonistic theology of Sunnī-Shīʿī relations, the Iraq-Iran war in the 1980s and the Gulf War in 1990–91 brought home a realization that even secularly based imported ideologies like nationalism and socialism could not advance the cause of pluralistic, tolerant political culture. The imported ideologies, to be sure, were enforced from above without the people's rational consent or political participation. Hence, they flagrantly failed to generate the necessary consensus for change in conservative Muslim societies. Whether in Algeria, Afghanistan, or Pakistan, the endless violent confrontations between different groups, all waving the banner of *jihād*, have raised a serious question about the ability of Muslim theology to stop demonizing competing Islamic factions as nonbelievers and apostates, deserving of death. Moreover, Muslim social ethics has not been able to provide the moral and spiritual weapons needed to combat oppressive state force and to generate civic participation or communal cooperation.

Individual Interests versus Collective Good

The Koran does not teach that humanity has fallen through the commission of original sin. But it constantly warns human beings about the egocentric corruption (*istikbār*) that can weaken the determination to carry out divine purposes for humankind. Human pride can infect and corrupt undertakings in politics, scholarship, everyday conduct, and theology. The last is the most sinful aspect of egocentric corruption because it is done in the name of God. Pride in matters of religion corrupts the message as well as the adherent beyond reform. The devastating effect of this kind of corruption in an individual has social implications: such people impair their natural relationship with God, which functions as a constitutive principle for all social relationships among the creatures of God. The Koran reminds humankind that, had it not been for their creation by God through a single soul through whom he created the first human couple, the very source of human relations to one another, people would not have realized the greatest good of establishing interpersonal justice in their relations:

> Humankind, be aware of your duties to your Lord, who created you of a single soul, and from it created its mate, and from the pair of them scattered abroad many men and women; and be aware of your duties to God [through whose relationship] you demand one of another, and the wombs [that relate you]; surely God ever watches over you. (K. 4:1–2)

Besides stressing the "noble nature" (*fiṭra)* that promotes human sociability and positive bonds between people because of their common ethical responsibility toward one another, this passage emphasizes the mutual expectations and relations fostered by a universal parentage. The family is the primary natural relationship in human society, and, hence, the Koran commands people to honor their parents:

> Thy Lord has decreed you shall not serve any but Him, and to be good to your parents, whether one or both of them attains old age with thee; say not to them "Fie" neither chide them, but speak unto them words respectful, and lower to them wing of humbleness out of mercy and say, "My Lord, have mercy upon them, as they raised me up when I was little." (K. 17:26)

The importance given by the Koran to interpersonal relationships evidently points to the institutions and culture that promote the creation of a spiritual-moral community made up of individuals willing and able to take up the challenge of working for the common good. It is for this reason that the moral performance of an individual in society is to be measured not so much by reference to some ingrained noble nature as by the religious-moral institutions through which history has shaped the community's ethical aspirations. The doctrine of the noble nature (*fiṭra*) in the Koran is properly anchored in the history of the human struggle toward discovering what it is to be properly human.

What of the claim that tolerance leads to the compromise of religious truth? By encouraging tolerance among its members, the community might claim that its transcending quality and its unique relation to truth are sacrificed to pragmatism. As discussed in chapter 2, theological differences about matters in the revelation are difficult, perhaps impossible, to resolve. Yet, the spirit of accommodation and tolerance certainly demands that a common ground should be sought for implementing the common good in society. Working for the common good without insisting on imposing the beliefs and desires each holds most dear can result in a legitimate public space for diverse human religious experience. Can this public space be realized without interfering with the ability of each person to work out his or her own individual salvation?

The debate has its origin in ideas about the highest ends of human existence on the earth. Can they be accomplished through communal cooperation for the collective good or for widely different and even irreconcilable individual interests? How can a religious community remain neutral and noninterventionist on ethical issues that, from the individual's point of view, might run counter to one's sense of the highest ends in life? As members of a democratic society, individuals are free to endorse various religious views or none at all. Religious pluralism is a prerequisite for a peaceful accommodation of the differences in the individual and the communal sense of the highest good.

The secular prescription of Western democracies seems to suggest that religious toleration can be achieved only when the idea of freedom of conscience is institutionalized in the form of a basic individual right to worship freely, to propagate one's religion, to change one's religion, or even to renounce religion altogether. In other words, the principle of toleration is equated with the idea of individual freedom of conscience.[35] Moreover, it delimits the role of conscience to the domain of private faith, which is clearly demarcated from the public realm—hence the separation of church from state. Whereas one has the freedom to choose between competing doctrines and pursue one's belief in private religious institutions, one is linked in common citizenry in public state institutions. This is the secularist foundation of a public order in which, in pursuit of freedom of conscience, all considerations drawn from belief in God or other sacred authority in one's private life are excluded from the administration of public life.

I will later return to the question of freedom of conscience in the Koran. Here, it is important to consider a nonsecularist model of religious tolerance offered by a public sphere founded on religious considerations, a society founded on the belief that God alone provides the center of gravity for developing a sense of loyalty to a comprehensive political life.[36]

The belief in God as the principle of unity (*tawḥīd*) presupposes a link between this world and the next world in such a way that faith becomes the essential medium for the comprehension of the norm that guides the collective life of socially responsible selves. Moreover, the socially binding character of this belief in transcendence transforms the act of commitment to a faith into a vision of the ideal social order. With common roots, the branches of revealed truth and life conduct differentiate within a single organism—a normatively conceived community.

Islam, as a systematic religion that propounds a set of beliefs and practices, embodies a public dimension in which the integration of the private and public spheres is grounded in the contract between two parties: the Muslims who emigrated in 622 from Mekka to Medina under the Prophet's guidance and the Medinan tribes. The political society that emerged through this contractual agreement did not originate so much from a formal acknowledgment of the Prophet's political leadership, but it resulted inevitably from his prophetic function. It integrated the tribal mechanisms of organization and decision making into a formal acknowledgment of belief in one God on whose behalf Muḥammad, the Prophet of God, was speaking. A prophet, according to Islam, is one who utters whatever messages are revealed to him through a supernatural source. The new community of the faithful did not simply transcend the tribal society in its principle of organization, which was essentially founded on kinship; it constructed the umma on the principle of equality among believers, who through their personal commitment to Islamic faith undertook to realize interpersonal justice. In the absence of a mediating religious institution like a church to represent God's claims, the community felt justified in insisting upon individual responsibility in constructing and maintaining an ethical order as a collective response to the Prophet's call of obedience.

Abrahamic traditions are characteristically founded upon the Scriptures that favor not merely a chiliastic projection of the future appearance of a restorer or redresser (messiah, *mahdī*) of mutilated justice or a purely esoteric stress on the disciplining of the believer on the path (*ṭarīqa*) of realizing the true calling of human beings; rather, they emphasize the divine-human covenant that locates justice in history through community. This ideal of justice in a divinely ordained community is a natural outcome of the belief in an ethical God who insists on justice and equality in interpersonal relations as part of the believer's spiritual perfection. The indispensable connection between the religious and ethical dimensions of personal life inevitably introduces religious precepts into the public arena. In other words, church and state are closely linked, requiring the involvement of the religious community in taking responsibility for law and order. All human beings are called on to support the community, the norms of which—defined as exclusive, comprehensive, universal, and uncompromising—form the boundaries for the individual's spiritual life. There is one true faith represented by the religious body, and all else is false. Hence, the tendency for people to be divided among the confessional religious bodies, belonging exclusively and decisively to one or the other of them, is strong. Hence, the organization of the entire population of a region into many mutually exclusive rival communities defined more by religious identity than by territorial claims. For an individual it is as socially unthinkable to be associated with two or more such communities as it would be to be associated with none.

Islam: A Comprehensive Social-Spiritual System

Muḥammad, the Prophet, was a remarkable leader who unified into one religious community (*umma*) most of the populace of the lands from the Nile to the Oxus. The essential characteristic of this community was its acceptance of not merely the moral demands of the Creator but also the political leadership of Muḥammad himself. The historical experience of the community conformed to the Koran's requirement that leadership under the Prophet link the private individual conscience to the concrete relationships of the collective order. This linkage between a transcendent universality embedded in the human conscience and the horizontal relationships of the community provided Muslims an opportunity to build the new social order demanded by God. The development of the individual's conscience was tied to social behavior. The Koran also established a new model of the moral order based on the autonomous individual, functioning as a moral agent, newly freed from the past Arab solidarities of kinship and clan.

As the initial Koranic model of political society moved from tribal to settled and agrarian cultures, the fusion of the religious and the political, which is structurally appropriate and indeed unavoidable in a tribal setting, created severe problems for the early Muslim empire. Muslims inherited some of their solutions to the problems of the interdependency of the religious and political realms from both the Byzantine and Sassanian empires. Under both these imperial powers, some sort of differentiation of the religious and political spheres was recognized as essential. This distinction did not eliminate the tensions between the spiritual and temporal realms but enabled the state to create a complex mechanism for resolving inevitable the power struggle between them. The caliphal state experienced similar tensions and stood more as a mundane imperial power, no longer based directly on Islam. It was supported internally as well as externally by a particular complex of military and physical power that was partially supported, in turn, by religious faith.[37] Since this development was seen by the religious-minded, to some extent rightly, as a lapse not only from the precedent set by the Prophet but also from the ideal of a just and equitable society, it was not accepted as legitimate.[38]

The subsequent Muslim community, however, failed to develop any workable alternative to the solution worked out by the Umayyads (660–748). Instead, the growing religious opposition simply reasserted the original prophetic model based on a responsible and egalitarian social commitment through the acceptance of Islam rather than the Arab descent. The ʿAbbasid caliphate (748–1256) was in part the result of this movement of religious dissatisfaction with the Umayyads, and it can be seen as the classic effort to put the Islamic ideal of religious-political fusion into effect in a large-scale empire.

The fundamental reason for its failure is that the ʿAbbasid revolution relied on public relations rather than on structural innovation. The ʿAbbasids turned their backs on the religious ideals cultivated by the pious Muslims, whose disillusionment followed rapidly upon a realization that the ʿAbbasid were merely cloaking an all-too-familiar absolutist Persian and Byzantine monarchical system in claims of religious legitimacy; these devout Muslims adopted either a radical Shīʿī ideological position that rejected the ʿAbbasid compromise or a relatively apolitical Sunnī position that recognized the validity of the general community experience, notwithstanding its imperfections. The post-ʿAbbasid period, then, saw a de facto differentiation of religion and politics punctuated by an occasional outburst of religious-political movements emerging from the provincial garrison towns in disruptive but largely ephemeral military conquests.

The de facto situation, however, was never accepted as fully legitimate. Muslim political thinkers from al-Māwardī (d. 1058) through al-Ghazālī (d. 1111) to Ibn Taymiyya (d. 1328) increasingly tended to legitimate any political regime that would guarantee a modicum of protection to Muslim institutions.[39] Political power remained suspect not only to rural activists but also to urban ulema, who viewed it as a necessary evil. In this situation, the state and the political realm in the Islamic world failed to develop an inner coherence and integrity. The state as a legitimate realm of thought and action, with its indispensable role for the citizen, failed to emerge. The Muslim community itself, even though lacking any effective means of exercising power, continued to express the only legitimate political self-consciousness in the society, and the role of adult Muslim believer, not that of citizen, was the only inclusive political role. The classical notion of citizenship—with its concomitant values of membership and participation in collective life, which played so important a role in the political development of the modern nation-state in Western Europe and North America[40]—was nearly absent in the Muslim world until it came into contact with European colonialism.[41]

The proposals offered by religious elements in the Muslim community since the end of the eighteenth century are summed up as government according to the Koran and Sunna. But what this might mean in particular social and historical situations has depended on each group's retrieval and interpretation of these two sources. The Koran is clear enough, but it was not an adequate guide to the day-to-day contingencies of autonomy and mutuality within the boundaries of modern nation-states. The crux of the problem lay in defining the political terms of reference in the Koran and the Tradition. Was the political mission of Islam particularistic, with a limited goal of defining the place of Islam in an ethnically bound community? Or was it more universalistic, presenting a comprehensive Islamic vision for a society of transnational and transcultural Muslims?

Buried under the traditional interpretations of Islamic revelation—the pretext of the established practice of the pious elders (*salaf*)—there lies the Koranic vision of individual dignity, personal liberty, and freedom from arbitrary coercion. That all Muslims ought to be treated on an essentially equal basis was clearly established through the Prophet's own treatment of his followers. The policy of discriminatory treatment of the non-Muslim populations under Muslim political dominance is traceable neither to the Koran nor to the early community. Yet the classical Muslim jurisprudence that deals with "conquered and subjugated peoples" and their legal status under Muslim political dominance explicitly rules that non-Muslims cannot have the same rights, obligations, and liberties as Muslims. Hence, the traditional rulings provide no help in resolving the problems raised by the modern political thinking about citizenship.

The value of the Islamic tradition as a resource for policy in the modern world still awaits intelligent articulation. The Islamic impulse toward a just society, which has expressed itself in every Islamic century, resonates powerfully with the needs of modern society. But the formalization of that ethical imperative in the vast body of the Sharīʿa, though it has succeeded in providing a rallying point for the unity of the umma through the ages, has grown increasingly inflexible in the face of the major problems now facing the Muslim peoples. Unfortunately, in the social and political context within which Islamic jurisprudence developed, the Koranic provisions about civil society were ignored; it was the post-Koranic precedents that became effective in the formulation of the rulings dealing with non-Muslims in a Muslim state. The rethinking of this tradition must emanate from within the Muslim community and must proceed with unremitting honesty and integrity.

The Koran and History as Sources for the Development of a Civil Society

In this section I intend to articulate the Koranic provisions that reflect a more universalistic political direction for humanity. The Koran's vision for the Muslim community was founded on a new locus of social solidarity that replaced distinctions based on tribal allegiance. Each individual was now endowed with personal dignity and liberty as part of his or her *fiṭra*, standing in direct relationship with God, the Creator, the Master of the Day of Judgment. This unmediated relationship, this covenant between God and humanity, suggested a new autonomy and agency of individuals sharing a set of beliefs and ideological commitments to the transcendent power and authority of God:

> And when thy Lord took from the Children of Adam, from their loins, their seed, and made them testify touching themselves, "Am I not your Lord?" They said, "Yes, we testify"—lest you should say on the Day of Resurrection, "As for us, we were heedless of this." (K. 7:172)

This is the covenant regarding the *fiṭra* and the belief of humanity, which is presented as a proof of God's lordship, of humanity's acceptance of that lordship, and of its obedience to the divine plan for human beings.[42]

The *fiṭra*, then, is the Koran's model of individual human responsibility and shared moral commitment with which a Muslim society is to be established. The model also affords a glimpse into the Koranic notion of universal human identity, both social and individual, constantly engaged in a *jihād* (struggle and striving) to locate the self in the spheres of existence and of just relationships with other human beings. The *jihād* for achieving fundamental equality of all human beings before God, regardless of their creed or race, is part of the dynamic of the *fiṭra*. The function of the *fiṭra* is to provide moral direction to individual and social activity by interrelating this and the next world in such a way that human religiosity finds expression in the perfection of public order and institutions. The Koranic vision of an ideal order is not based on the separation of private and public; rather, it is an integrated path that requires the perfection of both to render human struggle in this world soteriologically efficacious. In the integrated version of personal and public life, the Koran insists on the individual freedom of conscience as the cornerstone of existence and faith as they relate to the intra- and intercommunal life. Without the focus on the autonomous individual conscience located in the *fiṭra*, it is difficult to gauge the strong impetus that the Koran provided to the social and institutional transformation from a tribal, kinship-based-society to a cosmopolitan community in which the nature of social and individual identity and meaning were determined by shared moral commitments (*al-maʿrūf*).

The Koranic terms for social existence must be defined by the profound secularity of the *fiṭra*. By secularity of the *fiṭra*, I mean the this-worldliness of human nature in which, by its very creation, human *fiṭra* recognizes its limitations in matters that enhance religious life, without becoming entangled in claims of the superiority of one path over the other except in moral action that can be objectified. Accordingly, the *fiṭra* sits in judgment to determine the moral value of human action but avoids judging the rightness or wrongness of human faith. And, although *fiṭra* has the capacity to relate and integrate individual responsibility with spiritual and moral awareness (*taqwā*), its divinely ordained mandate is to engage in ethical purification through moral awareness: "By the soul, and That which shaped it and inspired it [with conscience of] what is wrong for it and [what is] right for it. Prosperous is he who purifies it, and failed has he who seduces it" (K. 91:7–10).[43]

According to these verses, the Koranic moral order was founded upon the moral behavior of each individual, who carries within the potential for prosperity, as well as for corruption. And, although faith was the defining term of the normative order and of participation therein, in matters of coexistence among several faith communities, it was personal morality founded upon the dictum of "competing with one another in good works" that defined the ultimate human community. The Koran weaves religious and civil responsibilities into an integrated pattern of human interaction and socialization on which it built its unique version of a civil society.

Christianity developed the inherent split between the sacred and secular in a monastic ideal of radical withdrawal from the world, particularly the familial and political world, which was quite alien to the Old Testament way of thinking. Islam under Muḥammad made an extraordinary leap forward in social complexity and political capacity. When the political society that took shape under the Prophet was extended by the early caliphs to provide the organizing principle for a world empire, the result was, for its time and place, remarkably modern in the stress on individual commitment, involvement, and participation in shaping the destiny of the community. The effort of modern Muslims to depict the early community as a prototype of egalitarian participant nationalism is by no means an entirely unhistorical ideological fabrication.[44]

The high degree of social and political commitment and participation of these individuals provided a unique form of universal mutuality that bound them to one another in the way that "civil religion" does in the context of the U.S. national character.[45] The Koranic doctrine of the *fiṭra* integrates the law of nature and the divine command to build a just society for humans qua humans. Natural law in Islam is ontologically related to the Koranic notion of *fiṭra* and its essential function in perceiving God, the source of both natural law and the revelation. *Fiṭra* thus becomes the background for a discussion of freedom of conscience and religion as prerequisites for an ethical order based on the Koran.

Freedom of Conscience and Religion in the Koran

Freedom of conscience and religion has been correctly recognized as the cornerstone of democratic pluralism.[46] Any pluralistic social order requires the active articulation of rational as well as revelational sources of protection for individual autonomy in matters of personal faith within a society as part of the divine-human covenant. The questions of individual autonomy and human agency might seem peculiar to the modern vision of a public order in which a group of individuals shares core ideas, ideals, and values geared toward maintaining a civil society;[47] yet living together in a society not only requires mutuality in matters of commerce and market relations, but it also presupposes a shared foundation of morality and binding sentiments that unite autonomous individuals who are able to negotiate their own spiritual space—and these criteria apply to all societies in all eras.

In general, by virtue of the natural human urge to sociation, diverse groups fell back on their religious teachings to derive and articulate the rules affecting public life. The recognition and implementation of the religious values of sharing and mutuality created a civil religion that encouraged coexistence with those who, even when they did not share the dominant group's particular vision of salvation, could share in a concern for living in peace with justice. There is nothing modern or liberal about such an acknowledgment of individual autonomous dignity and the human need for moral and spiritual nourishment—such yearnings are evident throughout history. A rudimentary terminology or an unsophisticated discourse in theology, ethics, or politics in no way implies that earlier cultures were unfamiliar with notions of civil religion or society based on freedom of conscience. On the contrary, the existence of similar human conditions in other cultures and the universally recognizable laws of nature that regulate interaction between religion and history, faith and power, ideology and politics, suggests the common moral and spiritual terrain that human beings tread in their perennial search for solutions to the problems of injustice, oppression, and poverty. Hence, as I shall contend, the concern for human autonomy—especially freedom of worship (or freedom not to worship)—is as fundamental to the Koranic vision of human religiosity as it is to that of other civilizations. The Koran requires Muslims to sit in dialogue with their own tradition to uncover a just approach to religious diversity and interfaith coexistence. Moreover, a rigorous analysis of the Koran will demonstrate that without recognition of freedom of religion, it is impossible to conceive of religious commitment as a freely negotiated human-divine relationship that fosters individual accountability for one's acceptance or rejection of faith in God, commitment to pursue an ethical life, and willingness to be judged accordingly.

The ability to accept or reject faith and to pursue an ethical life presupposes the existence of an innate capacity that can guide a person to a desired goal. This innate capacity is part of the human nature—the *fiṭra*—with which God shapes humanity (K. 91:7–10). This innate capacity encompasses the faculty of moral reasoning. Conscience in the Koran is connected with the source of ethical knowledge because its point of reference is the *fiṭra* and the *fiṭra*'s inherent ability to shape laws of conduct. Conscience, then, is a God-given ability to judge values and obligations.

Is human conscience capable of uncovering first principles without the help of revelation? By revelation I mean the guidance that comes to human beings through a divine act of creation, both in human nature as well as in the prophets, the carriers of the divine message in word and deed. In other words, universal guidance through the *fiṭra*, the prerevelatory part of human nature, is "a mode in which things previously unknown are added to things already known, making a different pattern but including many elements that were the object of anterior knowledge."[48] There is a correlation between the epistemes gleaned from the prerevelatory guidance in the *fiṭra*, and the revelatory guidance conveyed through the prophets because, according to the Koran, their source is one and the same: God. Hence, God's perfect revelatory commandments regarding justice, for instance, are also apprehended in general (*bi-l-ijmāl*) by the *fiṭra*, though the justice of everything He has commanded might not be apprehended in all its detail (*bi-l-tafṣīl*) until it unfolds in experience.

Conscience in the Koran is connected with the idea of *fiṭra* created by God as a necessary locus of universal guidance. The relationship between this general guidance and conscience is reflected in one's voluntary acceptance or rejection of faith in guidance through the Prophet. God has endowed human beings with the necessary cognition and volition in their *fiṭra* to further their comprehension of moral truths. Moreover, the distinction between evil and good is ingrained in the human personality in the form of a prerevelatory, natural guidance with which God has favored human beings. It is through this natural guidance that human beings are expected to develop the ability to perform and judge their actions and to choose that which will lead them to prosperity without any fear of external sanctions, immediate or eschatological.

Guidance from God is an exaltation of individual conscience as opposed to forcible, collective conformism; hence, the responsibility for the salvation of each Muslim lies in his or her own hands rather than in any religious authority. God provides a general direction, a spiritual predisposition that can guard against spiritual and moral peril (if a person hearkens to its warnings); this natural guidance is further strengthened through prophetic revelation. The Koran repeatedly shows the path to salvation to emphasize the fact that this form of guidance is universal and available to all who aspire to become godfearing and prosperous.

Because of their freedom of conscience and self-subsistent moral values, human beings can reject this form of guidance; they cannot, however, produce any valid excuse for the rejection of their inborn nature. Their rejection of revelatory guidance, moreover, does not necessarily deprive conscience of its cognitive capacity and practical impact. Thus, when God denies guidance to those who do not believe in divine revelation (K. 19:104), the denial pertains to the procurement of the desirable end of becoming godly, and not to the initial guidance that is originally engraved upon the hearts of all human beings through the *fiṭra*. "And We guide them to a straight path" (K. 19:104) points to the guidance that signifies the procurement of a good end. It implies that this guidance is available to an individual after that person has consented to lead a life of uprightness (*taqwā*). In another place, the Koran makes it even more explicit that this latter aspect of guidance makes it possible for a person to achieve that which is desirable:

> Whomsoever God desires to guide, He expands his breast to *islām* [to submit himself or herself to the will of God in order to procure the desirable goal]; whomsoever He desires to lead astray [because of a personal choice not to submit] He makes his/her breast narrow, tight, as if he/she were climbing to heaven. So God lays admonition upon those who believe not. (K. 6:125)

The Koran is thus speaking about two forms of guidance: prerevelatory and revelatory guidance. The first form is the one located in the *fiṭra* by means of which an individual becomes morally and spiritually aware; the second is the one that God bestows after the attainment of moral consciousness (*taqwā*). This latter guidance helps the individual to remain unshakable when encountering unbelievers and hypocrites. *Taqwā*, which is "keen, spiritual and moral perception and motivation," is a comprehensive attribute that touches all aspects of faith, when it is put into practice.[49]

It is important to note that the Koran considers "misguidance" or "leading astray" to be God's response to unsatisfactory actions or attitudes on the part of individuals who have chosen to reject the faith. Such individuals deserve their fate:

> How shall God guide a people who have disbelieved after they believed. . . . God guides not the people of evildoers. (K. 3:86)

> Surely those who disbelieve after they have believed and they increase in unbelief—their repentance shall not be accepted; those are the ones who go astray. (K. 3:90)

These passages imply human responsibility for being led astray. Human beings are given the choice to accept or reject the faith, and they bear the consequences of their choice.

But there are other passages in the Koran that impute the act of leading astray to God. In order to explain the contradiction between individual autonomous will and divine predeterminism, the Koran exegetes have distinguished between two kinds of misguidance as causes of human culpability. The first kind results from the use of demonstration and evidence, both faculties of human reason, to reject extrarevelatory guidance. Corrupt attributes such as disbelief and hypocrisy are symptoms of this kind of misguidance. The second kind results from the rejection of revelatory guidance from the prophets, which results in further entrenchment of the corrupt attributes. This is the point of the following verse: "In their heart is a sickness, and God has increased their sickness, and there awaits them a painful chastisement for that they have cried lies" (K. 2:10).

The heart (*qalb*) in the Koranic usage relates to conscience because of the possibility of describing it as sick (*marīḍ*) or sound (*salīm*): "Degrade me not upon that day when they are raised up, the day when neither wealth nor sons shall profit except for him who comes with a sound heart (*qalb*^{in} *salīm*)" (K. 26:89).[50] Hence, the first kind of sickness that conscience suffers is the result an individual's willful act, while the second stage is the result of the divine withdrawal of guidance. This means that God does not guide people who have neglected to respond to that universal guidance ingrained in the human personality (K. 91:7), by means of which they could have helped themselves to understand their true role on earth.

From the foregoing observations about guidance and misguidance, it would be accurate to visualize people who possess *taqwā*—"keen, spiritual moral consciousness and motivation"—as being situated between universal guidance and revelatory guidance. In other words, being equipped with the necessary cognition and volition, they are ready to follow the commands of God to attain prosperity (*falāḥiyya*). On the other hand, unbelievers and hypocrites can be visualized as being situated between the two forms of misguidance. By having allowed the heart (conscience) to become sick, they have allowed their native sense of correct judgment and their sense of personal responsibility, which are theirs by nature (*fiṭra*), to atrophy.

Since the question of guidance is related to the question of the source of knowledge of ethical values in both classical and modern works of Koranic exegesis, it is on this point that theological differences, as pointed out earlier in my brief remarks about the Muʿtazilite and Ashʿarite theological standpoints, are rooted in conflicting conceptions of human responsibility. The Muʿtazilites, who emphasized the complete responsibility of human beings, upheld the concept of human free will in responding to the call of both natural guidance and guidance through revelation. By contrast, the Ashʿarites, who upheld the omnipotence of God, denied the human will any role in responding to divine guidance. As a matter of fact, according to them, it was impossible for an individual to accept or reject faith unless God willed it. The Shīʿites maintained that the Koran contains a complex view of human responsibility.

It allows for both human decision and divine omnipotence in the matter of guidance.[51]

In the context of the present work, the concept of universal guidance has wider implications than merely demonstrating the human potential for volition (K. 91:7) in the development of a keen sense of spiritual and moral perception and motivation. It appears that the Koran regards humanity as having been one community under universal guidance before the specific revelation sent to prophets:

> The people were one community; then God sent forth Prophets, good tidings to bear and warning, and He sent down with them the Book with the truth, that He might decide between the people touching their differences. (K. 2:213)

Universal or extrarevelatory guidance treats all human beings as equal and as potential believers in God before they are sorted into membership in various religious communities.

In the Koran, universal guidance entails natural-moral grounds of human conduct. The relevant passages refer to an objective and universal moral nature—the *fiṭra*—on the basis of which all human beings are to be treated equally and held equally accountable to God. In other words, certain moral prescriptions follow from a common human nature and are regarded as independent of particular spiritual beliefs, even though all practical guidance ultimately springs from God. In chapter 2, I used the term *al-maʿrūf*, meaning the 'well-known,' 'generally recognized,' and even 'universally accepted,' to designate the moral prescription that no human being with sound reason can fail to recognize:

> Prescribed for you, when any one of you is visited by death, and he leaves behind some goods, is to make testament in favor of his parents and kinsmen in goodness (*al-maʿrūf*) [i.e., in a generally recognized way]—this is an obligation on the godfearing [i.e., those who possess *taqwā* (spiritual and moral awareness)]. (K. 2:180)

"Goodness" in this passage is understood as the Arabs understood it conventionally, before the Koran was revealed to supplement the common ethical sense of *al-maʿrūf*.

The Koranic passages concerning *al-maʿrūf* demonstrate an important point: goodness in revelation denotes moral virtue, which cannot become intelligible without reference to an objective state of affairs. Indeed, the notion of goodness logically appeals to that universal objective value "ingrained in the human soul" (K. 91:8); as such, it becomes comprehensible. This is the significance of the passage with which I opened this chapter. In this extremely important passage, the Koran recognizes in moral virtue (goodness) a universality and objectivity that transcend religious differences; humankind is admonished "compete with one another in good work."

The Ashʿarite theologian-exegete al-Rāzī, in line with the Ashʿarite proclivity toward predeterminism, interprets *fiṭra* as that which compels a person to affirm the unity of God (*al-tawḥīd*). Such an interpretation rules out the notion that human beings can freely affirm religious faith, since it does not allow for personal responsibility in developing *taqwā*, that sharp moral consciousness spoken of earlier.[52] On the other hand, al-Zamakhsharī, in conformity with the Muʿtazilite theory of individual autonomy and agential nature, interprets *fiṭra* as '*khilqa*,' that is, 'natural disposition,' in the sense that God has created in humans a capacity to affirm freely God's unity and submit to God's will. This interpretation, contends al-Zamakhsharī, is valid on the grounds that there is a concurrence between the *fiṭra* and moral reasoning, and a harmony between *fiṭra* and sound opinion (*al-naẓar al-ṣaḥīḥ*). In other words, *fiṭra* is as objective and universal as moral reasoning is, and, as such, *fiṭra* is the capacity to exercise rational choice in the matter of faith. This view of *fiṭra* is corroborated by the Koranic notion that guidance by means of revelation is preceded by a universal guidance available to humanity as originally created by God. Thus, when God commands human beings to set their purpose according to the original nature (*fiṭrat allāh*) of humans (K. 30:30–1), this leaves no doubt that *fiṭrat allāh* is that innate disposition and inherent capacity that enable a person to accept or reject faith.

The Koranic notion of *fiṭra* makes it imperative that Muslims take a fresh look at the verse that explicitly states: "No compulsion is there in religion" (K. 2:257). This verse is quoted by Muslim apologists as pointing to the Koranic notion of individual freedom of religion under the Sharīʿa. Yet, as I have discussed in the context of Muslim theology for the twenty-first century, it is the politically conditioned exclusionary legal decisions that actually bypassed the *fiṭra*-based Koranic spirit of freedom of conscience. What are the religious justifications for undertaking an offensive *jihād* in order to call people to faith or to deny their basic right to worship freely?

If the function of religious guidance through revelation is to provide precepts and examples to all men and women in worshipping God, and in dealing justly with their fellow humans, then it presupposes individual responsibility that flows from an inward stance, a natural faith (*al-imān al-fiṭrī*)[53] that lies at the heart of any religious and moral commitment. The Koran refers to this inward stance as an essential prerequisite for religious submission: "The Bedouins say: 'We believe.' Say: 'You do not believe; rather say, "We surrender," for belief (*īmān*) has not yet entered your hearts'" (K. 49:14). This passage clearly differentiates between *islām* (submission) and *īmān* (faith), that is, between a formal submission to the sacred authority—which could be the mere utterance of the formula of faith without any real commitment to uphold God's commands—and the faith born of the voluntary consent of conscience, free of external coercion, developing from a keen spiritual and moral awareness and motivation.[54] The faith that has "entered the heart" is the result of a choice innately available to all human beings, which is then strengthened and assisted by revelation. In this sense, faith is freely and directly negotiated between God and human being and cannot be compelled.

This is an extremely important observation about individual autonomy in matters of faith. The Koranic utterance "No compulsion is there in religion" (K. 2:256) seems to be saying that a person cannot be deprived of civil rights on account of religious conviction, no matter how distasteful it might be to the dominant faith community.

I view the "No compulsion" passage as the Koran's profound statement on basic individual religious freedom. In fact, Sayyid Quṭb regards the verse as "the manifestation of God's favor toward humankind," because the message upholds human dignity and respect for individual autonomy in the matter of guidance and error in belief.[55] ʿAllāma Ṭabāṭabāʾī regards the verse as the negation of enforced religion, because true faith abides in conscience, a domain unreachable by compulsion or enforcement.[56]

Curiously, a number of exegetes have interpreted the verse as implying that only the people of the Book—Jews, Christians, and Zoroaṣtrians—should be left to practice their religions, assuming that they pay the *jizya* (poll tax); by contrast, Arabs bereft of a revealed religion must be forced to accept Islam at the point of a sword. Ṭabarī, in his traditional exegesis, *Jāmiʿal-bayān*, cites several reports on the authority of the early associates of the Prophet that authorize tolerating only the people of the Book. But he does not agree that the "No compulsion" verse was abrogated by the verses that ordained *jihād* (K. 2:216ff.). Ṭabarī argues that while it was the practice of the Prophet not to force the people of the Book to accept Islam, he did condone compelling the idol worshippers among the Arabs and the apostates (*al-murtaddun*) to accept the faith.

In support of his contention, he relates a story of a Muslim belonging to the tribe of Sālim b. ʿAwf of Medina, whose two sons had embraced Christianity before Islam was preached. When the sons came to visit their father in Medina, their aggrieved father asked them to convert to Islam. The two refused to do so. The father brought them before the Prophet and asked him to intervene in the controversy. It was precisely on this occasion, according to Ṭabarī, that the "No compulsion" verse was revealed, and the father, apparently on the advice of the Prophet, left his two sons alone. The Ashʿarite exegete, Rāzī, agrees with Ṭabarī's conclusion that tolerance in the matter of religion was to be afforded only to the people of the Book and that others were to be coerced into converting to Islam.[57]

On the other hand, Zamakhsharī, the Muʿtazilite exegete, maintains that God does not permit faith through compulsion and coercion, as the Ashʿarites believe. Rather, he allows faith through strengthening a person with *fiṭra* and free choice (*al-ikhtiyār*). Zamakhsharī goes on to quote K. 10:99 in support of his assertion: "And if thy Lord had willed, whoever is in the earth would have believed, all of them, all together. Wouldst thou [O Muhammad] then constrain the people until they are believers?" Thus, Zamakhsharī says, if God had willed he would have compelled them to believe; however, he did not do this and instead allowed people to have free choice in the matter of faith.[58] The implications of the "No compulsion" verse for Zamakhsharī are in conformity with his overall rationalist view. Not only are the people of the Book not to be coerced into converting to Islam; all human beings must have the basic right to exercise free choice in this matter. Accordingly, the verse does not set a limit, such that "No compulsion in religion" is to be applied exclusively to the people of the Book. Moreover, the story cited in support of the interpretation of Ṭabarī and others does not end with a declaration from the Prophet that only the people of the Book were to be spared in the matter of accepting Islam by coercion. Indeed, the story appears to confirm my conclusions about the role of *fiṭra* and its implications for religious belief.

The Concept of *Fiṭra* in the Context of Freedom of Conscience

The *fiṭra*, the locus of natural guidance, if unimpaired (e.g., by unsatisfactory actions or attitudes), will lead to the strengthened faith of revealed guidance. More importantly, only a carefully nurtured and unimpaired *fiṭra* can establish human responsibility for heeding the directives of universal guidance. This responsibility is implicit in the Koranic teaching about the Day of Judgment, when God will not punish anyone for an act for which he or she is not responsible.

To keep the *fiṭra* in a sound state, then, is the responsibility of a free human agent. Failure to guard it results in the "hardening of the heart." The heart (*qalb*, plural *qulūb*) in Koranic usage is the "seat of consciousness, thoughts, volitions and feelings." Hence, the heart is the physical locus of the *fiṭra*, that inherent capacity that is affected by the choice made in the matter of faith. When a person rejects faith, the heart becomes veiled and is deprived of its ability to understand the moral situation. The heart thus functions as a faculty for distinguishing truth from falsehood, good from evil, the beneficial from the harmful. It discovers the benefit of revealed guidance, which reminds it that God commands that good be done and evil be avoided and ordains obedience to the religious and moral ordinances.

The heart in the Koran thus signifies the instrument of religious and moral perception that has the ability to make ultimate judgments in keeping with the *fiṭra*. So understood, the heart is *al-ḍamīr*, the conscience. Having discerned universal religious and moral truths established in the *fiṭra*, it is able to guide a person through religious and moral dilemmas. When the heart responds to revelatory guidance by embracing faith, it becomes the pure or sound heart that has been softened and made healthy by God's inspiration. On the other hand, when it fails to respond to revelation, it becomes a sick heart that is hardened to God's direction.

In some important ways, the heart, with its seat in the *fiṭra*, draws upon the ethical axioms available to it naturally and undertakes to resolve practical and spiritual dilemmas. If the Western/Christian idea of conscience involves the resolution of practical conflicts through judging degrees of personal responsibility and the merits of alternative courses of action,[59] the heart appears to play an analogous role in Koranic thought. According to the Koran, an individual will "call to mind what he has been striving for" (K. 79:35) and the way his choices are affected by his preoccupation with short-term, selfish, narrow, and material concerns at the expense of the loftier requirements of a life of devotion and righteousness (K. 69:19–29). This "calling to mind" is often pricked by certain painful emotional experiences, parallel to the Western/Christian pangs of conscience. Finally, an individual has the opportunity, by means of a conative disposition, to seek what the heart believes to be good and to shun what it believes to be evil, and to begin, at least, to achieve the goal of life—final prosperity.[60]

The Koran, by means of its notion of a universal guidance embedded in human nature, teaches that individuals are in possession of dispositions that make room for voluntary consent to faith, including the free embrace of the prophetically revealed truths, such as the doctrine of God and the Day of Judgment.

Undergirding the opportunity for human volition is a set of Koranic assumptions regarding the existence of objective and universal moral truths and their availability to free and rationally governed human thought and action. For his part, God, according to the Koran, has promised that he will abundantly bestow on all his creatures different forms of guidance to nurture them until they attain the desirable goal. Besides the aforementioned two forms of guidance—universal and extrarevelatory on the one hand, and revelatory on the other—four other types of guidance, bestowed by God in an act of benevolence toward humanity, have been identified by Muḥammad ʿAbduh (1849–1905), a prominent Sunnī theologian-exegete:

1. Guidance that comes though natural mental forces and an innate propensity or natural disposition and whose locus is the *fiṭra*. This is what I have identified above as the universal, extrarevelatory guidance.
2. Guidance that is provided through sensory perception, and that functions as an effectuation or development of the first form. This form also falls under the universal, extrarevelatory guidance available to all God's creatures.
3. Guidance that is created in the rational faculty. Since human beings live in society, their innate propensities need to be cultivated through an ability to reflect on and intuitively reason about the consequences of their acts, to correct errors of perception and explaining their causes.
4. Guidance that comes through religion, that is, through the message proclaimed through the prophetic medium. This guidance is subsequent to the universal *fiṭra*. Whereas universal guidance is fallible, religion based on revealed guidance is capable of unerringly showing people where they have gone wrong, thereby demonstrating the limits of reason. Revelatory guidance is thus the light that brings a person out of the darkness of innate, imperfect human judgment: "God is the Protector of the believers; He brings them forth from darkness into light; and the unbelievers—their protectors are false deities, that brings them forth from the light into the darkness" (K. 2:257).

Religion also makes one aware of the hereafter, the second life, wherein lies one's permanent abode. It is for this reason, says ʿAbduh, that God has bestowed religious guidance in addition to the three aforementioned forms of guidance.

Thus, concludes ʿAbduh, the meaning of guidance in the Koranic passages is directing (*al-dalāla*), which is analogous to aiding people at the crossroads of success and failure. It provides a full explanation of the consequences that accrue from choosing one path or the other. This guidance is given to all human beings equally, whereas additional guidance is given particularly to those who have voluntarily chosen to tread the path of success in order to speed their journey on the path of good and prosperity. This latter, enhanced guidance is not bestowed on all human beings alike, as is guidance given through the senses, rational faculty, and innate disposition. It is precisely for this reason that a person should ask for this superior guidance, as the Koran prescribes in K. 1:5. Since human beings encounter errors and are misled in their perceptions, they are in need of special aid, which God can confer through prayer. "Guide us in the straight path" (K. 1:5) means "Help us by divine aid so that we remain protected from being misguided and committing errors."[61]

Muhammad ʿAbduh's view of guidance, systematically extracted from the Koranic passages and their presuppositions, assumes that because certain objective and universal values are imprinted upon the human psyche, people can acquire the knowledge necessary to assume personal responsibility and reckon with its consequences. Such assumptions hardly leave room for compulsion in the matter of religion.

Just as there is a tension between rationalist objectivism and theistic subjectivism as modes of ethical knowledge, so there is a tension in the question of tolerance of what the Koran calls a "sick" (erroneous) heart, one that has not submitted to the "only straight path to God" (K. 16:9), that is, Islam. According to the Koran, only the path that acknowledges that God is of importance in leading human beings to prosperity is the straight path. All other paths are deviant, and detrimental to the unity of mankind (K. 6:160ff).

The Koran acknowledges the diversity of the paths adopted by different people, despite the unity of their origins; on the other hand, it declares the superiority of "the true religion with God [which] is *islām* ('submission')" (K. 3:19). In other words, the unity of the path is at the level of universal guidance, that which is imprinted upon human beings by God, by virtue of which they are all one nation. At the same time, diversity exists at the level of the specific guidance proclaimed by the prophets. Accordingly, humankind comes to be divided into various religious communities as its members adhere to one or another revelation. As discussed in the previous chapter, this diversity is a divinely approved mystery: "Had thy Lord willed, He would have made humankind one community; but they continue in their differences excepting those on whom thy Lord has mercy" (K. 11:118).

The differences to which the verse refers are related to religious claims of exclusive truth and are the result of the people's being "insolent one to another":

> The people were one community [under universal guidance]; then God sent forth the prophets, good tidings to bear and warning, and He sent down with them the Book (i.e., the particular revealed guidance) with the truth, that He might decide between the people touching their differences [in matters of religion]; and only those who had been given it (i.e., the revelation) were at variance upon it, after the clear signs had come to them [through the prophets], being insolent one to another; then God guided those who believed to the truth, touching which they were at variance, by His leave; and God guides whomsoever He will to a straight path.
> (K. 2:213–214)

Still, differences in matters of faith, although deplored as originating from human insolence, are tolerated by God. In a specific verse, even the Prophet is advised to show tolerance toward those who did not accept his message and opposed him: "And if thy Lord had willed, whoever is in the earth would have believed, all of them, all together. Wouldst thou [O Muhammad] then constrain the people, until they are believers?" (K. 10:99).

Submission to the will of God must come through voluntary consent, prompted by the universal guidance that is engraved upon the human heart. Thus, compulsion and external interference in the matter of sincere devotion to God would appear to be the antithesis of Islamic faith.

The necessary underpinning of the preceding passages is the absolute claim of the Koran that guidance, both revelatory and extrarevelatory, is the function of God and that it is he alone who can touch the hearts of those who have rejected divine guidance. Moreover, human insolence causes God to deprive human beings of the truth. So the burden of being misguided lies on human shoulders, for despite their inherent knowledge of the moral requirement to "compete with one another in good works" (K. 5:48), some human beings choose to turn their backs upon all guidance received from God (K. 9:38).

Thus, the Koran prohibits abuse of those who have not accepted divine guidance and, of course, any coercive conversions of such nonbelievers. Above all, there is the assurance that the final judgment in the matter of faith rests with God alone:

> Had God willed, they were not idolaters; and We have not appointed thee a watcher over them, neither art thou their guardian. Abuse not those to whom they pray, apart from God, or, they will abuse God in revenge without knowledge. So We have decked out fair to every community their deeds; then to their Lord they shall return, and He will tell them what they have been doing. (K. 7:107–108)

The Koran emphatically denies any human being the right to take it upon herself or himself to forcibly steer others onto a spiritual path. Such coercion is exclusively the domain of the "Master of the Day of Doom" (K. 1:4).

The Koranic notion of religious pluralism, even when the right path is conceived as the only basis on which God has decreed the unity of humankind, rules out the intolerant claims that religious communities frequently make. By recognizing the capacity for universal righteousness in the *fiṭra*, the Koran sets forth a fundamental principle of freedom of religion.

The difference between a moral and religious obligation is critical here, especially in relation to the two forms of guidance: the universal and the particular. On the basis of universal guidance, it is appropriate to demand uniformity because an objective and universally binding moral standard is assumed to exist that guarantees true human well-being. In enforcing that basic moral standard, resort to compulsion is legitimate. On the basis of particular guidance, it is crucial to allow human beings to exercise their volition in matters of personal faith because any attempt to enforce it would lead to its negation. And although the comprehensive nature of particular guidance provides the "thick" description of ideal human life on earth that is consonant with the historical and cultural considerations of community life in Islam, it removes the God-human relationship from human jurisdiction.[62] So construed, the aspect of revelatory guidance that regulates the God-human relationship is concerned with reminding and warning people to heed the divine call through submission to God's will. As the head of the community, the Prophet could not use his political power to enforce a God-human relationship that is founded upon individual autonomy and human agency. In fact, the Koran repeatedly reminds the Prophet that his duty was simply to deliver the message without taking it upon himself to function as God's religious enforcer:

> Your Lord knows you very well; if He will, He will have mercy on you, or, if He will, He will chastise you. We have not sent you [O Muḥammad] as a guardian (*wakīl*) over them. (K. 17:54)

> We know very well what they [unbelievers] say; you are not a compeller (*jabbār*) over them. Therefore remind by the Koran him who fears My threat. (K. 50:45)

The Koran provides a substantial basis for freedom of religion. Not only does it maintain the idea of universal and objective moral values that are cognitively accessible to human nature; it also upholds the notion of a fallible conscience. This notion results in the toleration of human autonomy in matters of religious choice.

Freedom of Religion in the Context of Islamic Public Order

The Koran deals not only with individual religious freedom, but also with the creation of a just social order. I have shown elsewhere how under certain conditions the Koran gives the state, as the representative of society, the power to control "discord on earth," a general state of lawlessness created by taking up arms against the established Islamic order.[63] The eradication of corruption on earth, taken in light of the Koranic principle of commanding good and forbidding evil, is a basic moral duty to protect the well-being of the community. In the Islamic polity, where religion is not divorced from the public agenda, leaving adherents of competing doctrines free to pursue their beliefs engenders an inherent tension between religious communities that has to be resolved through state regulation. The millet system in the Muslim world provided the premodern paradigm of a religiously pluralistic society by granting each religious community an official status and a substantial measure of self-government. The system based on the millet, which means a "religiously defined people,"[64] was a "group rights model"[65] that was defined in terms of a communitarian identity and hence did not recognize any principle of individual autonomy in matters of religion. And, this communitarian identity was not restricted to identifying non-Muslim *dhimmis*;[66] the millet's self-governing status allowed it to base its sovereignty on the orthodox creed officially instituted by the millet leadership. Under the Ottoman administration, this group status entailed some degree of state control over religious identification, overseen by the administrative officer responsible to the state for the religious community. In addition, the system allowed the enforcement of religious orthodoxy under state patronage, leaving no scope for individual dissent, political or religious. Every episode of the individual exercise of freedom of conscience was seen as a deviation from the accepted orthodoxy maintained and enforced by the socioreligious order.

Although the Koranic respect for the founders of the other Abrahamic religions created a relatively more tolerant attitude among Muslims, the policies of discrimination against the millets in the Muslim world remained in force because the Sharīʿa never accepted the equality of believers and nonbelievers. Contrary to the pluralistic spirit of the Koran, Muslim jurists encouraged a state-sponsored institutionalization of the inferiority of non-Muslims, including the monotheist *ahl al-dhimma*, as necessary for the well-being of the Muslim public order. For legal scholars, unbelievers had willfully spurned the offer of Islam. Hence, their inferiority was not imposed but freely chosen.

It was precisely this kind of evaluation of the religious other that led to the contemptuous attitude toward non-Muslim minorities in Muslim societies. But this negative attitude, arising from the spirit of enforced uniformity in the community, also extended to fellow believers who failed to meet the criteria of pure faith, unsullied by the accretions and innovations that the ultrapious believed had corrupted the authentic Islam of the Prophet and his companions.[67] The pious restoration of the faith meant intolerance toward individual freedom of conscience and hence the removal of the cornerstone of Koranic pluralism. Heresy (*ilḥād*, that is, questioning the orthodox doctrinal position) and apostasy (*irtidād*, that is, changing one's socioreligious affiliation) were promulgated as punishable crimes in the Sharīʿa. Given the Koran's endorsement of pluralism and individual autonomy and agency in matters of faith, one must wonder whether the Muslim penal code's provisions on apostasy lead to an enforced religiosity that runs counter to the letter and spirit of the Koran.[68]

Is Apostasy a Religious or Civil Offense in Islam?

Muslim jurists have not engaged in a conceptual investigation of the ethical-legal presuppositions of certain commandments in the Koran. For instance, the Koran assigns Muslim public order the obligation of controlling "discord on earth." This phrase is part of a long verse that prescribes the severest penalties for rebellion:

> The punishment of those who fight against God and His Messenger, and hasten to do corruption, creating discord on earth: they shall be slaughtered, or crucified, or their hands and feet shall alternately be struck off, or they shall be banished from the land. This is a degradation for them in this world; and in the world to come awaits them a mighty chastisement, except for those who repent before you lay your hands on them. (K. 5:33–34)

As noted earlier, eradication of corruption on earth is a moral commandment to protect the well-being of a community. But this need not contradict the freedom afforded to individual conscience in matters of faith. Not only is this essential distinction between the civil and moral absent in the exegetical literature on the foregoing verse, but also it is lacking in the classical juridical corpus.

In Islam, the distinction between the religious and the temporal or between the moral and the civil is not de jure but de facto. The categorization of religiously ordained God-human (*ʿibādāt*) and interhuman (*muʿāmalāt*) relationships in Islamic sacred law, the Sharīʿa, is perhaps the most explicit expression of the two realms of the religious and the temporal in human activity on earth. Whereas God-human relations are founded on individual autonomy under the divine regulation, interhuman relations are within the jurisdiction of human institutions founded on political consensus with the purpose of furthering justice and equity in society. The same distinction rules out the authority of the Muslim state to regulate religious matters except when the free exercise of religion for any individual is in danger.

That the Koran presents comprehensive commandments in which moral and civil are not always easy to distinguish is demonstrated by the equal gravity under civil law accorded to moral and religious transgressions by Muslim jurists. The conceptual distinction aside, Islamic law treats these transgressions as affecting not only humans, but also God. There is a sense in which both humans and God may have claims in the same infringement, even if the event seems to harm only one of them. Although punishment of crimes against religion is beyond human jurisdiction, the juridical body in Islam is empowered to impose sanctions only when it can be demonstrated beyond doubt that the grievous crime included an infringement of a human right (*ḥaqq ādamī* = private claim). There are six transgressions that are treated as crimes against religion and society and for which the law prescribes specific *ḥadd* (defined) punishments:

1. illicit sexual relations
2. slanderous allegations of unchastity
3. wine-drinking
4. theft
5. armed robbery
6. apostasy (*irtidād*)

The underlying principle in the penal code is that the punishment should fit the crime and the character of the offender, because the purpose of punishment is the prevention of any conduct that might undermine public order. The supreme duty of the Muslim ruler is to protect the public interest, a function for which the law afforded him overriding personal discretion to determine how the purposes of God might best be achieved in the community.

Since criminal law in Islam was a system of private law that fell under the ratifying and enforcement powers of the established political regime, prosecutions for offenses like false accusation of unlawful intercourse or theft, crimes that offend against both God's will and just human relations, take place only if initiated by the victim, and the plaintiff must be present at both the trial and the execution. In the case of unlawful intercourse, the witness plays a crucial role. There must be four witnesses to the actual act of intercourse. Moreover, at the time of punishment, if the witnesses are not present (and, if the punishment is stoning, if they do not throw the first stones), the punishment is not carried out. If the thief returns the stolen object before an application for prosecution has been made, the prescribed punishment lapses; repentance for highway robbery before arrest causes the punishment to lapse; and if an offense is treated as a misdemeanor (*jināyāt*) and the complainant is willing to pardon the offender, blood money may be paid instead of the punishment or the punishment may be remitted altogether. In the cases of offenses against religion that are not sanctioned by specific punishments—apostasy, for example (for which there is no definite punishment in the Koran)—the effects of repentance are even more far-reaching.

The treatment of apostasy as an impingement on the rights of God and humanity in Islam presents an interesting case of interdependency between the religious and civil in the laws that govern the Muslim community.

To begin with, there is a fundamental problem in rendering the Arabic word *irtidād* as 'apostasy.' The term *irtidād*, meaning 'rejection' or 'turning away from,' was historically applied to the battles that were fought against those

Muslims who had refused to pay taxes to the Muslim political authority after the Prophet's death. Hence, the *murtaddūn* were those who had rebelled against the established order. Compare this with the way the term *apostasy* is understood in Christianity, where it suggests historically an abandoning of one exclusive and institutionalized religion for another.[69] In this sense, apostasy occurs when different religions compete with one another in one public arena. *Irtidād*, on the other hand, occurs within the communal order in the form of internal subversion, which is no longer merely a religious offense. I have dealt elsewhere with the problem of the legal definition of apostasy in Islamic jurisprudence.[70] Here, I am once again confronted with the complexity of the question of apostasy in Islam, especially in the light of consistent and obvious Koranic treatment of that offense as being beyond human jurisdiction. It is evident that the Koran supports full freedom of religion, not merely tolerance of religions other than Islam. The *irtidād* or *ridda* of the Koran is apparently a turning away from God and hence is punishable by God alone; in jurisprudence, the *irtidād*, depending on its public manifestation and its adverse impact on the Muslim public order, denotes turning away from the community, in which case the determination of the gravity of the offense is strictly under the jurisdiction of the legitimate Muslim public order. The extent of punishment depends on the civil interpretation of the act by the political and juridical authority.

Consequently, although classified as a capital offense (*ḥudūd* crime) in the Islamic penal code, apostasy was and remains the only crime that presents Muslim legal authorities with a serious dilemma. The verse of the Koran that provides the jurists with the original ruling unambiguously characterizes apostasy as a noncapital offense. The Koran says: "And, whosoever turns (*yartadid*) from his religion, and dies disbelieving—their works have failed in this world and the next; those are the inhabitants of the Fire; therein they shall dwell forever" (K. 2:217).

Clearly, the problem is that while the Koran favored an overall tolerance of religious pluralism, the social ethics delineated by the Muslim jurists regarded pluralism as a source of instability in the Muslim public order. The so-called wars of apostasy (*ridda*) in the aftermath of the Prophet's death served as a grave reminder to the jurists to provide measures that would deter disruptive activity in the community.

Moreover, in an Islamic context, the Muslim political authority is solely responsible for determining that the act of *ridda* (as in the rejection of or turning away from the Muslim public order) is regarded as meriting certain punishment. The reason is that in the absence of the church and the ecclesiastical body, it is the responsibility of the civil authority to determine the *ridda*'s criminality and take appropriate action to deal with it. Since its determination as *ridda* was restricted to the political authority required to protect the common good of the community, a number of Muslim jurists classified *irtidād* as part of the *ta'zīr* (chastisement, deterrence) crimes that "infringe on private or community interests of the public order," and for which punishment is instituted by the legitimate political authority. Consequently, the burden is placed on the public authority to lay down rules that penalize all conduct that seems contrary to the public interest, social tranquility, or public order.[71]

Hence, civil considerations surrounding the question of sedition have shaped the interpretation of the act of apostasy in Islam. The harsh treatment of apostates in Islamic law was promulgated without making an indispensable distinction between the Koranic doctrine of freedom of religion, which insists that no human agency can negotiate an individual's spiritual destiny, and legitimate concerns about the Muslim public order. As long as apostasy remains a private matter and does not disrupt society at large, there is no particular punishment in the Koran. However, when it violates sanctity and impinges on the rights of Muslims to practice their belief, then it is treated as a physical aggression toward the faith. At that point, it is no mere apostasy; it is, rather, treated as an act of sedition that causes discord and threatens the unity of Islamic community. It is only in this case that apostasy is punishable by the severest penalties, framed as self-defense against a violent rebellion against God and the Prophet, to be countered, in turn, with violence if necessary.

There is a self-evident problem in any Islamic criminalization of apostasy defined in the strict sense of public abandonment of an institutionalized religion for another; a mere expression of religious dissent against the established community, which the Koran grants as a basic individual right, cannot constitute a criminal act punishable in this world. The Muslim civil authority has the ultimate responsibility for using its discretionary power to assess the level of discord created by a public declaration of an apostasy and to lay down the appropriate measures to deal with it.

4
Forgiveness Toward Humankind

O believers, the law of fair retribution is prescribed for you in cases of murder [with the following conditions]: a free man for a free man; a slave for a slave; and a woman for a woman. But if [one of those seeking to avenge the victim] should wish to pardon the murderer, then let the pursuing be honorable, and let the payment be with kindliness. [The Divine ruling serves to lessen the severity of retribution:] it is a manifestation of the mercy and compassion of your Lord [for the murderer]. Whoever exceeds the limits of this law [or reverts to the laws of the Age of Ignorance] shall receive painful chastisement. (K. 2:178)

In the last two chapters, I have tried to prove that the Koran and the Tradition provide Muslims with fresh opportunities to develop a new theology of interreligious and intrareligious relations in working toward a social and political system that regards human dignity as the sole criterion for equal membership in Muslim political society. At the same time, I have demonstrated the obstacles that stand in the way of developing such an inclusive theology, chief among which is the successful political history of past Muslim empires and their persistent grip on the imaginations of Muslims who dream of a universal caliphal state. Such yearnings are steeped in the piety of the future success promised in the messianic tradition. This piety, steeped in real past political successes and imagined future ones, has made it all but impossible for

Muslim fundamentalists to accept any notion of intercommunal ethics based on the Koranic principles of peace with justice for all human beings. In contemporary fundamentalist discourse about implementation of the Sharīʿa norms, there is barely any room for building intracommunal relationship between the Sunnī and the Shīʿī Muslims, much less between Muslims and the peoples of the Book. Fueled by futuristic piety, there is a real danger that in exclusionary discourse, retaliation will eclipse rehabilitation. The Sharīʿa norms are founded upon the moral realism of the Koran, which does not view human weakness as sin. It is viewed as a disease that needs to be cured through regenerative faith and rehabilitative relationships.

In Muslim culture, restoration of relationships has traditionally required some measure of retribution, tempered with pardon. The Koran and the Tradition have treated retribution as a prerequisite for restoration. However, in the process of constructing a system to regulate interpersonal relations, Muslim scholars of the Sharīʿa have overemphasized vengeance to the extent that the Koranic corrective has led to ostracization of individuals and groups regarded as apostates or heretics, abject victims of fundamentalist intolerance. In creating and maintaining relationships that would lead to a just society, the principle of coexistence among individuals and communities requires Muslims to rediscover and implement a missing dimension in a political society: restoration through forgiveness and compassion.

In this chapter, I will again explore foundational ideas and precedents to demonstrate to Muslims that the claim that "Islam is the solution" today, as in the past, implies a responsibility to present Koranic ethics in a way that grapples with the contemporary realities of a multicultural and multifaith global society. The need to recognize the freedom to believe and practice any religion is a prelude to the development of a democratic system in which shared civic responsibility rather than religious doctrine determines citizenry. Religion functions as both an open and a closed system. It is open in the sense that it invites all to join the community of the faithful; it is closed in the sense that it excludes those who reject the invitation. It does not stop with a threat of exclusion; it nurtures an antagonistic attitude toward the other, sometimes leading to the other's outright condemnation to hell. At other times it leads to a call for *jihād*—a holy war, or retribution for slighting the invitation of the dominant faith community. It is evident that the denial of a God-given right to religious freedom has fostered antipluralistic attitudes among religious extremists.

The intensification of interreligious violence through retaliation and retribution among these groups raises a serious question about their interpretation of the sacred texts, which are skewed to perpetuate a culture of violence. How far are such interpretations derived from the Koran? To this end, I start with retributive justice in the Koran and the critical role played by forgiveness in rehabilitating humans in relationships.

Retributive Justice in the Koran

In our collective essay entitled "World Religions and Conflict Resolution" in *Religion, the Missing Dimension of Statecraft*,[1] we struggled with the dismal historical record of intolerance among religious communities—Hindu, Buddhist, Jewish, Christian, and Muslim—in order to prove to our readers that despite this disheartening record, there were untapped resources within these traditions for preventing future deadly interreligious conflicts. In view of religious fundamentalists' strong exclusionary tendencies and their ability to mobilize violent forces, conflicts have persisted among them around the globe. Muslim fundamentalists, as discussed in chapter 2, have systematically interpreted the Islamic tradition as sanctioning harsh, even violent, treatment of those who are outside the Islamic faith. To be sure, this selective retrieval of the Tradition has, unfortunately, cast Islam and its practitioners in a harsh and inhumane light. Where are those instructions of the Prophet and the early leaders of the community, some of which were cited in chapter 2, to treat human beings as equals?

The task of mining these untapped resources for opposing meaningless violence has assumed even greater urgency in the face of those laws inspired by the Old Testament spirit of retaliation and retribution. Most of the time, the heirs to the biblical ethos of "eye for an eye" justice seek to justify their militant approach to religious conflicts with the notion that retribution is the surest method of correcting social evils. Moreover, this perspective regards humans as capable of the kind of wrongdoing best addressed by punitive measures designed to combat threats to the social fabric.

Finding a just level of retribution has proved difficult, however. While Biblical and Koranic law prescribe only "an eye for an eye," the human tendency has been to exact measureless revenge. To be sure, notions of fairness and justice, although in some general ways derivable from universal moral values, are deeply rooted in specific cultural contexts whose diversity makes it impossible to envision a single definition of crime and of just and effective punishment. In many cultures, the seriousness of a crime is measured in terms of its impact on society, especially when the harm or injury moves from the individual to the community. At that point, as many contemporary anthropological studies have shown,[2] because of the variable cultural and psychological scales of determining societal harm, the appropriate measure of collective punitive response becomes even more difficult to calculate. Whatever the level of punitive response, it is socially desirable that for the sake of its own preservation, no group should perpetuate retribution endlessly without seriously engaging in a restorative process.[3] Restorative justice seeks to encourage the offender to recognize the harm the wrong has caused to the victim so that a repaired relationship between offender and victim can reinstate the dignity of both.

In pre-Islamic Arab culture, tribal relations were regulated by the sense of just vengeance as the solution for wrongdoing; carried to excess, this outlook proved more detrimental than helpful to the commonweal. At the time of the emergence of Muḥammad as the Prophet (CE 610) intertribal relations in Arabia were dictated by blood feuds in which retributive measures always exceeded what was due. Such excesses led to abuses by powerful tribes whose social status depended upon their military prowess. In fact, as historical accounts dealing with pre-Islamic Arabia bear out, retaliation of "a life for a life" led to escalations in violence and loss of life.

The endless and malicious cycle of wrong answered by wrong was the social-cultural context for the previously cited verse, K. 2:178. The passage, which deals with the law of fair retribution in cases of murder and the exhortation to pardon and eschew revenge, underscores the Koranic concern to curb excessive violence through fair dealing in retribution. The ruling seeks to lessen the severity of retributive justice, manifesting God's mercy and compassion for the murderer by offering an alternative to violence in order to redress a wrong committed against another person. More important, it shows retributive justice as a cultural phenomenon that governed Arab tribal society's approaches to conflict resolution. The passage concludes the prescription with a stern reminder about the evil consequences of perpetuating the extremes of the pre-Islamic tribal culture of conflict.

By regulating retribution, the Koran evidently wanted to underscore two socially related goals: to put moral-legal restrictions on the natural human tendency to an excessive penalty and to suggest an alternative to retribution and a potential cycle of violence through an acceptance of blood money as compensation or forgiveness. The alternative to retributive justice assumes that no peace can result from retaliatory measures until forgiveness enters to provide the healing process needed to restore human relationships. Forgiveness is a human capacity that makes genuine social change possible;[4] it can also effect a just and peaceful political order by bringing individuals, families, and groups closer together. In interreligious relations, when a dominant group ill-treats minorities, forgiveness rather than an endless cycle of violence can restore relationships among enemies. Whenever the Jews and the Palestinians in the West Bank or the Sunnīs and the Shīʿītes in Pakistan have resorted to retaliation and retribution, the result has been deadly and endless cycles of carnage, the chief victims of which are often innocent civilians.

The overarching message in Abrahamic Scriptures is of God's forgiving power to compensate for human shortcomings, whether in dealing with oneself or others. God's forgiveness leads to restoration of self-respect, which can lead to better human relationships. There is a deep moral insight in the following verse of the Koran:

> Your Lord has made bestowal of Mercy incumbent upon Himself: if any of you commits an evil in ignorance, and then repents and mends his ways, [he will be certainly forgiven]. Be sure that He is All-forgiving and All-merciful. (K. 6:55)

On the one hand, humankind is assured of God's forgiving nature; on the other, humans are required to demonstrate their predisposition to moral humility in reforming and restoring membership in society. In order to earn divine forgiveness, humans must act responsibly toward one another. They must take the responsibility for wrongdoing in a personal and social way. Acknowledgment of harm or injury caused to others or to oneself is the first and key step in seeking forgiveness:

> Say [O Muḥammad]: "O my people who have been excessive against yourselves, do not despair of God's mercy; [if you turn to God in repentance] surely God will forgive sins altogether; surely He is the All-forgiving, the All-compassionate. Turn unto your Lord and submit to Him, before the chastisement comes upon you, [for then it will be too late and] you will not be helped." (K. 39:53)

How can one be "excessive against oneself"? Can one cause injury to oneself? According to the Koran, wrongdoers who harm others also harm themselves (*ẓulm al-nafs*) in their acts of sin. Hence, the harm comes inescapably as punishment for these sinful acts.[5]

Repentance is a turning to God to earn divine mercy and forgiveness; it is a withdrawal from behavior injurious to oneself. "Turn unto your Lord" establishes a special and direct relation between God and a human being in those moments of desperation when one has fallen short in carrying out the religious-moral duties. Acts of disobedience involve a kind of injury to one's self-respect, which needs to be healed if a person wishes to function as a full member of a society. It is for this reason that "turning to God in repentance" serves as the most important means by which a wrongdoer can distance himself from his wrongdoing.

Sayyid Quṭb reminds his readers that it is never late to "turn unto your Lord and submit to Him," since the gates of mercy and forgiveness are always open for those who are looking to establish peace within themselves and with others in society.[6] The order in which the restoration of peace takes place is remarkably instructive. The act of turning to God in the Koran is repeatedly recommended as a ritual of apology, of begging God for forgiveness (*ghufrān*) for one's wrongdoing.[7] This ritual, however, is a form of symbolic communication with one's own conscience, a recognition of the need to withdraw from one's past immoral behavior. Without first sincerely humbling oneself, one cannot restore the inner peace to repair one's self-respect. According to the Koran, it is unthinkable to regain the confidence of other humans without first working toward the restoration of one's vitiated sense of security and integrity.

Providing an inner sense of security and integrity is the function of faith—*īmān*—in Islam. *Īmān* is derived from the Arabic root *amn* which means 'to be at peace,' 'to be safe.' The idea is that faith bestows safety and peace. This meaning undergirds the most important Koranic notion concerning faith and its external projection in action. In order to gain security and tap their vast potentialities for creating an ideal public order, human beings can and ought to avoid moral and physical peril, individually and collectively. The destiny of every society depends on how faith shapes the quality of individual and collective behavior. Genuine faith in God sharpens the human ability to know that wrongs done to others are more profoundly wrongs done to oneself.

It is for this reason that individuals and societies cannot ignore any immoral acts that lead to fragmentation and destruction. Acquiescence in personal immorality or public injustice is regarded as the major cause of degradation of self and others. As flagrant moral depravity edges toward the satanic, it invites divine wrath. Disbelief in God's activity leads to self-deception, narrow-mindedness, rejection of truth (*kufr*), and a total privation of moral energy. The crucial human defense against such self-abasement is vigilance against the self-deception that arises from all myopic interests, whether individual or collective. Although the Koran frequently emphasizes God's mercy, pardon, and forgiveness, it requires human beings to respond to their divinely ordained *fiṭra*—that inner disposition that gives humans the ability to extricate the self from self-deception. Interpersonal human justice depends on one's ability to realize a moral injury done to others and to work toward wiping the slate clean. Divine mercy and pardon, as Ṭabāṭabā'ī explains, await those who care deeply about others and their relationships with them and who seek their forgiveness. The humility expressed through genuine repentance and surrender to God restores our self-respect in the community.[8]

Human Arrogance as a Source of Conflict

What stops human beings from self-reform, from turning toward God, seeking divine forgiveness, and working toward the betterment of society? Two grievous sins in Islam are arrogance (*istikbār*) and jealousy (*ḥasad*). Religious arrogance has been one of the major causes of antagonism across cultures. As an important source of identity and meaning, religion has been used to promote violent inter- and intrafaith conflicts. Abrahamic religions, as traditionally interpreted, have strong exclusivist tendencies that can give rise to serious conflicts.[9] Religious self-righteousness has functioned as the most pervasive instrument of demonizing others and legitimizing violence against them. A religiously inspired sense of superiority and attendant arrogance have led to a "ritualization of violence"[10] against the demonic other. As a consequence, religious approaches to resolving conflicts through forgiveness and mercy have been pushed to the background. Powerful political and religious institutions in some parts of the world have ironically worked hand in hand to institutionalize hatred in the name of God and to suffocate any attempt to pave the way for better understanding among different religious communities.

Since a major cause of these conflicts is arrogance, it is important to understand this human trait in some detail. *Istikbār* (arrogance) is derived from *kibr* (pride), a psychic state in which a person feels a sense of superiority and behaves high-handedly. Arrogance is fed by feelings of self-importance, superiority to others, and grandiose entitlement. Imam Jaʿfar al-Ṣādiq (d. 748) describes the way arrogance disgraces a person in the eyes of his or her fellow human beings:

> There is no person who does not have a harness on his head, and an angel who attends to it. Whenever he is arrogant, the angel says: "Be humble, lest God should disgrace you." Thus, in his own eyes he is the greatest of human beings, whereas in other people's eyes he is the smallest of creatures.[11]

Arrogance leads to a trampling of the rights of others and thus often engenders violent conflicts. The reasonable way of averting conflicts that arise out of divergent interests among individuals or groups of individuals is to insist that individuals and groups recognize the aspirations of others as a social principle of human interdependence.[12]

The other grievous sin in Islam, jealousy (*ḥasad*), is also a source of arrogant behavior. Jealousy leads to aggressive behavior: inflicting physical, psychological, or social harm on others. Is there a way to overcome this behavior, which is often more harmful to the perpetrator than to the victim? Muslim ethicists regard jealousy as a self-cultivated vice and, therefore, remediable.[13] The antidote to jealousy is social interaction, which fosters a sense of interdependence, thereby reducing violence among individuals. Furthermore, it requires them to realize that intentional wrongdoing prompted by resentment degrades others and causes them moral injury. Hence, an essential and effective remedy for such behavior is an act of sincere repentance and public apology. Such moral humility can serve as a religious prelude to the just resolution of the conflict caused by the moral injury inflicted upon those whose well-being should be the concern of the entire community of the faithful.

"Your Brothers in Religion or Your Equals in Creation"

Throughout this book, I have emphasized the role of religion in fostering norms, attitudes, and values that can enhance peaceful relations among different ethnic and religious communities. A number of anthropological and sociological studies have demonstrated the potential of a religious worldview for reducing tensions and providing nonviolent solutions to the conflicts in different cultural settings.[14] This is especially true of traditions like Islam that have articulated the idea of responsible government as a prerequisite for an ethical public order. The exercise of authority without accountability is inimical to the notion of "enjoining the good and forbidding the evil." This injunction, which requires Muslim authorities to work actively for the good of the whole community, is, according to Muslim scholars, founded above all on reason and confirmed in the Koran (K. 3:104, 110, 114). In order to attain this purpose, one must enjoin good and forbid evil with heart, tongue, and hand. Although fulfilling this obligation could be done with heart and tongue by any believer, the use of force could be employed only by the state. Because the use of force can result in the spilling of blood, it must guarantee a desirable result. It is, moreover, the duties of enjoining and forbidding that have provided the basis of the idea of an Islamic public order capable of mediating between the force of the state and the just needs of the people.

With moral and religious justifications for the legitimate use of physical force easily available to the state, the concentration of power in a few hands and its abuse is a danger more in ideological states than in nonidealogical ones. The early Muslim polity was founded on a religious belief that demanded some kind of uniformity and consistency among its membership. This demand by its very nature excluded those who do not share the norms and institutions of the community represented by the state. Depending upon those in power, members of other religious communities living among Muslims were debarred from full participation in the civil life that the state claimed to protect.

The Prophet and his immediate political successors, the caliphs, were aware of the fact that concentration of power in the hands of powerful military leaders and governors in distant provinces was open to abuse. Consequently, to forestall the unnecessary use of force against their subjects, they provided these officials with detailed guidelines in statecraft founded on concern for justice and fairness. The following instructions emphasize the importance of mercy and forgiveness in governance. The document was written by ʿAlī b. Abī Ṭālib (d. 660) when, as the caliph, he appointed Mālik al-Ashtar as governor of Egypt and its provinces. He wrote:

> Infuse your heart with mercy, love and kindness for your subjects. Be not in face of them a voracious animal, counting them as easy prey, for they are of two kinds: *either they are your brothers in religion or your equals in creation*. Error catches them unaware, deficiencies overcome them, (evil deeds) are committed by them intentionally and by mistake. So grant them your pardon and your forgiveness to the same extent that you hope God will grant you His pardon and His forgiveness. For you are above them, and he who appointed you is above you, and God is above him who appointed you. (emphasis added)[15]

Since authority engenders arrogance, Imam ʿAlī advises his governor as follows:

> If authority you possess engenders in you pride or arrogance, then reflect upon the tremendousness of the dominion of God above you and His power over you in that in which you yourself have no control. This will subdue your recalcitrance, restrain your violence and restore in you what has left you of the power of reason. Beware of vying with God in His tremendousness and likening yourself to Him in His exclusive power, for God abases every tyrant and humiliates all who are proud.[16]

Justice is the counterweight to arrogance. Whoever wrongs people becomes God's adversary, and God renders null and void the argument of whoever contends with Him. Such a person will be God's enemy until he desists or repents. It is important to emphasize that people in the foregoing document are not simply categorized as members of the faith community and as those who are outside it. Rather, they are related as "brothers" in faith and "equals" in creation. This is the foundation of Muslim civil society: the privilege of citizenry attaches to Muslim and non-Muslim alike, both sharing equally in God-given dignity. Imam ʿAlī's categorization of people under his government makes it a violation of law and religion to discriminate against a fellow citizen simply because he or she happens to be a non-Muslim.

If this is the teaching of Islam, then where does this religiously generated discrimination against the other come from? According to the Koran, the source of this socially depraved conduct is the worship of Satan, who was the first being to utter the statement that has become the source of all human conflicts: "I am better than he!" (K. 38:76). The Koran warns all humanity against succumbing to this evil claim of superiority, which disrupts the peace and security attained through faith: "Children of Adam! Did I not make covenant with you that you should not serve Satan? [Did I not tell you that] he is your sworn enemy? And that you should serve Me, for this is a straight path" (K. 36:61–62).

"Serving Satan" (literally, worshipping Satan) in this passage has been interpreted as following Satan's path of arrogance and zest for conflict, which were demonstrated at the time of human creation when Satan swore that he would entrap human beings and drag them to perdition (K. 17:63) by instigating them to rebel against God's order. "Serving Me," that is, God, restores the original state of creation through the *fiṭra*, that natural inclination toward obedience and doing good, the straight path.[17] Muslim ethicists describe levels of restorative "service of the Divine" through repentance (*tawba*), through which the arrogant and jealous self, melted in the furnace of self-reproach, re-forms in remorse and a turning toward God by seeking the forgiveness of one's fellow humans. Again, to quote Imam ʿAlī's instruction to those who exercise authority over the people:

> Nothing is more conducive to the removal of God's blessing and the hastening of His vengeance than to continue in wrongdoing, for God hearkens to the call of the oppressed and He is ever on the watch against the wrongdoers.[18]

Although, in Islam, there are rights that accrue to God qua God (*ḥaqq allāh*), and human qua human (*ḥaqq al-ʿibād*), it is religiously and morally the latter set of rights that must either be redressed, if they are violated, or forgiven by the possessor of the right, if they are impossible to restore. The rights of God are forgiven by God in response to active repentance, but repentance has no effect on the amicable settlement of crimes that involve infringing on a human right. Crimes against fellow humans are also treated as crimes against religion because they violate the sanctity of the dignity bestowed by God on humankind without distinction. In other words, the rights of human beings are treated with such gravity that even if a person repents a thousand times, his slate is not wiped clean without a concrete demonstration that the violated rights of the wronged person have been restored. Muslim jurists of different schools are in agreement that the rights of human beings are not forgiven by God nor are they dismissed by Him, unless the aggrieved party forgives or dismisses them first.[19] While it is true that people harm one another, they cannot live in isolation, because of their inherent social nature. In order to restore human relations, they must forgive one another. Reconciliation flows from forgiveness and willingness on the part of the victim to forgo retribution as an end in itself. From the Koranic admonition to forgive and accept compensation, it seems that retributive punishment is worth pursuing only to the extent that it leads to reconciling (*shifāʾ al-ṣudūr* = 'healing of the hearts') the victim and the wrongdoer, and rehabilitating the latter after his or her acknowledgment of responsibility:

> The law of fair retribution is a source of life: [by adhering to it you may be restrained from desiring the death of those who murder and instead be content with compensation]. This point We clarify so that you may fear God [and exercise caution when seeking revenge]. (K. 2:179)

All the commentators point out that the phrase "retribution is a source of life" in this passage invites people to consider retributive justice as a process of rehabilitation rather than as a cycle of violence of the sort common in the pre-Islamic Arab tribal culture of revenge. The desire for revenge must be overcome by considering the physical, as well as the psychological, harm caused by it. Retributive justice, according to the Koran, should aim at redressing the wrong by making the offender acknowledge responsibility and encouraging the victim to consider alternatives to the perpetuation of violence through retribution.[20]

Moral Restrictions on Retributive Justice

The purpose of Koranic legislation pertaining to retributive justice, as ʿAllāma Ṭabāṭabāʾī and Sayyid Quṭb remind their readers, is to instill in human beings a readiness for forgiveness and restitution and to explain to them the public good that can be accomplished through them in their practicing compassion (*raḥma*) and altruism (*īthār*). Yet retributive punishment is important to maintain justice in society because the notion of the wrongdoer's responsibility for his wrong cannot be fully realized without it.

The contemporary Muslim world is caught up in serious violations of peoples' basic social and political rights. In order to correct these political injustices peacefully, Muslims must search for historical precedents for the idea of peaceful reconciliation through instituting restorative justice, a process that, I believe, can restore to the people their God-given dignity through the *fiṭra*.

The Koranic *Jihād*: Between Ideal and Reality

Reflection on historical precedents set by the founder of Islam, Prophet Muḥammad, have enabled subsequent generations of conscientious Muslim leadership to elicit from their tradition ideas of peaceful coexistence among peoples of different faiths and cultures. There remains, however, one contentious political-religious term, namely *jihād*, an ambiguous designation for a just war undertaken as a religious duty to restore violated justice.[21] This highly charged idea has provoked various interpretations and implications for modern international relations as it echoes through the contemporary mass media.

In the context of Koranic retributive or restorative justice, the notion of *jihād* poses a challenge to Muslim pluralists. The requirement of *jihād* against unbelievers and hypocrites in the Koran seems to support the view that Muslims must destroy other faiths and peoples to create an Islamic society—*dār al-islām*.

In this section, I want to demonstrate that contrary to the generally accepted interpretation of *jihād* as a means to further the domination of Muslims over other peoples and religions, in its Koranic usage it denotes a moral endeavor to work for peace with justice—a component of the quest for restorative, not purely retributive, justice.

Jihād, in its ethical denotation, is part of the human struggle to establish a moral order on earth. It is one of the principal commandments in the Koran.[22] However, there is a tension in the Koranic insistence on freedom of human conscience in responding to the call of faith and the power invested in the state to create an ideal Islamic public order. In contrast to *jihād*'s technical meaning in political jurisprudence, which involves a struggle against a visible enemy, its purely religious signification includes struggle against one's own baser instincts. This inner *jihād* has been declared by the Prophet as the "greater *jihād*," whereas the external combat is identified as the "lesser *jihād*." The ability to forgive requires a *jihād* against one's anger and resentment in order to restore one's spiritual station by participating in the divine attribute of forgiveness.

Islam emerged in seventh-century Arabia as a moral challenge to humanity to rise above its personal grudges and pettiness and to respond to God by affirming belief in God's plan for the whole of humanity and working for its ultimate realization. Accordingly, Islam sought to create its own public order, which would translate the Islamic revelation into a religious-moral public order. In this sense, Islam inherently functioned as an active ideology within a specific social-political order that it constantly evaluated, calling upon its adherents either to defend and preserve or to overthrow and transform.

However, the use of force in creating the public order was regulated by taking into consideration the harm caused by human rejection of faith to the corporate well-being of the society. The Koran appeals to a moral-religious duty that godfearing people—people with *taqwā*—have in defending their homes and families threatened by the unbelievers (*kuffār*): "O believers, fight (*qātilū*) those unbelievers who surround you, and let them sense your harshness [and hostility toward them]; and know that God is with those who fear Him [and do good]" (K. 9:124).

In spite of its emphasis on forbearance and forgiveness, the Koran permits the use of force under specific circumstances in keeping with pre-Islamic Arab tribal culture, which had institutionalized the military to defend tribal security. In introducing the injunction legitimizing the limited use of force through the instrumentality of *jihād*, the Koran was thus responding to moral-religious and political conditions prevalent in seventh-century Arabia. Primacy among the tribes belonged to those that were able to protect all their clients and to avenge all insults, injuries, and deaths through their military strength. Aggressive expeditions were quite common in pre-Islamic Arabia. Against this background, the legitimate and morally restricted use of physical force endorsed by the Koran was an acknowledgment of the realities of human nature that underlie the alternations of peace and conflict in harsh and complex social and political conditions.[23]

Jihād as a Religious, Moral, and Cultural Phenomenon

When bloodletting in retribution is compared to the bloodshed in *jihād*, one is struck by the magnitude as well as the coercive nature of the war machinery mobilized to accomplish what are often ambiguous and morally questionable objectives. For instance, the use of *jihād* to impose doctrinal unity among Muslims in order to achieve social cohesion is religiously as well as morally troublesome. Religious commitment is freely negotiated between God and humanity. As such, it does not leave room for employing coercive measures to bring about doctrinal unity at the intra- and intercommunal levels. To achieve social unity for a well-ordered Muslim state, the Koran, as demonstrated in chapter 2, requires humanity to search for a common moral terrain. Knowledge about good and evil, according to the Koran, is imprinted upon the *fiṭra*, which makes humans moral agents endowed with volition. The Koranic assumptions are about human reasonableness and the potential for good citizenship. Then why is there a need for *jihād*?

To be sure, the Koranic legitimation of *jihād* as warfare is evident in verse K. 2:193, in which the commandment is declared in no uncertain terms: "Fight them (i.e., those who fight against you), till there is no persecution (*fitna*)[24] and the religion be only for God"; this is concerned with the problem of eradication of unbelief that causes a breakdown in the Islamic public order:[25]

> Fight in the way of God against those who fight against you, but begin not hostilities. Lo! God does not love those who transgress. And slay them wherever you find them, and drive them out of the places from where they drove you out, for persecution is worse than slaughter. (K. 2:190–191)

The permission to fight in this passage was a response to the problem posed by the powerful Mekkan tribes. The Koran indicates that although unbelief is a religious problem to be construed as one dimension of the work of God, unbelief can be and, in the case of the Mekkans, was malicious—a willful act on the part of human beings who seek to deceive God or to deprive God of God's rights.

Hence, a prescriptive measure was needed to deter general harm and to redress the wrongs suffered by the weak at the hands of those immoral, godless aggressors. In other words, the religious 'struggle' and the 'striving' (key meanings of the word *jihād*) by means of force were divinely sanctioned campaigns hostile to unbelief. It is not all unbelievers who are the target of force, but unbelievers who demonstrate their hostility to Islam by persecution of the Muslims. In other words, it is not merely the negative attitude to religion per se that sanctions the use of force; it is the hostility in general to which it leads that makes it a prior moral offense and that requires an armed response.

The need for the use of force first became evident when the Muslims, under the leadership of the Prophet, established the first Islamic polity in Medina. Muslim society defined itself under the umbrella of the state guided by the Prophet, to whom the Koran required obedience. Any plot to harm the Prophet was regarded as plotting to overthrow the Muslim state under him. Hence, the Prophet's Medina was more than an alternative to the pre-Islamic tribal society. It was the sphere that defined relations of comprehensive political-religious leadership, power, and the human connections inside and outside the community. In this sense, Islam was not just another religion in the region; it was the bearer of a new political culture in which human relationships were geared toward creating a radically new kind of social and political life to which the Mekkans of the seventh century were vehemently opposed. Like every religious community, early Muslims created and maintained the boundaries within which the antagonistic behavior of the unbelievers was treated as necessary grounds of exclusion. In addition, when unbelief took the form of a willful challenge that tore at the fabric of community cohesion, it became a problem with moral, as well as religious, dimensions. The Koran indicates that various kinds of action were appropriate for the Prophet and the community to deal with this situation. The more the Koran stresses the intercommunal ethic as a process of controlling the damage caused by Mekkan persecution of the Muslims and their expulsion of the innocent from their homes, the more the severest of the punishments are prescribed for punitive justice.

The use of force, then, as far as the Koran is concerned, is defensive and limited to the violation of interpersonal human conduct. The Koran emphasizes its defensive aspects as a weapon against rejection of faith. Nonetheless, in the historical development of the relationship between Islam and power, Muslim jurists regarded this explicitly Koranic principle of defensive warfare as abrogated. They maintained that fighting was obligatory for Muslims, even when the unbelievers had not initiated hostilities.[26] This accommodation with the historical practice of *jihād* is not uncommon in the works of the jurists.

What happens when unbelief among the people of the Book (Jews and Christians), who are otherwise tolerated as non-Muslim monotheists (*muwaḥḥidūn*), takes the form of disregard for the moral standards prescribed by the Islamic public order? The Koran says:

> Fight those who believe not in God and the Last Day and do not forbid what God and His Messenger have forbidden—such men as practice not the religion of truth, being those who have been given the Book—until they pay the tribute out of hand and have been humbled. (K. 9:29)

This is the only passage in the Koran that carries the implication that a merely defensive posture might be insufficient. Yet it is the moral clause in the verse ("do not forbid what God and His messenger have forbidden") that is public and within the jurisdiction of the community to assess its negative impact and respond accordingly. Although the Muslim community, according to the Koran, was one among many divinely guided communities sharing in their blessed Abrahamic origin, soon after the establishment of Muslim political power, a tradition evolved that viewed Islam as a political movement destined to vanquish and convert all other communities. Accordingly, Islam was to convey true and uncorrupted divine guidance to humankind, creating the worldwide society in which the Koran and the Tradition, the Sunna, would be the everyday norm of all the nations. This interpretation of Islam as a political ideology became the source of both creative social-political thinking and a vigorously contested exclusionary theology, changing the course of *jihād* forever.

Jihād from a Defensive to an Offensive Strategy

Long before the Muslim jurists undertook to provide a religious rationale for the historical practice of *jihād* by developing political-legal terminology like *dār al-islām* (the sphere of submission [to God]) and *dār al-ḥarb* (the sphere of war), the Koran had implicitly divided the world into *dār al-īmān* (the sphere of belief) and *dār al-kufr* (the sphere of disbelief). There is, however, a difference in the way the sacred law, the Sharīʿa, defined the two spheres and the way the Koran projected the realms of belief and disbelief. In Islamic law, the division of the world into the spheres of submission to God and war encompassed both the spatiotemporal and the religious hegemony of Islam; whereas for the Koran, the spatial division was stated in terms of the spiritual and moral distinction between the spheres of belief and disbelief.

For the Koran, the submission of the people to the Islamic order brought about the conversion of Mekka to the sphere of belief. A religious significance is thus attached to the spiritual-moral condition of the people but not necessarily to the land, to which everyone should aspire to return as part of the divine promise. While the Koran speaks about the holy land in connection with the Children of Israel, it prescribes no such notion of connection to a specific piece of holy territory for Muslims. More important, there are no divine guarantees that once the sphere of belief is established in any region of the world, it will not revert to the sphere of disbelief. The prevention of just such a regression is a collective responsibility laid upon the entire community. Furthermore, there is no covenant between God and Muslims that certain parts of the earth will enjoy immunity from corruption and injustice. The human response to the divine challenge of becoming morally and spiritually attentive would decide the degree of sacredness of any part of the earth.

Such an integrated conception of religious and political order for the entire world created an inevitable tension between the Koranic defensive conception of *jihād* and the more militant version, which was viewed as a means of calling (*al-daʿwa*) people to the divine path.[27] The tension, to be sure, is not between the City of God and the Earthly City, as conceptualized in the Augustinian rationalization of the Christian empire. Muslim public order theoretically admits no such distinctions between the two cities. Muslim structures of governance encompass all matters related vertically to God and horizontally to humans. Accordingly, as a manifestation of the divine will in its entirety, its scope covered spiritual as well as secular matters.

On the one hand, there was freedom to negotiate one's spiritual destiny without coercion from any human agency; on the other, the responsibility of living as a member of a political society with well-defined rights and obligations. Here was fertile ground for a growing tension over the use of force. There were conflicting opinions about personal conscience, conversion, and access to the resources at the horizontal level of societal relationships. Muslim jurists legitimized the *jihād* for purposes of calling persons to Islam—thus rendering it a form of holy war with the purpose of winning souls for Islam. In addition to the calling for conversion, tangible political advantages forced jurists to be pragmatic and realistic in their formulation of the justifications for undertaking *jihād*. This obligation was even more pronounced if the de facto rulers were, at least nominally, willing to regard the normative legal system as the law of a Muslim public order. In the process of providing a religious legitimation for the territorial expansionism of the Muslim rulers, the jurists overlooked those passages of the Koran that point toward moral justifications of defensive *jihād* (e.g., "fight until there is no persecution"). Consequently, their rationalization of the *jihād* as the means by which the entire world might be converted to the sphere of Islam obscures the Koran's pluralistic idea of permitting the development of a religiously diverse, well-ordered society based on a strong sense of justice and guided by appropriate principles and ideals.

The problem in extending the mandate of *jihād* to include matters that are beyond human jurisdiction has deep roots in defining the scope of legal and ethical categories in jurisprudence. At no point did Muslim jurists ever undertake to define the ethical-legal and religious foundations of Islamic legal thought as allowing for separate jurisdictions for religious and moral acts. All acts performed as part of one's obligations as a member of the community were thought to have a religious significance. And, since Muslim law and faith were interdependent, the religious and ethical coexisted in the Muslim polity. This interdependence led to a blurred distinction in Islam between moral law and civil, both of which were integrated to direct the community toward the realization of Islamic ideals in social relationships. The case of apostasy, as discussed in chapter 3, provides a clear example of the problem of an overlapping conception of religion and morality. Had there been conceptual clarity about distinguishing the moral from the religious, apostasy in its public manifestation would have been treated more as a civil than a religious offence. Muslim legal-moral discourse, which was governed by the ideal of the universal caliphal empire, failed to take note of the new contingencies presented by various Islamic states that were exercising political power without the juridically and morally legitimized bipolar division of the world into the sphere of Islam and the sphere of war. When this bipolar notion is applied to today's vastly changed social contexts, it often results in a conflict of values. Unless these inherited, ambiguous formulations are clarified to respond to new circumstances, the classical idea of *jihād* in the juridical corpus, with its fudging of moral and religious categories, will remain of limited value.

The promise of the creation under the normative Sharīʿa of a just and equitable public order that embodied the will of God was central to Islamic revelation and also to the social, political, and economic activity of the Muslim community. The connection between the divine will and the creation of such an order was fundamental in the jurists' evaluation of the *jihād* as an instrument in the realization of the ideal Muslim society. Moreover, it was not difficult to interpret the Koran in such a way that the relatively limited justification for *jihād* contained in the sacred text was broadened to include the notions of justice and divine guidance and the desire to secure the well-being of all humanity.

The possibility of offensive *jihād* as a means of converting people to Islam gives rise to the tension between pluralism and tolerance on the one hand and an active, militant opposition to unbelievers who endanger the well-ordered society under the comprehensive doctrines of Islam on the other. If the divine commandment in K. 8:39—to fight the unbelievers—is interpreted in the context provided by the general Koranic justification for engaging in *jihād* (as a response to aggression or moral wrong), it can be construed in terms of a moral-civil duty to fight persecution, which, according to K. 2:191 "is worse than slaughter." On the other hand, if the verse is interpreted in terms of the development of Muslim political power, then it may be said to provide a warrant for wars of expansion.

Offensive *jihād* must be understood within the notion of the human responsibility to strive for the success of God's cause, as consistently maintained by the Koran (K. 9:41). Accordingly, legitimizing the use of force against moral and political offenses does not contradict the Koranic notion of freedom of religion as expressed in the dictum "No compulsion is there in religion" (K. 2:256). The Koran justifies the use of force in the establishment of an order that protects the basic welfare of the Muslim community against internal and external enemies. The internal enemies include tyrants who, according to the Koran, "fight against God and His messenger, and hasten about the earth, to do corruption there" (K. 5:33). "Fight" or "take up arms" is taken to mean "subverting a Muslim public order under God and His Messenger," leading to "chaos and lawlessness." The external enemies include the "leaders of unbelief," who "break their oaths after their covenant and thrust at your religion" (K. 9:12) and who "do not forbid what God and His messenger have forbidden" (K. 9:29) and thereby obstruct the struggle to make "God's cause succeed."

Criteria for a Just War and for Violence

Islamic law requires the existence of a legitimate authority for carrying out capital punishment. Such an authority, in accordance with the doctrine of religious leadership in Islam, is empowered to exercise discretionary measures to oversee the administration of justice as required by the Koran. Since war, like retributive justice, involves the taking of human life, a legitimate representative of the Divine is essential.

Juridical formulations about *jihād* conceived of the Prophet not only as the representative of divine goals on earth but also as their interpreter, charged with making them relevant in situations where a human life is at stake—especially as regards *jihād*, in which the decision to engage in warfare was contingent upon the Prophet's authorization as the leader of the Muslim polity. As a matter of principle, the Koran required the Prophet to abide by its strictures against maleficence. No harm to human life is warranted if the religious-moral goals are unclear or if there is no guarantee that engaging in warfare will eradicate the causes of corruption.

The principle of nonmaleficence was an important factor in the Shīʿite ruling that required that a divinely appointed leader (the Imam) be involved in any triggering of offensive *jihād*. The Sunnī jurists, in contrast, did not consider it necessary that the leader of the Muslims be a divinely appointed Imam. Rather, they regarded any de facto Muslim authority as sufficient to declare an offensive *jihād*. This dispute is a symptom of deeper differences over the issue of legitimate authority; it also underscores the distinction between the historical *jihād* and the notion of *jihād* in the Koran, where the emphasis is on self-preservation of the polity rather than on conquest of other polities.

The major goal of the Koranic *jihād* under the right leader is to establish a united political community. The intent was internal integrity and purification, not external expansion. In this sense, the Koranic notion of *jihād* could justify the overthrow of an oppressive or corrupt government that impeded the establishment of a Muslim polity.

Historical *jihād*, as rationalized by the jurists, not only provided the de facto Muslim political authority with interpretive rationales for expansionist aims, but it also bolstered its political grip over the conquered peoples in the name of Islam. This political rationalization of *jihād* ran contrary to the Koran's view of a morally justifiable war. For a *jihād* to become a just war, the Koran requires that a prophetlike authority confirm the propriety of entering hostilities that would enlarge the boundaries of the Muslim polity.

This rationalization also clashed with the Sunnī jurists' view that in the area of constitutional affairs, the community should have a sovereign head in charge of all its affairs, including the declaration of *jihād*. The sovereign was, moreover, bound to rule in accordance with the sacred law. Under the Sharīʿa, the sovereign was required to consult the community and hear its pleas. Neither side was to act independently of the other or to impose its own point of view. Governance in accordance with the sacred norms was to be flexible, not rigid, able to adapt itself to changing circumstances. Hence, the legal system did not lay down hard and fast rules for consultation and representation. Nevertheless, a religious rationale was provided by the jurists for the historic practice of Muslim rulers, who were thus afforded a pretext for advancing their own interests rather than those of the community at large.

For the Shīʿites, offensive warfare required the presence of the just, divinely appointed Imam, not simply any de facto ruler. The Shīʿite jurists made an explicit distinction between the offensive *jihād* and the defensive *jihād*, which would protect the welfare of the Muslim community against aggression. The requirement of a just authority (in the case of offensive war) was supposed to guarantee that the *jihād* against the unbelievers would be waged strictly in conformity with the religious and ethical principles of Islam. In fact, it was only the just Imam who, by virtue of his divinely protected knowledge of Islamic revelation, could authorize a *jihād* against unbelievers; only he possessed wisdom enough to ensure that the shedding of blood truly furthered the sacred mission of Islam.

The Imam's authorization was not required for defensive warfare, because defense, the Shīʿites maintained, was a moral requirement founded upon Koranic passages such as K. 2:190–191. They argued that whenever Muslims are attacked by enemies and fear for the safety of the boundaries and peoples of Islam, it is their duty to defend themselves. The moral obligation of defense also implied the military obligation to fight in defense of the Muslim territory where Shīʿites live as a minority. This obligation extended to non-Muslim territories where the Shīʿites lived in peace and were able to practice their religion freely.[28] The duty of self-defense was regarded as universal enough to require all Muslims, Shīʿite or Sunnī, living under any government to undertake proper measures of self-preservation.

The Koran made it possible for Muslims to assert that the only just war is the one fought for defensive purposes under legitimate political authority. The reason is that the concern for peace that has led to the visions of a just society has also required proscriptions on the use of unnecessary force to procure that peace. A just war tradition, even in the West in general, is connected with the desire to strive and to achieve true peace by removing the causes of conflict. Accordingly, violent or nonviolent approaches to conflict in Islam have depended on the ultimate outcome of the struggle.[29]

Islam requires humankind to respond to its natural disposition, which is not only cognizant of the meaning of justice, but also endowed with the will to further it through legitimate *jihād*. No human being can make ignorance of the ingrained sense of wrong and right an excuse for undertaking a morally ambiguous war. Injustice toward fellow humans, whether they are part of one's religious community or not, is inexcusable. Legitimate *jihād* makes human relationships central for building an ideal polity. More important, *jihād* is divinely sanctioned only as a measure for enhancing the security and integrity of the Muslim polity. Hence, any *jihād* that leads to meaningless destruction of human life and ignores concerns for peace with justice is non-Koranic *jihād*.

The Ethics of Self-determination

The aforementioned criteria for legitimate *jihād* raise questions about irregular warfare in Islamic law. The issue of the people's right to mobilize against an unjust government is bound up with the legitimacy of rebellious movements in Islam. Muslim juridical formulations explicitly emphasize the necessity of a Muslim's unyielding obedience to a higher political authority; yet a legacy of uprisings and the sacred Scripture's emphasis on justice combine to cast what seems to be divinely sanctioned light on the idea of just rebellion. The testimony of Islamic history is decidedly mixed. The juristic rulings, reflecting the political might of the rulers, prohibits rebellion under almost any condition. The rulings also express the Koranic view that opposition to an unjust government should not result in greater discord than that which is being suffered.

Those supporting the right to rebellion have stressed the idea of government as an instrument for the common good, with its legitimacy hinging on its fulfillment of the religious-moral obligations of Islam. In discussing rebellion against a Muslim government, the law discusses the criteria relevant to rebellion (*al-baghy*), which serve to distinguish its participants from apostates and brigands. Muslim jurists define an insurgent (*bāghī*) as someone who commits an act of insurrection (*khurūj*) with a reason or interpretation (*ta'wīl*) while enjoying wide support or power (*shawka*). In the absence of a reason or power, the party in question is treated as a common criminal and not as an insurgent. A rebellion may be justified because of what is ascribed to the Prophet, who said: "If people see an oppressor and they do not hinder him, then God will punish all of them."[30] The tradition requires some communitarian response to oppression. Accordingly, the criterion of power functions as a safeguard against an individual or small faction undertaking to correct social and political ills. The insurgent group must demonstrate wide support in order to be recognized as having somewhat equal standing with the authority against which it is rising. The form of organization, leadership, and membership reduces the possibility that anarchy and lawlessness will arise from a corrupt person or group inventing a pretext for seizing power. This requirement is consistent with the Islamic concern for the community and the protection of Islamic order. In the case of collective rebellion, the group itself essentially functions as a community and is concerned with the preservation of Islamic values rather than motivated by individual self-interest. The action is undertaken by public mandate, not by private initiative. If the group's justification for rebellion is valid and the ruler concedes it, then, according to the law, the ruler is responsible for any ensuing disorder, not the rebels. Additionally, even though both sides of the conflict may have some legitimacy, Islamic law acknowledges the likely power discrepancy between the state and the opposition by exempting the rebels from liability for any harm to property or life that occurrs during the course of rebellion.[31]

However, the rebels should not exploit this power discrepancy as a way to justify the use of violence. There are some among Muslim jurists who, taking the side of the insurgent group, argue that the justness of the rebellion permits the use of any means necessary for victory, including terrorism. On the other hand, there are those jurists who support the state in reasoning that the legitimate authority of the state, faced with a violent internal threat, has the right to use necessary force.[32] Moreover, those engaging in guerrilla or terrorist practices commonly argue that their weaker position necessitates the use of such violent tactics. These arguments embody the concern evident in the debates about the *jihād*. In Islamic history, the emphasis on justifications for war has led to the relative neglect of limits on the use of violence. However, in the law of rebellion, the emphasis is on the means of resistance employed by rebels rather than on the ends they seek. After all, in essence, the law actually regulates rebellion by Muslims living under an Islamic order. The rebels are not legally classified as criminals and are required to observe moral restrictions in seeking redress to injustices. Thus, the primary concern of the entire community when rebellion occurs is to find ways of reconciling the contending parties and reestablishing order.

Overall, the laws of rebellion are concerned with justifying the use of state power to maintain a continuing affirmation of one common religious doctrine. Maintaining unity and stability in the community takes precedence over allowing factionalism based upon diverse claims about religious truth. Since, according to the Sharīʿa, one cannot resist an unjust tyrant without causing an even greater harm to the well-being of the civilians, the oppressive use of state power, if proportionally implemented, is justified. In granting the political legitimacy, however tacitly, of unjust rule simply because it is the lesser of two evils, this doctrine accords a monopoly of decision to use force to the prevailing power. Yet, the Sharīʿa cannot ignore acts of terrorism in which the rebels feel that they are beyond accountability. As a rule, the Sharīʿa views acts of terrorism against unarmed people as a grave violation of the people's integrity and as a goad to greater conflicts.

Muslim jurists have constantly evoked the rule against maleficence and the requirement of proportionality when dealing with persistent violence perpetrated by rebels; yet, they have neglected the principle of restorative justice demanded by the Koran:

> If two parties of the believers fight one another, make peace between them [by removing all the causes of conflict]; then, if one party of believers transgresses against another, [selfishly violating their rights,] then fight the transgressors until they obey once more God's commandment. Then, when the transgressors have submitted [their will once more to His], establish peace between them with fairness and justice, so that the rights of neither party are violated. Surely God loves those who act with fairness and justice. (K. 49:9)

This important passage of the Koran, which is regarded as the basis for intracommunal conflict resolution, points to the activist response demanded by the Koran to "make peace between them" through restorative justice without violating the integrity of the people. "Fighting the transgressors" is commanded only when restorative justice has failed to produce a fair outcome.

Addressing the root causes of rebellious movements can bring about a peaceful resolution to conflicts. Hence, recognition of the people's right to protest acts of injustice, within the limits imposed by concerns of proportionality and forewarning, gave rise to a new opinion among some jurists. According to this ruling, the victims of injustice no longer suffered the stigma of causing the greater harm by rising in rebellion. They had the right to resist. This outlook ran contrary to the generally held opinion, which was based on the doctrine of predetermination and its corollary of resignation in the face of injustice.

A number of Muslim theologians believed in the postponement of decisive judgment on a Muslim's belief or conduct until the Day of Judgment, when

God himself would deal with such individuals and reward or punish them for their behavior. This attitude led to a degree of moral complacency because what it meant was that a Muslim retains his or her membership in the community even if he or she fails to uphold the moral conduct prescribed by the faith. It also suggested that no one besides God can judge a person's real faith and conduct. In support of this attitude, many traditions attributed to the Prophet were circulated to justify the tyrannical rule of Muslim dynasties like that of the Umayyads (660–748). Most of these traditions, although accepted by the community at large, directly contradict the policies demanded by the Koran. In one such tradition, the Prophet is reported to have advised one of his close associates, Hudhayfa, as follows:

> After me there shall be political leaders who will not be guided by my instruction nor shall they follow my custom (*sunna*). Moreover, there shall rise among them men whose hearts shall be the hearts of the devil in the frame of human bodies.
>
> Hudhayfa asked: "What shall I do when I find myself in such a situation?"
>
> The Prophet replied: "You must listen and obey the political leader; even if he beats you on the back and confiscates your property, you must listen and obey."[33]

Such traditions were actually used to rationalize the concrete situation in the community and to argue for the prohibition of rebellion against an established state.

The admonition to avoid civil strife and sedition must be understood within the internal structure of the Muslim cultural values that encourage a religiously legitimized, passive attitude toward political injustice in order to avoid the greater evil that might come through irregular warfare. Peaceful resolution of conflicts, as the just cited verse K. 49:9 demands, is the result of applying restorative justice in a collective human struggle (*jihād*) to overcome the selfish violation of rights. Just as private individuals must engage in personal *jihād* and show proper restraint in self-defense, public officials must also wage their institutional *jihād* to ensure that social and political institutions reflect Koranic justice. Since conflict is always a possibility in oppressive situations, the Koranic prescription to "fight the transgressors until they obey once more the commands of God" and to establish "peace with fairness and justice" must be taken seriously by all responsible human societies on earth.

Restorative Justice in the Islamic Penal Code

The Islamic ideal of a political society united in affirming the comprehensive idea of justice under the sacred law, the Sharīʿa, opens a window to the ways in which the sacred law preserved Muslim identity and maintained its political community. To this latter end, Islam provides a complex relationship between the principles undergirding private acts of self-defense and the principles supporting public legal systems. It is important to bear in mind that even when concerns such as proportionality and self-preservation are present in different schools of legal thought within Islam, these principles vary in scope, weight, and practice. With the existence of an Islamic legal tradition that grants concessions to the accused beyond those of the presumption of innocence and the requirement to prove guilt beyond a reasonable doubt, it is incongruent to assume the reliability of the politically quietist traditions ascribed to the Prophet in the section on permissible rebellion in law.

The Koran and the Sharīʿa allow self-defense by appealing to the instinct of self-preservation. The agent who is empowered to save his life must do so without intending to harm or kill the attacker. With these moral strictures in place, it is difficult to maintain a pacifist position from the Islamic perspective. Nevertheless, some form of resignation as a consequence of the doctrine of predetermination in the Muslim community has led to political acquiescence when faced with unjust rule. The alternative to this attitude of resignation need not be *jihād*-oriented activism. Rather, the Muslim aspiration to live in accordance with the divine norms elaborated in the Sharīʿa has led to restorative and rehabilitative activism inspired by the penal code of Islam.

This restorative rather than retributive activism is based on the Sharīʿa's doctrine of balancing violence with the concerns of proportionality. The Koran acknowledges human ability to cause harm to others, and it therefore, as discussed, allows but does not require "eye for an eye" retaliation—and nothing beyond it (K. 5:45). The principle of legality requires that no one accused of a crime can be punished unless he has been forewarned of the criminal nature of his conduct.

There are four purposes for punishment in Islamic criminal law: prevention, deterrence, retribution/revenge, and restoration/rehabilitation through repentance.[34]

In the Islamic criminal justice system, the human instincts for vengeance and punishment compete with the religiously inspired qualities of compassion, empathy, and forgiveness. The Koran appeals to these qualities as one considers more immediate emotional and psychological reactions to a criminal act. It also prescribes forgiveness and restorative justice by making the criminal system responsive to both the personal and the communal needs of victim and offender. This essential connection between individual and society, personal and communal, and private and public is the dominant feature of Islamic criminal justice. The system is founded on a comprehensive religious and moral doctrine that promotes this connectedness and forges human interdependence by relating the painful criminal experience to the need for rehabilitating victims and offenders in the society.

Since crimes hurt both individuals and communities, deterrence is an underlying purpose in both private and public categories of crime. But retributive justice is connected to rehabilitation in, first, crimes that deserve retribution (*qiṣāṣ*) in order to redress a criminal wrong by restitution, and, second, crimes that deserve chastisement or deterrence (*ta'zīr*) for which discretionary punishment is instituted by the legitimate authority to deter the offender or others from similar conduct. According to the Koran, the death penalty, which falls under the *ḥudūd* (God's restrictive ordinances) applies to acts directly prohibited by God.[35]

There is also a religious element of Islamic criminal justice—the idea that a crime committed by an individual may affect not only humans and communities at large, but God as well. The willingness of the merciful and compassionate God to forgive the divine claims against human beings has made spiritual values connected with forgiveness and compassion assume a central role in the administration of justice in Islam. This divine-human connectedness ensures the healing process that should occur when the offender accepts responsibility for the harm and undertakes to repair it, and when the community provides the necessary support for this reparation.

In this sense, both humans and God may have claims in the same criminal act, even if the event seems to harm only one of them. Although the punishment of crimes against religion is beyond human jurisdiction, the juridical body in Islam is empowered to impose sanctions only when it can be demonstrated beyond doubt that the grievous crime included infringing a right of humans (*ḥaqq ādamī* = 'private claim').

The important consideration in the penal code is the intercommunal ethic as a process of restorative justice with room in it for proportional penalties. Here the supreme duty of the Muslim ruler is to protect the public, in whose interest the ruler is called upon to exercise wide discretion in determining how the religious norms might serve the restoration of social relationships.

Overall, there is a strong tendency in the penal code to restrict the applicability of capital punishment as much as possible, except in cases of false accusation of illicit sexual relations. But even in these cases, the applicability of capital punishment is circumvented by the requirement of four witnesses to unlawful intercourse.

The emphasis of the criminal justice system is on making amends by removing the causes of despicable social behavior. The key word in the Koran for this process is *iṣlāḥ*, 'putting things in order, restoring, making amends.' No lasting solution to social disintegration is possible without eliminating the causes that violate justice. The Koranic prescription conveys a universal significance because it uses moral categories like justice to demand humankind's commitment to it. Rigorous elaboration of these legal and ethical categories within the framework of intercommunal norms could make the restorative elements of the Islamic penal code an important source of conflict resolution. The unresolved case of apostasy in Islam, as I discussed in chapter 3, provides a paradigm through which the Islamic legal tradition can shape an approach to freedom of religion within the framework of international norms without succumbing to the political agenda of a specific government.

Retributive justice in Islamic legal thought is comprehensive in the sense that it covers all recognized values and virtues that inform the entire range of human relations. Its major concern is a well-ordered political society in which the individual is able to negotiate his or her vertical relationship with God voluntarily. But it is a closed society at the horizontal level; one cannot leave voluntarily without causing disruptions in interpersonal relations. At this point, the community exercises its collective will, backed by the legitimate political authority, in enforcing such restrictive ordinances. However, at no point does the Koran endorse the community's use of political power to compromise freedom of conscience, which is an inalienable right through the very creation of the *fiṭra* in humankind. The state would forfeit its claim to be Islamic if it were to coerce people in the matter of the God-human relationship. Consequently, the case of apostasy in sacred law must be reinterpreted to allow pluralism to emerge as a permanent feature of political life.

Violence to the Self in Achieving a Higher Goal

The legal heritage of Islam that deals with retributive/restorative justice demonstrates that as a political society, the Muslim community is constantly called on to 'strive' (*jihād*) for peace with justice in order to advance horizontal relationships. If the advancement of human relationships is the goal of this striving, can one endanger one's own life to realize this lofty objective of Islam? Where, if anywhere, does a willingness to kill and risk one's life fit into a struggle to repair and restore relationships fractured by violence?

The fervent seeking of death in *jihād* appears to be in conflict with the definition of death on the battlefield as a voluntary act of piety. Could the Sharīʿa's requirement of participation in *jihād* give rise to a desperate desire for martyrdom? Using the idea of *jihād* as justification for martyrdom has historically led to the perpetration of extreme violence in the name of God, especially in the case of rebellions against unjust, oppressive authorities—the rebel anticipates a guaranteed entrance to Paradise as a reward for his or her self-sacrifice. There is no doubt that, according to the Koran, the value of human life is relative to the believer's devotion to the community and God. The principle of proportionality determines whether such self-sacrifice or sacrifice of other human lives is worthwhile. The use of violence to achieve divine goals, as Islam teaches, could not justify indiscriminate destruction of human life. The readiness to use violent means and even to wage war to overcome obstacles to the public interest carries the burden of establishing the validity of one's religious claim and the ever present temptation of excluding others from having a share in that religious doctrine.

Every perception of truth is accompanied by its own characteristic defects. A unique test of Islam as an ethically driven, community-bound religion lies in explaining the supreme virtue of dedication to a goal beyond oneself, even to the point of readiness to give up one's life. Death in the service of divine goals leads to the reward of martyrdom in *jihād*. However, this ideal death must occur without falling prey to a spirit of exclusivity. The vision of exclusive salvation that finds expression in violent death carries with it a flawed perception of the divine truth.

Self-sacrifice through martyrdom in *jihād* becomes legitimate in Islam when the goal is to publicly heighten personal accountability to God and social responsibility to fellow humans. Its remembrance becomes a source of healing in a community torn by the criminal behavior of some, because through self-sacrifice martyrdom provides moral standards for a right relationship among people. Often, religions that begin with a spirit of openness to interested outsiders end up falling prey to dogmatic, exclusivist arrogance in their internal and external relations. The story of the Muslim community's internal struggles provides many instances of moral and spiritual leaders who rediscovered a spirit of inclusiveness through self-sacrifice.

As discussed in chapter 2, the paradigm of a good society, according to the Koran, is one in which distinct but interconnected communities learn to recognize people's inherent capacity (*fiṭra*) to find ways of living together in peace with justice. When communities become indifferent to their horizontal responsibilities, they forfeit their claim to be just. For any community, to remain just is a constant struggle. It requires individual as well as collective efforts to mobilize against forces that cause humans to despair and to underestimate their ability to heal and restore relationships through forgiveness and rehabilitation.

The Search for the Koranic Ideal of a Well-Ordered Society

The Islamic tradition offers a variety of answers to the question of balancing means and ends in the quest for the ideal social order. If retribution is a comprehensive system of justice to restore fractured human relations and provide punitive measures to deter human beings from violating one another's rights, then what need is there for warfare in establishing an ideal political society?

Why should the Koran endorse violent means of restoring justice when compassion and forgiveness characterize God's way of dealing with human defects? Why cannot human society emulate God's methods of treating socially alienated people through forgiveness and mercy? More poignantly—and I raise this question as a believer in divine intervention in human affairs—if God is omnipotent and omniscient, why does God not make humankind one community living in peace and harmony and save it from self-inflicted perdition?

The response to these questions would require a detailed examination of the Koranic philosophy of human existence on earth. Since the scope of this work is limited to searching for the Islamic roots of democratic pluralism, and since my search in the Islamic sources has led me to identify religious pluralism as one of the most important preconditions for the development of a democratic society in the Muslim world, I will limit myself to assessing the realization of a pluralistic society in the context of the legal and doctrinal heritage dealing with retributive and restorative justice.

Human existence on earth, according to Islam, is caught up in contradictory forces of light and darkness, guidance and misguidance, justice and injustice. Although not born in primordial sin, human beings are subject to weakness, temptation, arrogance, narrow-mindedness, and, self-interest. The key to combating these defects is a continual struggle to cultivate a guiding principle of selflessness, whence flow all those religious and moral values that conduce to the sense of justice and fairness, the cornerstone of an ideal society.

In this struggle, religion is the fount of inspiration. It inculcates ethical responsibility and personal accountability for one's actions. Furthermore, it generates incentives to correct one's social misconduct by emphasizing the consequences of moral choices. The religious belief in the hereafter prompts human beings to identify actively with the cause of justice and work for it.

The role of religion in the advancement of interpersonal justice is epitomized by the Sharīʿa. As discussed in the context of criminal justice, the Sharīʿa provides a comprehensive system for dealing with communitarian ethics as a process of restorative justice that recognizes the moral responsibility that an offender has toward the victim. Punitive criminal justice, while regarding the offender culpable and meriting blame and censure, does not rule out the efficacy of forgiveness in restoring social relationships, in both private and public settings. However, the system also does not rule out retribution as a right of the victim; it simply limits it by insisting on fairness and the need to renew interpersonal relations.

At any rate, adherence to the principle of proportionality in settling conflicts raises a serious ethical quandary: is the attainment of the general good ever worth the sacrifice of human life? The jurists view this question in relation to the seriousness of the threat to the social fabric. If a disruption threatened social cohesion, it had to be met with all necessary force. The power to make such judgments was vested in the legitimate authority. This was the situation in classical jurisprudence. However, at no time was human life to be destroyed without justification, because the Koran commanded time and again: "Slay not life that God has made sacred" (K. 6:152).

With its ideology firmly based on creating an ethical order that embodied divine will on earth, Islamic tradition provided a detailed vision of peace with justice. The commitment to peace with justice was the act of faith in working toward a perfect social order by promoting the divinely ordained scales of justice in the religious-moral law, the Sharīʿa. As such, peace was not possible in a society that disregarded the evil of injustice. The struggle against injustice was the sole justification for engaging in *jihād*.

Precisely at this crucial juncture in sanctioning violence, the role of the Prophet or the rightly guided Imam, as the interpreter of the divine purposes for which such a sacrifice was inevitable, becomes indispensable. Here, the Prophet or the Imam represents the institution of governance through whom humanity was expected to determine the proportionality and the appropriateness of endangering the sacred life for the greater good.

To be sure, the Muslim community did not always live under what the Muslims came to regard as the ideal leadership of the Prophet and his righteous successors. The time came when Islam and Muslims became entangled with unjust, even tyrannical, rulers who traduced the Islamic quest for the creation of a just order on earth. The Muslim community could choose to oppose and overthrow these rulers, tolerate them with patience until God intervened, or foster a distinct identity, independent of the unjust political system and dedicated to realizing the Sharīʿa's vision of an ideal Islamic polity.

The solution to individual cases of injustice through an aggressive response was an activist interpretation of the Islamic ideology that incited some of the most radical revolutions throughout the history of Muslim peoples. A quietist attitude of tolerance, on the other hand, was a solution favored and institutionalized by those whose interests were served by the changing basis of power in the expanding Islamic empire. A third alternative maintained sufficient ability to mobilize necessary force to put down opposition but also believed in social transformation through individual moral and spiritual reform. This was the Koranic activism that was expressed in terms of a religious commitment fostered by the Islamic revelation for the guidance of humankind and the practical policies of a cosmopolitan world.

It is important to emphasize that both the quietist/authoritarian and the activist postures were potentially radical solutions, awaiting the right time and conditions for their realization. But Islamic revelation, by its very emphasis on justice and equity on earth, calls upon its followers to evaluate a specific sociopolitical order and to defend and preserve it or to overthrow and transform it. The specific response to the existing social and political situation is obtained within a cultural setting. This setting provides powerful symbols that enable spiritual/moral leaders to articulate the subtle and even complex religious ideas in a language that speaks to ordinary people.

Islam, accordingly, has been a source for both a critical assessment of people's religious commitment to social harmony and peaceful living among different communities alienated through social custom and diverse doctrines, and a moral challenge to humankind to rise above personal self-interest in order to work toward a polity that reflects the divine concern for bonding humans through forgiveness and compassion. Nevertheless, recourse to violent retribution without uncompromising adherence to the twin principles of self-preservation and proportionality has remained a central problem of justice in Islam, as Muslims in the past have demonstrated a readiness to go beyond the Koranic mandate of retribution in ways that tore at the very fabric of communal ethics. In advancing a political community of people united under a single religious doctrine, Muslim leaders have succumbed to the temptation of a spirit of exclusivity and self-righteousness that has all too easily justified violent means, even though creative nonviolent methods of resolving problems of co-existence have been suggested in Islamic revelation. Is such violence an inevitable byproduct of social transformation? Not necessarily, if humanity would respond to the divine call to heed its own sense of preservation and justice. It is this submission to God's will that promises the peace and security to which humanity has aspired since its first representative, Adam, was put on earth. It is, undoubtedly, the search for peace and integral existence without submission that threatens the bonds of community of God's creatures.

5

Epilogue

You are the best community ever brought forth to human beings, commanding the good, and forbidding the evil, and believing in God. (K. 3:110)

I have tried to assess the challenge of an Islamic form of government as an alternative to modern systems. The crux of the problem, as I have shown, is the antipluralist posture adopted by fundamentalist Muslims who lead—or wish to lead—Islamic governments in modern nation-states. The subject of the development of civil society in the Islamic world has drawn much attention among Muslim scholars in the Middle East.[1] However, few Sunnī religious scholars from traditional institutions of Islamic learning have participated in these academic endeavors, which try to identify and analyze and retrieve religious sources of democratic pluralism that could be used to legitimize modern secular ideas of citizenship in the Muslim political culture. The situation is a little different among the Shīʿite scholars in Iran who have undertaken rigorous criticism of Western literature on these subjects to prove the validity as well as the superiority of Islamic political values.[2] Nevertheless, religious discourse on the subject of pluralism or democracy has often remained critical of these efforts by the academics as an exercise in surrendering to the Western imperialist view of Islam as inadequate to the tasks of administering a modern nation-state. In addition, according to the propounders of an Islamic alternative, these Western-inspired internal criticisms of Islam perpetuate a secular-Western ideological grip over Muslims.[3]

Traditionally educated religious leaders seriously doubt whether notions of religious pluralism or democracy are conducive to preserving Islamic values in public life. They have, accordingly, relentlessly attacked some forms of religious pluralism, which, they believe, relativizes Islam's claim to provide the exclusive source of public ethics. What if, they ask, institutionalization of this kind of pluralism leads to the endorsement of gay rights in Muslim society? What role, if any, remains for the revelation if divinely ordained religious norms are reduced to any opinions that can be legitimately made part of the public policy through a democratic process? More fundamentally, what is the utility of adhering to democracy if its emphasis on consensus building leads to the adoption of public policies that would result in the disintegration of Muslim familial and societal ethics?

These concerns do not in themselves appear frivolous when the point of reference in this kind of polemical discourse is the moral situation in the West, whether real or perceived. Do Muslims want to import the problems that accompany Westernization through secularization, such as the notions of extreme individualism and moral relativism? In other words, if these concerns are taken at their face value, the paradigm of democratic pluralism offered by the West lacks cultural legitimacy in the Muslim world. What is the alternative?

It is remarkable that no one in the Muslim world, including the fundamentalist leadership, disputes the need for an Islamic paradigm of civil society in which religious pluralism generates principles of coexistence among different religious and ethnic communities.[4] The difference in their discourse from the one that is heard in the universities in the Middle East lies in the methods employed in interpreting the Muslim tradition. The classical formulations are obviously influenced by the idea of a powerful Muslim empire as the sole broker of all human relations, including interreligious and intrareligious ones. In the pluralistic international order of a postempire world in which Muslim and non-Muslim nations share equal membership, classical juridical rulings have remained a sacred point of reference. Any community that treats past human intellectual endeavors of understanding and applying the revelation as sacred, and hence immutable, end up actually closing what Muslim scholars have aptly described as 'the gates of independent reasoning' (*ijtihād*) in matters of law. The function of independent reasoning in juridical sciences is to infer decisions from the revelation. Every age needed its Muslim scholars (*mujtahid*, the one who practices *ijtihad*) to freshly interpret the revelation without departing from its original message. In keeping with the dynamic nature of the juridical tradition, great classical scholars like Abū Ḥanīfa, Mālik, Shāfiʿī, and others did not regard their legal decisions as sacred or immutable. In fact, their religiously mandated humility ruled out such arrogance among these jurists. As such, the gates of independent reasoning have always remained open, until Muslim fundamentalist discourse began to attach finality and infallibility to legal decisions made by well-trained and well-meaning jurists of the past.

Most of the past juridical decisions concerning the treatment of non-Muslim minorities have become irrelevant in the context of the pluralism that pervades international relations today. The Koranic provisions reflect a more universalistic direction for its political mission for humanity than the subsequent tradition admits. They also present a model of individual human responsibility and shared moral commitment with which a just society can be established. Moreover, the Koran provides a rare glimpse into a universal human identity, rooted in its original nature—its *fiṭra*—that is constantly engaged in a struggle (the perpetual and greater *jihād*) to move away from self-centeredness and toward achieving the fundamental equality of all human beings. Following a long and well-established tradition of critical thinking among Muslim scholars, in this study I have reopened the gates of independent reasoning to present my theology of interreligious relations in Islam. I have ventured, sometimes radically departing from past interpretations but not from the actual text of the Koran, to expound religious plularism as a Koranic prescription for coexistence among peoples of diverse faiths. Maintaining the integrity of each religious tradition as a unique path to salvation, I have avoided relativizing religions to the point of creating an esperanto religion. More importantly, as a believer in universal moral values that touch all humans, notwithstanding their diverse cultural application, I agree with those scholars of religion who maintain that theological differences about any matter in the sacred Scriptures are difficult, perhaps impossible, to resolve. Yet, human beings need to live together in mutual respect and cooperation to implement the common good in society. Working for the common good without insisting on a shared comprehensive religious doctrine is possible by articulating the ethical imperative of each religious tradition. Religious inclusiveness will have to arise through the ethical demand of working toward a just society in which Muslims and non-Muslims have the same rights, obligations, and liberties.

The ethical imperative of the Koran—"to compete with one another in good"—can serve to overcome discrimination based on exclusive religious claims and entitlements and can provide humankind the vision of a global community bound together to achieve the common good for all citizens of the world. However, the verse cited in the beginning of the epilogue might lead to just the opposite of pluralism and acceptance of other religious communities as partners in the moral betterment of humanity. Is not the claim to be the "best community ever brought forth to human beings" a negation of all that the Koran teaches about human dignity and equality?

The Challenge of Claiming to Be the Best Community

My research in the Koran and the Tradition has led me to assert with confidence that the issue of interpersonal relations in Islam awaits a treatment equal to the challenge of contemporary society. The Koranic provisions about civil society allow a legitimate juridical judgment concerning inclusive political, civil, and social participation in the political community. Take, for example, the earlier cited verse about the "best community."

The Koranic statement "You are the best community ever brought forth to human beings" is constitutive of God's purpose of creating an ethical order responsible for "commanding the good and forbidding the evil." The statement does not connect the status of being the best with a self-righteous presumption of the need to convert others; rather, it ascribes the status of the best to a community charged with the responsibility of instituting good and preventing evil.

The new religion brought by the Prophet Muḥammad in the seventh century in Arabia laid the foundation of its universal community, the umma, as a religious-political society governed by the dictates of the divinely inspired law, the Sharīʿa. The earth was divided according to its spiritual condition into the sphere of faith (*dār al-īmān*) and the sphere of disbelief (*dār al-kufr*). The later juridical division of the world into the sphere of submission (*dār al-islām*), the territories administered by Muslim political authority, and the sphere of war (*dar al-ḥarb*), the territories to be duly subdued, was founded upon a rationalized vision of the historical success of the Muslim armies in bringing large areas of the world under the sphere of submission.

The universal idiom of the Islamic mission was underscored by the Koranic version of the Genesis story in which Adam, the first human, was sent as the vicegerent (*khalīfa*) of God on earth to exercise divine authority. But as the Muslim community began its journey toward the creation of the divine order on earth, it moved away from its original universalist ideal and toward a more immediate practical concern to create what was best for the followers of Islam in accordance with their history and culture. The process of cultural self-identification in the community was carried on through shared religious beliefs, practices, and attitudes. The religious commitment to a community-oriented belief system necessarily led to the formulation of an exclusivist theology in which all pre-Koranic revelations were considered superseded. Politically, this theology was not neutral; it led to the negation of pluralism, overshadowing the ethical mission of creating a just society founded on the universal obligation to call people to good and forbid evil. The community was tempted to succumb and did succumb to the abandonment of the ethical element in Abrahamic monotheism, which demanded attention to the concerns, needs, and capabilities of the common people irrespective of particular religious affiliation.

Pure religion, a vertical relationship with one's Creator, inherently defies any communal limitations imposed on individual spiritual autonomy. But such a universal conception of religion, innately and autonomously bound to humans' natural disposition, could not fulfill the exclusive needs of the historical community that was declared by the Koran to be the best. The dilemma of conflicting claims to restrictive salvation under a specific religious community had to be resolved if the new community was to prove its universal excellence as an ethical and spiritual paradigm. In other words, the claim to be the best community "ever brought forth to human beings" could be sustained only if Islamic revelation could provide an inclusive religious doctrine that would institutionalize the divinely ordained diversity of faiths. To create a just society in which peoples of different religions would coexist in peace and harmony was the responsibility of the best community.

The Koranic imperative to humankind to respond to its original nature is an ethical one, based on the objectivity of good and evil. This ethical cognition is fortified with faith in the source of all human cognition, namely, God. Accordingly, the criteria for the best community are both ethical and religious: ethical in enjoining good and forbidding evil, and religious in mandating belief in God. The ethical aspect is defined in terms of social-ethical responsibility to other humans, whereas the act of believing is strictly personal. Inasmuch as the fulfillment of other-regarding ethical obligations justifies and even requires institutional structures like government agencies that could use reasonable force to ensure justice and fairness in all interpersonal human situations, the self-regarding duty of faith is founded on a noninterventionist approach. It is an unmediated relationship of individuals through a covenant between God and humanity. The moment religion is coerced, it breeds hypocrisy.

At this juncture, the best community faces its greatest challenge: how can it create an inclusive political society if the guiding principle of its collective identity as a confessional community is strictly founded upon shared religious doctrine? How about the Koran's repeated reminder that if God had so willed, "whoever is in the earth would have believed, all of them, all together," and that people cannot be constrained "until they are believers" (K. 10:99)? Does this not contradict the emphasis on a comprehensive shared religious doctrine in a political society? Given the logic of divine wisdom in endowing humans with the freedom to believe, it is inconceivable that the foundation of this just society under the "best" community should be based on an exclusionary notion of mandatory uniformity in human religiosity.

The Koran severely criticizes the exclusive claims of the pre-Koranic communities, which led to hostilities among them and to destruction of life, including the lives of God's prophets, who were unjustly killed while calling people to serve God's purposes. In fact, to alleviate the negative impact of such behavior, the Koran went back to the very source of the monotheistic tradition, namely, "submission to the Divine Will." Essentially and fundamentally, it is the acceptance of the same Creator that determines the spiritual equality of the followers of diverse religious traditions. Nevertheless, this God-centered pluralism of the Koran was in tension with the historical, relative experience of the new political society, which regarded its own system as the best. This exclusionary conceptualization of historical Islam proved to be both a point of departure for the early community, affording it a specific identity as a Muslim community, and the beginning of a dialogue within the Muslim community about the Koranic commandment to create an inclusive, just order under divine revelation. The importance given to the moral duty to command good and forbid evil in verse K. 3:110 indicates the way the Koran conceived of ethics as the basis for interreligious cooperation, in a religiously oriented civil society, with equally shared responsibility for the moral well-being of the people.

The thesis that Islam does not make a distinction between the religious and the political requires revision in light of what has been argued in this volume. Even the all-comprehensive sacred law of Islam, the Sharīʿa, presupposes the distinction between spiritual and temporal, as it categorized God-human (*ʿibādāt*) and interhuman (*muʿāmalāt*) relationships respectively. God-human relations are founded upon individual autonomy and moral agency regulated by a sense of accountability to God alone for any acts of omission or commission. Interhuman relations, in contrast, are founded upon an individual and collective social-political life, with personal responsibility and social accountability as the means of attaining justice and fairness in human relations. This latter category of interhuman relations has customarily provided Muslim governments with the principle of functional secularity that allows them to regulate all matters pertaining to interpersonal justice. The same principle rules out the authority of Muslim governments to regulate religious matters except when the free exercise of religion for any individual is in danger. This is the purport of Imam ʿAlī's statement about shared "equality in creation." The foundation of a civil society in Islam is based on the equality in creation in which the privilege of citizenry attaches equally to Muslim and non-Muslim, entailing inclusive political, civil, and social membership in the community.

Functional secularity was well entrenched in the political thinking of the early community. A number of Arab tribes that had submitted to the Prophet Muḥammad felt themselves free of any further obligation when the Prophet died, and they refused to send any further taxes to Medina. They viewed their relation to the public order under the Prophet as null and void because of the death of the party to the contract. But some men had a more integrated conception of the Islamic polity and of the community Muḥammad had created. Islam was not merely a matter of each individual obeying God; it was a compact in which all Muslims and non-Muslims were bound to one another as well. This compact did not cease with the Prophet's death; the pattern of life he had instituted could be continued under the leadership of those who had been closest to him. Anyone who separated from the core of the Muslims at Medina was in fact backing out of Islamic polity; they were traitors to the cause of God for which Muḥammad and his followers had so long been fighting. That cause was still to be fought for and demanded a single chief to whom all would be loyal. The successors to Muḥammad are credited with persuading the Muslims of Medina to adopt this daring interpretation of a latent political membership as distinct from a religious membership. It is remarkable, when one studies the religious sermons that were delivered by the early Muslim leaders on Fridays or other religious holy days, that there are hardly any comments about getting rid of the non-Muslims as a threat to Islamic public order. Their treatment of their subjects is illustrated by their inclusive rather than exclusive political order.

But as Muslims began to expand the mission of Islam to create a worldwide society under their political domination, Islam was conceived as a political ideology that would first rule over and then supersede all other communities. The religious mission was actually obscured behind a political vision that sought to expand the sphere of Islam. From then on, the mission of the best community was the political success of the Muslim commanders. Muslim jurists, formulating their opinions under Muslim dominance, regarded the adoption of Islam by others as a religious duty, which, if resisted, required imposition by *jihād*. The sphere of war had to be brought entirely under Islam. The theoretical foundations of the pluralism of the Koran, then, were periodically ignored as the political notion of *jihād* for faith gained religious importance at the expense of the divine promise of making the Muslim community the "best" instrument of instituting good and preventing evil.

Concluding Remarks

This study has shown that Islam is not monolithic in its vision of a just society. The focus of the Islamic social message has been to make human beings aware of their true potential, to overcome self-cultivated weaknesses that prevent them from dealing with others with justice and fairness. Islam seeks to remedy these weaknesses by improving interhuman relations and emphasizing people's civil responsibilities toward one another. The challenge for Muslims today, as ever, is to tap the tradition of Koranic pluralism to develop a culture of restoration, of just intrareligious and interreligious relationships in a world of cultural and religious diversity. Without restoring the principle of coexistence, Muslims will not be able to recapture the spirit of early civil society under the Prophet. The principle of "equals in creation" can serve as the cornerstone of Muslim civil society. The principle must be implemented globally to restore fractured human relations through forgiveness and compassion.

As an important source of private and public values, Islam in the twenty-first century can become a model of religion that furthers interpersonal justice in society. It is built on a legal-ethical system that inculcates moral responsibility and personal accountability for what one does to oneself and to others. Furthermore, with its emphasis on the need for just governance in human affairs, it generates incentives to correct social misconduct by highlighting the consequences of moral choices. Finally, with its doctrine of the final Day of Judgment, when all people will have to face their Lord to account for their deeds during their sojourn on earth, it prompts human beings to learn to forgive and renew social relationships in order to be forgiven by God and restored in eternal bliss. Islam's overlapping social and religious ideals can inspire the creation of pluralistic, democratic institutions in a best Muslim global community of the twenty-first century.

Notes

Chapter 1

1. In her article "Toleration and the Law," in *Toleration and Integrity in a Multi-faith Society*, ed. John Horton and Harriet Crabtree (London: Interfaith Network, 1992), pp. 50–52, Therese Murphy critically evaluates the legal implications of the "disestablishment" law in secular societies for promoting mutual tolerance among communities of the faithful. Disestablishment "privatises religion . . . building a wall of separation between church and state."

2. Armando Salvatore, *Islam and the Political Discourse of Modernity* (London: Ithaca Press, 1997), pp. 54–55, distinguishes between "political society" and "civil society," the latter being "too deeply influenced by the Western liberal-individualist tradition and conceived as the emanation of private relationships." "Political society," on the other hand, is "sustained by a diffuse sense of legitimate publicness" that makes it "thoroughly functional to modern rules of public communication exercised in the name of intellectual distinction."

3. As distinguished from the orientalism that perpetrated the notion that Islam promoted despotism and political submission, neo-orientalism promotes the idea that Islam, by its emphasis on universal spiritual egalitarianism, refuses to legitimize political authority, thereby weakening the ability of the state to emerge as a strong cohesive entity (Yahya Sadowski, "The New Orientalism and Democracy," in *Political*

Islam: Essays from Middle East Report, ed. Joel Beinin and Joe Stork [Berkeley: University of California Press, 1997], pp. 33–50). Neo-orientalism, based on its thesis about the absence of the trappings of a modern state in Islamic history, moreover, refuses to recognize the possibility of the emergence of a "civil society," a prerequisite for democratic pluralism (Salvatore, *Islam and the Political Discourse*, p. 73).

4. The epitome of this approach is the highly acclaimed work of a French Jewish scholar, Bat Ye'or, *The Decline of Eastern Christianity under Islam: From Jihad to Dhimmitude*, trans. M. Kochan and D. Littman (Madison, NJ: Fairleigh Dickinson University Press, 1996). This work claims "not to be about Islam" but ends up formulating the "theology" of *dhimmitude*, justified by the Koran. Aside from the methodological problems connected with the use of "documents" produced by the "victims" of Islamic *jihād*, the entire book suffers from a hegemonic approach to the study of the cultural and religious other, an other who is thoroughly dehumanized and demonized. Far more objective and methodologically sound research on the treatment of Jews under Christendom and Islamdom is Mark R. Cohen, *Under Crescent and Cross: The Jews in the Middle Ages* (Princeton: Princeton University Press, 1997). The work is solidly based on documents without the diabolism of Ye'or's study. For an evenhanded treatment of the entire question of dechristianization of the conquered territories under Muslim rulers, see: Youssef Courbage and Philippe Fargues, *Christians and Jews under Islam*, trans. Judy Mabro (London: I. B. Tauris, 1997).

5. I have adopted the term as used by David Little in his unpublished paper "Secularity, Islam, and Human Rights." He clearly makes a distinction between *secularity* and *secularism*. Whereas the latter term signifies "the well-being of mankind in the present life, to the exclusion of all considerations drawn from belief in God or in a future state," the former implies "a condition of state self-limitation." In other words, secularity simply regulates matters pertaining to this world, without negating or disregarding nonsecular or spiritual affairs.

6. See, for instance, the widely distributed and widely read work by al-Qāḍī al-Shahīd ʿAbd al-Qādir ʿAwda, *Al-Aʿmāl al-Kāmila* (Cairo: al-Mukhtār al-Islāmī, 1994).

7. Some of the critical articles on the epistemological crisis that faces Muslim scholarship on Islam and Sharīʿa are in ʿAbd Allāh Fahd al-Nīfisī, ed., *al-Ḥarakat al-islāmiyya: ruʾya mustaqbala awrāq fi naqd al-dhātī* (Cairo: Maktabat al-Madbūlī, 1989). Also of significance are some of the most scholarly presentations of the way Sharīʿa has been abused by the so-called fundamentalists who want to see the Islamic system promulgated as it was formulated in the classical age. See in particular Muḥammad Saʿīd al-ʿAshmāwī, *Uṣūl al-sharīʿa* (Cairo: Dār al-Kitāb al-Maṣrī, 1979), and *al-Islām al-siyāsī* (Cairo: Sīnā li al-Nashr, 1987).

8. T. Ball, J. Farr, and R. L. Hanson, eds., *Political Innovation and Conceptual Change* (Cambridge: Cambridge University Press, 1989), editors' introduction, pp. 1–5.

9. D. G. Jones and R. E. Richey, eds., *American Civil Religion* (New York: Harper and Row, 1974), p. 3.

10. The closing decades of the twentieth century saw new interest in the potential of traditional religious values to solve global concerns about cultural identity in the

modern world. Throughout the world, people turn to their ancient Scriptures or myths in search of ideas and values that encourage, for example, a protective attitude toward nature. There is also widespread concern to restore an ethically viable balance between human beings and their relational needs in a highly technicalized society. See: *The Assissi Declarations: Messages on Man and Nature from Buddhism, Christianity, Hinduism, Islam, and Judaism* (Gland, Switzerland: WWF International, 1986); A. Giddens, *The Consequences of Modernity* (Stanford: Stanford University Press, 1990); Hans Küng, *Global Responsibility: In Search of a New World Ethic* (New York: Crossroads, 1991).

11. Jacob Neusner, "Can You Be "Religious in General"? *Religious Studies and Theology* 12 (1992), pp. 69–73.

12. T. Luckmann, *The Invisible Religion: The Problem of Religion in Modern Society* (New York: Macmillan, 1967).

13. Gerald Parsons, ed., *The Growth of Religious Diversity: Britain from 1945*, vol. 1: *Traditions* (London: Routledge, 1993), in a comparative study of diverse religious and ethnic groups in the United Kingdom and with reference to other parts of Europe and the United States, indicates cognitive as well as practical obstacles and solutions in the path of the religiously and culturally pluralistic reality of modern society.

14. In this connection see: John L. Esposito, *The Islamic Threat: Myth or A Reality?* (New York: Oxford University Press, 1992); Bruce Lawrence, *In Shattering the Myth: Islam beyond Violence* (Princeton, NJ: Princeton University Press, 1998).

15. David Heyd, ed., *Toleration: An Elusive Virtue* (Princeton: Princeton University Press, 1996), in several scholarly essays brings out the "elusiveness" of the virtue of "tolerance." See, in particular, the introduction, pp. 3–17.

16. Gerrie Lubbe, "The Role of Religion in the Process of Nation-building: From Plurality to Pluralism," *Religion and Theology* 2 (1995), pp. 159–170.

17. The concept of the clash of civilizations was introduced by Bernard Lewis before the final collapse of Communism in "The Roots of the Muslim Rage," *Atlantic Monthly* September 1990, p. 60. In 1993, Samuel P. Huntington popularized it in an article and his subsequent book, *The Clash of Civilizations and the Remaking of World Order* (New York: Simon and Schuster, 1996). The clash deals with more than the reaction of the West to the final demise of the Soviet Union. It conveys the dismay of some Western scholars who realize that non-Western civilizations are not willing to accept the superiority of Western liberal ideas because of some inherent incompatibilities of "other" cultures and civilizations. See, for an incisive critique of Huntington's thesis, Shireen T. Hunter, *The Future of Islam and the West: Clash of Civilizations or Peaceful Coexistence?* (Westport, CT: Praeger, 1998); also of interest in tracing the genesis of the clash is Bernard Lewis, *Cultures in Conflict: Christians, Muslims, and Jews in the Age of Discovery* (New York: Oxford University Press, 1995).

18. *Fundamentalism* in this work has been used to describe the phenomenon that represents an alternative ideology to different forms of secular modern ideologies, such as communism, socialism, nationalism, and so on. In describing an activist response to religious impulse in Islam, I have decided to stick to this term rather than to adopt

the more ideologically problematic *Islamism* or *political Islam*, which are in no sense more neutral than *fundamentalism* or *religious radicalism* in the works of American social scientists. See chapter 2.

19. Ḥasan ʿAbad Allāh al-Turābī, "Al-shūrā wa al-dīmuqratiyya: ishkālāt al-muṣtalaḥ wa al-mafhūm," in *al-Mustaqbal al-ʿArabī wa al-qaḍiyat al-filastiniyya baʿda azmat al-khalīj*. Ed. Ibrāhīm Saʿduddīn (Cairo: Markaz Ittiḥād al-Muhāmīn al-ʿArab, 1991) pp. 4–22.

20. John Dunn, *Western Political Theory in the Face of the Future* (Cambridge: Cambridge University Press, 1993), p. 2.

21. Such is the opinion of Abū al-Qāsim al-Khūʾī, *The Prolegomena to the Qurʾan*, trans. with an introduction by Abdulaziz Sachedina, (New York: Oxford University Press, 1998). This opinion has been adopted and critically examined, in light of opinions expressed in earlier works by Western scholars of the Qurʾan, by John Burton, *The Collection of the Qurʾan* (Cambridge: Cambridge University Press, 1977), chapter 10.

22. Rudolf Bultmann in his essay "Is Exegesis without Presuppositions Possible?" in *The Hermeneutics Reader: Texts of German Tradition from the Enlightenment to the Present*, ed. by Kurt Mueller-Vollmer (New York: Continuum, 1992), regards the historical understanding of the text on the basis of a "life-relation" to it as the existential encounter because it "grows out of one's own historicity." I have used the term *life-orientation* in a similar sense to express the Muslim encounter with the Qurʾan as a paradigm for the creation of the ideal Muslim society.

23. The question of "authorial pretext" or "author's intentions" and contextual significance and their relation to a broader context for historical understanding of a text is taken up by Jeffrey Stout in his article "What Is the Meaning of a Text?" *New Literary History: A Journal of Theory and Interpretation* 14 (1982–83), 1, pp. 1–12.

24. *Nahj al-Balāgha*, ed. Muḥammad ʿAbduh (Beirut: Dār al-Maʿrifa, n.d.) vol. 2, p. 17.

25. George F. Hourani, *Islamic Rationalism: The Ethics of ʿAbd al-Jabbār* (Oxford: Clarendon, 1971), p. 3.

26. Ibid.

Chapter 2

I have used two translations throughout this book: A. J. Arberry, *The Koran Interpreted* (New York: Macmillan, 1955), and Colin Turner, *The Quran: A New Interpretation* (London: Curzon Press, 1997). In some cases I have added my explanation in brackets or revised these two translations to conform with the original.

1. In addition to K. 2:213 cited in the beginning of this chapter, see: K. 5:48, 10:19, 11:118, 16:93, 21:92, 23:52, and 42:8. I have preferred "community" to "nation" as the translation of the word *umma*. The reason is that the principle that directs the creation of *umma* is moral-spiritual affinity rather than birth, which the word *nation* suggests.

2. Muslim commentators have argued about the time when humankind was all one community. Was it the community that lived between Adam and Noah? Were humans united until that time and then divided? Since there is no indication in the Koran or the Tradition as to the time of the unity or the time when the first discord occurred in that community, I take the passage as a matter open for reflection and interpretation. For the views of different commentators in classical as well as modern times, see: Mahmoud M. Ayoub, *The Qur'an and Its Interpreters* (Albany: State University of New York, 1984), 1, pp. 215–216.

3. Most Muslim commentators believe that the introduction of "the Book" in singular form in spite of the plurality of the prophets suggests the generic nature of the revelation, sharing essential unity and function as a source of spiritual guidance and prescriptive conduct for organizing communities and regulating the intercommunal affairs "touching their differences." See: Bayḍāwī, *Anwār al-tanzīl* (Cairo, 1887), p. 45; Ṭabāṭabā'ī, *al-Mīzān fī tafsīr al-qur'ān* (Beirut: Mu'assasa al-A'lamī, 1972), vol. 2, pp. 128–129.

4. Marshall G. S. Hodgson, *The Venture of Islam: Conscience and History in a World Civilization* (Chicago: University of Chicago Press, 1977), vol. 1, p. 336.

5. The term "rite" or "legal school" is the translation of *madhhab*—a system of rules that covers all aspects of the human spiritual and moral obligations (*takālīf*, plural of *taklīf*) that a Muslim must carry out as a member of the community. Four *madhhab*s, Mālikī, Ḥanafī, Shāfi'ī and Ḥanbalī, were ultimately accepted as legitimate by the Sunnis; the Shī'ites formulated and followed their own rite, known as Ja'farī.

6. I have treated the matter of freedom of conscience from the Qur'anic point of view in an essay in a work I coauthored with David Little and John Kelsay, "Liberty of Conscience and Religion in the Qur'an," *Human Rights and the Conflict of Cultures: Western and Islamic Perspectives on Religious Liberty* (Columbia: University of South Carolina Press, 1988), pp. 53–100.

7. See chapter 1, n. 17. Armando Salvatore, *Islam and the Political Discourse*, part 3, p. 117, deconstructs the Western treatment of "political Islam" and traces the ideological and hegemonic epistemology and its transition from a monodimensional "essentialized" view of Islam maintained by the orientalists, where the "political is considered derivative of religion," to a bidimensional hermeneutics adopted by social scientists, where the "political acquires the status of an additional and autonomous dimension grounded on a concern of the observer."

8. Abdullahi Ahmed An-Na'im, *Toward an Islamic Reformation: Civil Liberties, Human Rights, and International Law* (Syracuse: Syracuse University Press, 1990), on the basis of the thesis propounded by Maḥmūd Ṭāhā, the Sudanese reformer, has argued that it is the Mekkan sections of the Koran that are tolerant and pluralistic because they capture the minority status of the Muslims who had to learn to coexist with the hostile world around them. Such a view is untenable in light of a number of important verses in the Medinan sections that deal with the universal humanity within the activity of God in the sphere of ethics and its function in sustaining the world. This moral connection in humanity is underscored in Medina, where the first Islamic

political society was already in place. See also similar views held by Mohamed Khalil, as reported in *Islam and Democracy: Religion, Politics, and Power in the Middle East* (Washington, DC: U.S. Institute of Peace Press, 1992), chapter 2. He, like An-Na'im, uses Ṭāha's thesis for his critique of the so-called Muslim fundamentalists. Khalil is, however, right about the way Muslims have misused the principle of abrogation (*naskh*) to repeal the pluralistic teaching of the Koran. But this is not a modern problem connected with the fundamentalists. It goes back in history to a time when the legal rulings in the classical sources that justified the early territorial expansionism in the name of *jihād* were formulated. See chapter 3 in this volume.

9. The Koran uses the phrase to describe Jews and Christians, whose founders had brought the divine message to guide the conduct of their respective communities and prepare them for the hereafter. However, technically, even Muslims are part of the "peoples of the Book." See my article "Jews, Christians, and Muslims According to the Qur'an," *Greek Orthodox Theological Review* 31 (1986), 1–2 pp. 105–120.

10. I have rendered *sunna* with capitalized *T* in the translation for this technical term (Tradition), meaning all that is reported as having been said (*aqwāl al-rasūl*), done (*a'māl al-rasūl*), and silently confirmed (*taqrīrāt al-rasūl*) by the Prophet; whereas the translation of *ḥadīth* (the vehicle of the *sunna*, through which it is related) is rendered with lower case *t* (tradition) or simply '*ḥadīth*-report.' The Tradition in the religious sciences is comprised of the major compilations of the *ḥadīth*-reports, which include the six officially recognized collections of the *Ṣiḥāḥ* (sound traditions) among the Sunnī Muslims, and the four *Kutub* (books) among the Shī'a.

11. In the context of the traditional sources dealing with the prescriptive rulings, indicative of the ways in which the Koran and the Tradition are employed to formulate juridical propositions, it is necessary to develop an interpretive process that could go beyond the textual and contextual analysis to take into consideration the intertextual dimension of the legal discourse in Islam. Issues related to the treatment of religious minorities in Muslim culture must go beyond the traditional interpretive assumptions based on official texts to include oral transmissions that reflect intertextual negotiations between dominant Muslims and the self-governing minorities in Muslim societies. The need for such an inter-textual analysis, without mentioning the word *intertext*, is suggested by Derrida in his *Margins of Philosophy*, trans. Alan Bass (Chicago: University of Chicago Press, 1982). For the actual discussion on intertext and Derrida, see: Vincent B. Leitch, *Deconstructive Criticism: An Advanced Introduction* (New York: Columbia University Press, 1983), pp. 87–163.

12. Ibn Manẓūr, *Lisān al-'arab* (Beirut: Dār Ṣādir, n.d.), vol. 13, p. 365.

13. The "global ethic" concept is used by Hans Küng and is described as the fundamental consensus relating to binding values, ultimate standards, and basic personal attitudes between the religions that enable them to lead the way for society as a whole by their good example. See: Hans Küng and Karl-Josef Kuschel, eds., *A Global Ethic: The Declaration of the Parliament of the World's Religions* (London: SCM Press, 1993), p. 21.

14. What follows is an expanded version of my earlier article "Is Islam an Abrogation of Judeo-Christian Revelation?" in *Concilium International Review of Theology: Islam: A Challenge for Christianity*, ed. Hans Küng and Jürgen Moltmann (London: SCM Press, 1994), pp. 94–102.

15. The Arabic term *naskh* actually means 'abrogation' or 'repeal.' Although its usage is limited to legal matters, it has been extended to include abrogation of the pre-Koranic revelations. For the full discussion of abrogation as supersession see: Jane D. McAuliffe, *Qurʾanic Christians: An Analysis of Classical and Modern Exegesis* (Cambridge: Cambridge University Press, 1991).

16. Historically, Muslims, like other religious groups, have demonstrated far greater intolerance toward dissenters within their own ranks than outside them. Muslim history is replete with instances of intrareligious violence, not only between the majoritarian Sunnī and the minority Shīʿite communities, but also among the Sunnī adherents of different legal rites, such as the Ḥanafī and the Ḥanbalī schools. See Benjamin Braude and Bernard Lewis, eds., *Christians and Jews in the Ottoman Empire: The Functioning of a Plural Society* (New York: Holmes and Meier, 1982), pp. 1–34; G. R. Elton, "Introduction," in *Studies in Church History* vol. 21: *Persecution and Toleration*, ed. W. J. Shields (Oxford: Basil Blackwell, 1984), pp. xiii–xv.

17. McAuliffe, *Qurʾānic Christians*, has done extensive work on the verses dealing with Muslims' perceptions of Christians through the exegetical works produced by both Sunnī and Shīʿite commentators, from the classical to the modern period. Her study concludes accurately that the issue of the prophethood of Muḥammad remained an important element in affording non-Koranic peoples of the Book a share in salvation. However, in the midst of this exclusivist soteriology, there have been Muslim commentators, more in the modern period of interfaith hermeneutics, who have regarded the promise in K. 2:62 as still important in constructing an inclusive theology founded on belief in God, the hereafter, and right action as overriding criteria in attaining salvation.

18. Al-Khūʾī, *The Prolegomena to the Qurʾan*, pp. 186–253; also, John Burton, "Introductory Essay: 'The Meaning of Naskh,'" in Abū ʿUbaid al-Q̱āsim b. Sallām's *K. al-nāsikh wa-l-mansūkh*, ed. with a commentary by John Burton, E. J. W. Gibb Memorial Series, New Series, XXX (Suffolk: St. Edmundsbury Press, 1987).

19. For the classical exegetical formulations that dominate the intolerant and exclusivist attitude toward the peoples of the Book based on the notion of abrogation of the tolerant K. 2:62 by K. 3:85, see: Muḥammad b. Jarīr al-Ṭabarī, *Jāmiʿ al-bayān ʾan taʾwil āy al-qurʾan* (Cairo: Dār al-Maʾārif, 1954), 2: pp. 155–156, where he cites the exclusivist opinions and then rejects the view that God will exclude those who had lived in faith and acted righteously, because he finds it incongruent with the divine promise; Ibn Kathīr, *Tafsīr al-qurʾān al-ʿaẓīm* (Beirut: Dār al-Fikr, 1970), vol. 1, p. 103, limits salvation to the people of the Book before Muḥammad became the prophet; Rashīd Riḍā, *Tafsīr al-qurʾān al-ḥakīm al-shahīr bi-tafsīr al-manār* (Beirut, Dār al-Maʿrifa, 1970), vol. 6, p. 479, however, grudgingly, does concede the validity of salvation for the people of the Book.

20. Ṭabari, *Jāmiʿ al-bayān*, vol. 2, pp. 155–156.

21. Ibn Kathīr, *Tafsīr*, vol. 1, p. 103.

22. For the theological problems faced by early Christianity in declaring its originality and working out its relation to Judaism, see: Marcel Simon, *Versus Israel: A Study of the Relations Between Christians and Jews in the Roman Empire* (*AD 135–425*) (New York: Oxford University Press, 1986), in particular chapter 3.

23. Ibn Kathīr, *Tafsīr*, vol. 1, p. 180, vol. 2. p. 67.

24. Rashīd Riḍā, *Tafsīr al-manār*, vol. 1, p. 339.

25. Ibid., vol. 1, p. 336.

26. Ṭabāṭabāʾī, *al-Mīzān fi tafsīr*, vol. 1, p. 193.

27. Avishai Margalit, "The Ring: On Religious Pluralism," in Heyd, *Toleration*, pp. 147–157.

28. Margalit, "The Ring," p. 151.

29. Wilfred Cantwell Smith, *The Meaning and End of Religion* (New York: Macmillan, 1962), p. 113.

30. Ibn Kathīr, *Tafsīr*, 2:68.

31. Sayyid Quṭb, *Fī ẓilāl al-qurʾān* (Beirut: Dār Iḥyaʾ al-Turath al-ʿArabī, 1971), vol. 1, pp. 625–627.

32. This section is based on the earlier version of the paper I presented at the conference on Christian-Muslim Relations, sponsored by the Center for Muslim-Christian Understanding at Georgetown University in 1994.

33. A fairly detailed analysis of the Islamic and Western systems appears in David A. Westbrook, "Islamic International Law and Public International Law: Separate Expressions of World Order," *Virginia Journal of International Law* 33 (1993), pp. 819–897. Westbrook has examined critically the works of various Muslim thinkers who have expounded their versions of Islamic international order and has provided a rare corrective to the Western perception of Islamic order.

34. In my article "Islam and Muslims in Diaspora," *Bulletin of the Institute of Middle Eastern Studies*, 7 (1993), pp. 109–146, I demonstrated that the Koran sees the world as one stage of a struggle between the forces of faith (*īmān*) and disbelief (*kufr*), with the promise that the latter will ultimately succumb to the former. However, in Muslim legal writings, the world is divided between the "domains of Islam and war" (*dār al-islām* and *dār al-ḥarb*), with the implication that the latter sphere has to be subdued by the former to establish Muslim hegemony over the entire world. This legal conception of global territory is not supported by the Koran. It should be seen as part of the Muslim political jurisprudence to justify territorial expansion without peacefully converting the world to the "domain of faith."

35. This is *dīn al-fiṭra* in theology, comparable to Augustinian *religio-naturalis*, which is God's gift through creation to all human beings. In this connection the Prophet is reported to have said, "Every child is born in the *fiṭra*; it is his parents who make of him a Jew or a Christian or a Parsee" (*Ṣaḥīḥ Muslim*, *bāb al-qadar*, *ḥadīth* 22; *Ṣaḥīḥ*

Bukhārī, bāb al-tafsīr, Sūra 30, section 1; *bāb al-qadar*, section 3). The word *fiṭra* signifies the "original state of things" and serves as a universal recognition of God's sovereignty before people become obligated to their specific *dīn* (paths of conduct) brought by the prophets. See: A. J. Wensinck, *The Muslim Creed: Its Genesis and Historical Development* (London: Frank Cass, 1965), pp. 214–216.

36. Fazlur Rahman, *Islam and Modernity: Transformation* of an Intellectual Tradition (Chicago: University of Chicago Press, 1984), introduction.

37. See n. 7.

38. It is not an easy task for any conscientious Muslim intellectual in the Muslim world or in the West to undertake this critical task without endangering his or her life. The intolerance exhibited by the religious establishment in some Muslim countries and more recently in Muslim communities in Europe and North America, which feels threatened by the rational assessment in the universities of religious texts in their historical context, has forced these scholars to abandon their religious and moral responsibility to their own community. In some cases, these scholars have been forced to go underground and seek asylum in the West. As is well known, both Jewish and Christian academicians, in the early days of their entry into the academic world, encountered similar reactions from their respective religious authorities and congregations around the world. For Muslims in general, and their communities in the West in particular, the academic study of Islam is a new phenomenon that causes them, because of deep-felt insecurities in their faith, to react strongly against anything that appears to challenge their long-held belief system.

39. Joseph Schacht's edition of Tabarī's *Kitāb ikhtilāf al-fuqahā'* remains one of the best editions of the work, published by E. J. Brill in 1933. The work is comprehensive in that Ṭabarī cites all the major Sunnī opinions on the matter of *jihād*, attributing them rightly to the individual jurists rather than to legal schools, as later authors were to do.

40. Ibid., p. 199.

41. The reference is to the *ḥunafā'* (plural of *ḥanīf*), who are mentioned in the Koran as the 'upright' people among the contemporaries of Muḥammad in Mekka. They were also monotheists who had rejected idol worship. Some of them practiced the asceticism of eastern Christianity.

42. This definition was developed by Marty Martin, the project director of comparative fundamentalisms.

43. Bruce Lawrence, *Defenders of God: The Fundamentalist Revolt Against the Modern Age* (New York: Harper and Row, 1989).

44. Fazlur Rahman, "Roots of Islamic Neo-Fundamentalism," in *Change in the Muslim World*, ed. Philip H. Stodard (Syracuse: Syracuse University Press, 1981), p. 23.

45. Wilfred Cantwell Smith, *Islam in Modern History* (Princeton: Princeton University Press, 1977), p. 41.

46. Ibid.

Chapter 3

1. Ann K. S. Lambton, *State and Government in Medieval Islam* (Oxford: Oxford University Press, 1981), pp. 203–204.

2. Ibn Saʿd, *al-Ṭabaqāt al-kubrā* (Beirut: Dār Ṣādir, 1380/1960), vol. 1, p. 358.

3. Aḥmad b. Yaḥya al-Balādhurī, *Futūḥ al-buldān*, ed. M. J. de Goeje (Leiden: E. J. Brill, 1866), pp. 106, 147. English trans. Philip Khūri Ḥitti, *The Origins of the Islamic State* (New York: Columbia University, 1916), vol. 1, p. 109. Muḥammad b. Ismāʿīl al-Bukhārī, *Ṣaḥīḥ* (Beirut: ʿĀlam al-Kutub, 1986), *Kitāb al-jihād*, *ḥadīth* 275, mentions the instructions given to Muʿādh and Abū Mūsa when the Prophet sent them to the Yemen: "Treat the people with consideration, and not with harshness; fill them with glad tidings, and not with repugnance. Follow each other and do not differ."

4. Muḥammad b. Jarīr al-Ṭabarī, *Taʾrīkh al-rusul wa al-mulūk* (Cairo: Dār al-Maʿārif, 1960, vol. 1, p. 2922, cites ʿUmar's disapproval of harsh measures against the subject populace on account of the land tax (*kharāj*), on the basis of the *ḥadīth*-report according to which the Prophet said, "If someone causes people to suffer in this world, God will cause him to suffer on the Day of Judgment." Such reports abound in all historical sources and in the works of *ḥadīth*, indicating concern on the part of Muslim rulers about the excesses that were being committed against non-Muslims.

5. *Dhimma*, the 'pact' or 'covenant' that was accorded by the Muslim state and community to the followers of other monotheistic religions living under their rule, granted them protection and certain restricted rights, and even discriminatory provisions, in exchange for their recognition of Muslim power. *Ahl al-dhimma* or *dhimmi* refers to the people gathered under such a covenant. See the article *Dhimmī* in the *Encyclopaedia of Islam*, 2d ed.

6. Ṭabāṭabāʾī, *al-Mīzān*, vol. 1, pp. 52–54, argues that the words *kuffār* (infidels) or *alladhīna kafarū'* (those who disbelieve) in the Koran, without exception refer to the Mekkan Arabs at the beginning of the Prophet's mission, unless there are contextual aspects to suggest otherwise.

7. The document is preserved in Muḥammad b. al-Walīd al-Ṭurṭūshī, *Sirāj al-mulūk* (Cairo: al-Dār al-Miṣriyya al-Lubnāniyya, 1994), pp. 229–230. The English translation is adapted from Bernard Lewis, *Islam: From the Prophet Muḥammad to the Capture of Constantinople, vol. 2: Religion and Society* (New York: Oxford University Press, 1987), pp. 217–219.

8. Hodgson, *Venture of Islam*, vol. 1, p. 269; Lambton, *State and Government*, p. 203.

9. Most of the major historical sources that deal with the caliphate of the Umayyad ʿUmar b. ʿAbd al-ʿAzīz (717–720) and of the ʿAbbasid al-Mutawakkil (847–861) mention carrying out such measures against the people of the Book. The latter is also well known for his persecution of the Shīʿites.

10. Aḥmad b. Abī Yaʿqūb, *Taʾrīkh al-yaʿqūbī*, ed. Muḥammad Ṣādiq Baḥr al-ʿUlūm (Najaf: al-Maktaba al-Ḥaydariyya, 1394/1974), vol. 2, p. 135.

11. For the translation of the text, see Lewis, *Islam*, vol. 2, pp. 219–223.

12. Balādhūrī, *Futūḥ al-buldān*, p. 162.

13. Bukhārī, *Ṣaḥīḥ*, *Kitāb al-jihād*, *hadīth* 287.

14. Translation of the text by Lewis, *Islam*, vol. 2, pp. 217–218.

15. Lewis, *Islam*, vol. 2, pp. 221–222. Originally published in Muḥammed b. Idrīs al-Shāfiʿī, *Kitāb al-umm* (Cairo: Dār al-Shaʿb, 1321/1903), vol. 4, p. 118–119.

16. This has been a cry connected with the establishment of Islamic government. The awakening of Islam in modern times as an alternative to secular ideologies has been conceived in terms of the implementation or promulgation of the Islamic Sharīʿa. See Muḥammad Saʿīd al-ʿAshmāwī, *al-Sharīʿa al-islāmiyya wa al-qānūn al-miṣrī* (Cairo: Maktaba Madbūlī, 1988); al-Nafīsī, *al-Ḥarakat al-islāmiyya*, especially essays by Tawfīq al-Shāwī and Fatḥī ʿUthmān.

17. Ibn Kathīr, *Tafsīr*, vol. 2, p. 588, cites Bukhārī, *Ṣaḥīh*, as the source for the tradition of the Prophet.

18. Karl-Josef Kuschel, *Abraham: Sign of Hope for Jews, Christians, and Muslims* (New York: Continuum, 1995), p. 190.

19. Cohen, *Under Crescent and Cross*, p. 26; Simon, *Versus Israel*, especially chapter 3.

20. Ibn Kathīr, *Tafsīr*, vol. 2, p. 589, mentions another opinion that regards the audience of the passage to be the Muslim community. However, the subsequent subjunctive clause beginning "Had God willed" clearly makes its audience communities under different prophets.

21. Thus, for instance, Ibn Kathīr, *Tafsīr*, vol. 2, p. 589, regards the *khayrāt* as referring to obedience to God through obedience to his law brought by Muḥammad, whose revelation has abrogated all previous laws. On the other hand, Sayyid Quṭb, *Fī ẓilāl al-qurʾān*, vol. 2, p. 903, in his endeavor to prove that it is only one Sharīʿa that is to dominate all other religions, has treated K. 5:48 most superficially. The Shīʿī commentator Ṭabāṭabāʾī, *al-Mīzān*, vol. 5, p. 353, regards *al-khayrāt* as *al-aḥkām* (the ordinances) and *al-takālīf* (moral-religious duties).

22. Paul Mendes-Flohr, *From Mysticism to Dialogue: Martin Buber's Transformation of German Social Thought* (Detroit: Wayne State University Press, 1989), p. 27, introduces the term in the context of Georg Simmel's sociological paradox in human interaction in everyday life. By virtue of "feeling bound to others," sociation or social life based on interaction between individuals constitutes "a unique and autonomous form of existence."

23. David Little, "The Nature and Basis of Human Rights," in *Prospects for a Common Morality*, ed. Gene Outka and John P. Reeder, Jr. (Princeton: Princeton University Press, 1993), pp. 73–92, has developed a convincing argument in support of moral intuition as part of contemporary moral discourse, which is torn between the two opposing camps of the "particularists" and the "universalists," who either deny or support the "equal and inalienable rights of all members of the human family," based on certain ethical theories.

24. I have adopted the phrase and its referent from Alan Gewirth, "Common Morality and the Community of Rights," in *Prospects for a Common Morality*, ibid.,

pp. 30–31, in which he defines a "common morality" as a positive concept of morality that consists of a "set of rules or directives for action that are upheld as categorically obligatory," in contrast with a normative concept that "consists in the moral precepts or rules or principles that are valid and thus ought to be upheld as categorically obligatory."

25. Sayyid Quṭb, *Fī ẓilāl al-qur'ān*, vol. 4, p. 2241, relates the *karam* to the very first quality with which a human becomes human: autonomous in orientation (*ḥurriyat al-ittijāh*) and individually responsible (*fardiyyat al-tabī'a*). 'Allāma Ṭabāṭabā'ī, *al-Mīzān*, vol. 13, p. 156, regards *takrīm* as a special endowment and honoring of human beings that no one else among God's creatures possesses. It is different from *tafḍīl* (esteem) in that *takrīm* is related to the person by making him dignified with self-respect.

26. Sayyid Quṭb, *Fī ẓilāl al-qur'ān*, vol. 6, p. 3917, explains the theory of human creation with a twofold nature: capable of doing good and evil and of being guided and misguided; endowed with the capacity to distinguish between the two. This is a concealed power in human existence that the Koran introduces sometimes as inspiration (*ilhām*) and at other times as guidance (*hidāya*). It is concealed in one's innermost being in the form of a potential that external factors may arouse from time to time, sharpening and orienting humans in this or that direction. However, humans cannot create this twofold potential, because it is created in the *fiṭra*. 'Allāma Ṭabāṭabā'ī, *al-Mīzān*, vol. 20, pp. 297–299, treats the question of inspiration (*ilhām*) in the context of ethical epistemology. He regards inspiration as the medium through which God presents knowledge in the form of conception or confirmation and instructs the human soul about its ethical responsibilities. God provides the knowledge of both good and evil related to the same act, such as consuming wealth: consuming the wealth of an orphan is wrong, and consuming one's own wealth is right. Hence, *ilhām* about the wrongness and the rightness of an act is perfected in practical reason through the divine command regarding "human by nature upright" in K. 30:30–31.

27. Sayyid Quṭb, *Fī ẓilāl al-qur'ān*, vol. 5, p. 2767, explains the relationship between human nature and the nature of God's religion, which are both created by God. Both are in accordance with the laws of creation and are symmetrical in nature and orientation. God creates the human heart, where he reveals this religion so that it can judge a person, direct his attention, and cure him from the diseases that are caused by sinful deviation. In this sense, both the *fiṭra* and the *dīn* are unchanging. When the person deviates from *fiṭra*, the only thing that can bring *fiṭra* back in harmony is the religion. 'Allāma Ṭabāṭabā'ī, *al-Mīzān*, vol. 16, pp. 178–179, regards religion as a tradition of life that humankind must follow to reach the goal of happiness. The *fiṭra* empowers human beings to reach that goal.

28. Scholars of *uṣul al-fiqh* do not deal with ethical issues separately from legal ones in the juristic application. In line with their theological positions, the role of human reasoning is evaluated in terms of understanding ethical principles, whether they are cognitively placed in the nature with which God creates human beings or are extracted from the commands and prohibitions in the revelation. For various theological opinions as they relate to the legal-ethical deliberations, see Muḥammad b. Muḥammad al-Ghazālī, *al-Mustaṣfā min 'ilm al-uṣūl* (Cairo: Būlūq, 1322/1904), vol. 1, pp. 55–60.

29. The Koran made no attempt to lay down a comprehensive moral system, because it treated morality as "the known," *al-maʿrūf. Al-maʿrūf*, in the meaning of moral behavior in the Koran, signifies "goodness," a "good quality or action," "gentleness in any action, or deed," whose goodness is known by reason and by revelation. *Al-munkar* (the censured, blamed) signifies the contrary of *al-maʿrūf.* In the case of divorced women, for instance, the Koran says: "And for the divorced women there shall be a provision with moderation, or right and just aim, and beneficence (*bi-l-maʿrūf*)" (K. 2:242). *Al-ʿamr bi-l-maʿrūf* (commanding the good = the "known") and its opposite, *al-nahy ʿani-l-munkar* (forbidding the evil = the "abominable"), are classified among the social responsibilities collectively or representatively (*bi-l-kifāya*) required of the community. See: E. W. Lane, *An Arabic-English Lexicon* (Beirut: Librairie du Liban, 1968), vol. 5, p. 2014.

30. This is John Rawls's method of narrowing "the range of disagreement" in matters related to securing democratic liberty and equality, in order to include "our considered convictions at all levels of generality," on due reflection or "reflective equilibrium," without regarding any particular level of abstract principle or judgment in particular cases as "foundational." Rawls uses the example of convictions about the desirability of, for instance, religious toleration and rejection of slavery, achieved through a process of "reflective equilibrium" to "organize the basic ideas and principles implicit in these convictions into a coherent political conception of justice," without giving the foundational voice to either the convictions or principles in determining the ultimate judgment. See his *Political Liberalism* (New York: Columbia University Press, 1993), p. 8.

31. In Muslim philosophical sciences, the unknown is called *al-maṭlūb*, 'that which is sought,' and the known is called *muqaddima*, 'premise'; in the traditional sciences, which include theology and ethics, the unknown is called *farʿ*, 'branch' or 'derivative,' and the known is called *aṣl*, 'root' or 'paradigmatic precedent.' I have used *maṭlūb* in its philosophical, as well as its lexical, sense to indicate the analogical reasoning (*qiyās*) that depends on both the traditional sources as well as human reasoning to deduce new decisions in the area of social ethics. See: Harry Austryn Wolfson, *The Philosophy of Kalam* (Cambridge, MA: Harvard University Press, 1976), pp. 6–7.

32. For details, see Hourani, *Islamic Rationalism*, 103–104.

33. A. James Reichley, "Religion and American Democracy," in *Morality and Religion in Liberal Democratic Societies*, ed. Gordon L. Anderson and Morton A. Kaplan (New York: Paragon House, 1992), pp. 201–222.

34. Ṭabarī, *Taʾrīkh*, vol. 3, pp. 1389–1390.

35. John Rawls, "The Priority of Right and Ideas of the Good," *Philosophy and Public Affairs* 17, 4, pp. 251–276.

36. Will Kymlicka, "Two Models of Pluralism and Tolerance," in *Toleration: An Illusive Virtue*, ed. David Heyd (Princeton: Princeton University Press, 1996), pp. 81–105, has critically evaluated the Rawlsian liberal, secular model of religious tolerance based on the twin principles of justice and autonomy. Kymlicka, in agreement with the importance of individual freedom of conscience as a human right, has shown

another model of religious toleration, in which a dominant religious community, committed to a particular belief system in its comprehensive political life, could provide a system that would ensure harmonious intercommunal life in a multifaith society. In spite of the fact that Islam recognizes the centrality of autonomous human conscience in negotiating its spiritual destiny, it is the second model proposed by Kymlicka that has historically provided the Muslim state and its legal system the means to foster some semblance of modern citizenry.

37. Hodgson, *The Venture of Islam*, vol. 1, p. 218.

38. Ibid., p. 252.

39. See: Lambton, *State and Government*, chapters 6–9.

40. Adam B. Seligman, *The Idea of Civil Society* (New York: The Free Press, 1992), chapter 3.

41. Hamed Enayat, *Modern Islamic Political Thought* (Austin: University of Texas Press, 1991), chapter 3.

42. Sayyid Quṭb, *Fī ẓilāl al-qur'ān*, vol. 3, pp. 1392–1393, regards this as the most unique passage of the Koran: the divine lordship is asserted in light of the covenant between the children of Adam and their Creator until the Day of Judgment. The locus of this covenant is human nature, the *fiṭra*, which runs through the generations to confirm the autonomous human relation to God. Ṭabāṭabā'ī, *al-Mīzān*, vol. 8, pp. 306–309, regards this verse as humankind's testimony of its own commitment to fulfill its own need to be perfected. How can human beings go against their own testimony about their need and disbelieve in God's lordship established through the covenant that God made before they were physically created? The covenant also separates each individual and makes those individuals testify against themselves and confess God's lordship. In the following verse, human beings are warned, "Lest you say, 'Our fathers were idolaters aforetime, and we were seed after them. What, wilt Thou then destroy us for the deeds of vain-doers?'" (K. 7:173).

43. Sayyid Quṭb, *Fī ẓilāl al-qur'ān*, vol. 6, p. 3917, explains the theory of human creation with a twofold nature. See n. 26.

44. Robert Bellah, "Islamic Tradition and the Problems of Modernization," in *Beyond Belief: Essays on Religion in the Post-Traditional World* (New York: Harper and Row, 1970), p. 150.

45. The unique interweaving of religious and civil traditions that characterized the civil society tradition in the United States, according to Robert Bellah, is the consequence of "a genuine apprehension of universal and transcendental religious reality as seen in or revealed through the experience of American people" ("Civil Religion in America," *Daedalus* 96 [Winter 1967], pp. 1–21). In this civil religion, the law of nature and the law of revelation, though in different channels, flow from the divine source. The Muslim experience of the integrated civil and moral law, in some specific ways, shares the characteristic of a civil religion in that there is a correlation between the two in directing human society toward its earthly goal.

46. Rawls, "Priority of Rights and Ideas," pp. 260, 265.

47. Seligman, *The Idea of Civil Society*, chapters 1 and 2, traces the development of the idea in Europe and the United States. The work is not comparative in any sense and therefore does not deal with similar developments in other societies. But, as pointed out in this work, Muslim societies are heir to both biblical and Greek ideas of individual, private, and public realms of human activity. Hence, some of the characteristics that are now identified as being consonant with a civil society have been present in all cultures in which people had to learn to live in harmony.

48. James Barr, *Biblical Faith and Natural Theology* (Oxford: Clarendon Press, 1993), p. 195, speaks about God's revelation to a specific person and God's revelation in creation (*fiṭra* lexically conveys the meaning 'creation,' as it is used in other places in the Koran) and regards the former as a continuation rather than a correction of the latter, in a manner more consistent with the spatial and temporal circumstances of the people for whom the revelation is intended.

49. I have adapted various translations of the term *taqwā* in this section from Fazlur Rahman, *Major Themes of the Qur'an* (Chicago: Bibliotheca Islamica, 1980), making sure that they conform to their lexical meanings in Arabic. On page 29, Rahman has equated the term *taqwā* to "conscience." This is not possible according to its Koranic usage, because whereas conscience becomes impaired through its unsatisfactory response to the normative human nature, *taqwā* does not. Moreover, conscience loses the "capacity to ask right questions," whereas *taqwā*, as "keen [spiritual and] moral perception and motivation," is a permanent state of the human mind that is attained by responding positively to universal guidance.

50. Sayyid Quṭb, *Fī ẓilāl al-qur'ān*, vol. 5, pp. 2604–2605, connects the sound heart, conscience, to sincerity, which is totally committed to God in upholding the moral values that lead to perfect health and salvation in the hereafter, when no amount of wealth or number of children will avail. Ṭabāṭabā'ī, *al-Mīzān fī tafsīr*, vol. 15, pp. 288–289, 292–293, cites a tradition going back to Sufyān b. ʿUyayna, who explained the sound heart as one in which there is none but God. Any heart that associates something with God or entertains doubt begins to waver. In another tradition, the Imam Jaʿfar al-Ṣādiq is reported to have said that such a sound heart is safe from the love of this world, confirming what the Prophet said: "Love of this world is the root of all crimes."

51. Abdulaziz Sachedina, *Islamic Messianism: The Idea of Mahdi in Twelver Shīʿism* (Albany: State University of New York Press, 1981), pp. 120–121.

52. Fakhr al-Dīn al-Rāzī, *al-Tafsīr al-kabīr* (Cairo: al-Matbaʿa al-Bahiya, n.d.), vol. 25, p. 121ff.

53. I have adopted the phrase from Rāzī, *Tafsīr*, vol. 25, p. 120, where he believes this to be sufficient for the proper affirmation of the unity of God as explained in the revelation.

54. Ṭabāṭabā'ī, *al-Mīzān*, vol. 18, p. 328, and Quṭb, *Fī ẓilāl al-qur'ān*, vol. 6, p. 3349, make a distinction between a deeper commitment through *īmān* and formal submission through *islām*. As Quṭb points out explicitly: "This external Islam is the one that has not as yet fused with the heart in order to become transformed into a

trustworthy and dependable faith." And, although God accepts this Islam because he is most forgiving and merciful, it is not the expected ideal faith.

55. Quṭb, *Fī ẓilāl al-qur'ān*, vol. 1, p. 291.

56. Ṭabāṭabā'ī, *al-Mīzān*, vol. 2, pp. 342–343.

57. Ṭabārī, *Jāmi' al-bayān*, vol. 3, pp. 10–12; Rāzī, *Tafsīr*, vol. 4, pp. 15–16. For a variety of interpretations of the verse to circumscribe its general meaning, see: Ayoub, *The Qur'an and Its Interpreters*, vol. 1, pp. 252–255.

58. Maḥmūd b. 'Umar al-Zamakhsharī, *al-Kashshāf 'an ḥaqā'iq al-tanzīl wa 'uyūn al-aqāwil fī wujūh al-ta'wīl* (Cairo: Musṭafā al-Bābī al-Ḥalabī, 1966), vol. 1, p. 387.

59. David Little, "Duties of Station vs. Duties of Conscience: Are There Two Moralities?" in *Private and Public Ethics: Tensions Between Conscience and Institutional Responsibility*, ed. Donald G. Jones (New York: Edwin Mellen Press, 1978), p. 136.

60. C. D. Broad, "Conscience and Conscientious Action," in *Conscience*, ed. J. Donelly and L. Lyons (New York: Alba House, 1973), p. 8.

61. Rashīd Riḍā, *al-Manār*, vol. 1, pp. 62–65.

62. I have adopted "thick" in the way Michael Walzer, *Thick and Thin: Moral Argument at Home and Abroad* (Notre Dame: University of Notre Dame Press, 1994), pp. x–xi, uses it in reference to the thickness of "particularist stories" across different cultures, which also possess "a thin and universalist morality" that they share with different peoples and cultures. The "thickness" and "thinness" of the moral tradition of particular peoples and cultures also lead us to recognize the "maximalist" and the "minimalist" meanings, respectively, in those traditions, with a clear understanding that "minimalist meanings are embedded in the maximal morality, expressed in the same idiom, sharing the same . . . orientation" (p. 3). I have introduced "universal" and "particular" guidance in the Islamic tradition in a similar conceptual framework, where the universal provides the minimalist and thin description of the moral principles and the particular provides the maximalist and thick description of culturally integrated moral language that responds to specific purposes.

63. Abdulaziz Sachedina, "Justifications for Violence in Islam," *War and Its Discontents: Pacifism and Quietism in the Abrahamic Traditions*, ed. J. Patout Burns (Washington, DC: Georgetown University Press, 1996), pp. 122–160.

64. Benjamin Braude, "Foundation Myths of the *Millet* System," *Christians and Jews in the Ottoman Empire: The Functioning of a Plural Society* (New York: Holmes and Meier, 1982), p. 69.

65. Kymlicka, "Two Models," p. 82.

66. Braude, "Foundation Myths," pp. 69–72.

67. Sayyid Quṭb, *Fī ẓilāl al-qur'ān*, vol. 1, pp. 293–296, undertakes to justify the need for *jihād*, to reinstate the original Islam without the corrupt accretions introduced by the tyrannical order (*al-niẓām al-ṭāghiya*), which would be replaced with a just Islamic order. He does this in the context of the "No compulsion" verse (K. 2:257), which requires tolerance toward those who have not accepted the faith and which had

been used by Muslim modernists as well as orientalists to maintain the view that the obligation of *jihād* was in abeyance. For the modernist view on *jihād* see: Muḥammad Sa'īd al-'Ashmāwī, "al-Jihād fi al-islām," in *al-Islām al-siyāsī* (Cairo: Sīnā li al-Nashr, 1987), pp. 95–109.

68. This question has been raised by a number of Muslim scholars in recent decades, especially in the light of the basic individual right to freedom of religion. See: al-'Ashmāwī, *al-Sharī'a al-islāmiyya*, pp. 73–90.

69. See the article "Apostasy" in *Encyclopedia of Religion*, vol. 1, p. 353ff. and n. 20.

70. Abdulaziz Sachedina, "Freedom of Conscience and Religion in the Qur'an," in Sachedina, Little, and Kelsay, *Human Rights and the Conflict of Cultures: Western and Islamic Perspectives in Religious Liberty*, (Columbia: University of South Carolina Press, 1988), pp. 53–90.

71. A. A. Mansour, "Hudud Crimes," in *The Islamic Criminal Justice System*, ed. M. Cerif Bassiouni (New York: Oceana Publications, 1982), pp. 195–196.

Chapter 4

1. Harvey Cox, with Arvind Sharma, Masao Abe, Abdulaziz Sachedina, Harjot Oberoi, and Moshe Idel, "World Religions and Conflict Resolution," in *Religion, the Missing Dimension of Statecraft*, ed. Douglas Johnston and Cynthia Sampson (New York: Oxford University Press, 1994), pp. 266–282.

2. See, for instance, R. K. Dentan, *Semai: A Nonviolent People of Malaya* (New York: Holt, Rinehart and Winston, 1968); L. E. Sponsel and T. Gregor, eds., *The Anthropology of Peace and Nonviolence* (Boulder, CO: Lynne Reinner, 1994); K. Avruch, P. W. Black, and J. A. Scimecca, eds., *Conflict Resolution: Cross Cultural Perspectives* (Westport, CT: Geenwood Press, 1991).

3. Walter J. Dickey, "Forgiveness and Crime: The Possibilities of Restorative Justice," in *Exploring Forgiveness*, ed. Robert D. Enright and Joanna North (Madison: University of Wisconsin Press, 1998), p. 107, defines restorative justice as justice that undertakes "restoration to wholeness of those whose lives and relationships have been broken or deeply strained by a criminal offense." Dickey rightly points out that restorative justice has much in common with forgiveness. "It is not forgetting; it is not condoning or pardoning; it is not indifference or a diminishing of anger; it is not inconsistent with punishment; it does not wipe out the wrong or deny it. Indeed, it relies on recognition of the wrong so that repair can occur. It also relies on taking of the responsibility for the wrong in a personal and social way" (p. 108).

4. Donald W. Shriver, Jr., *An Ethic for Enemies: Forgiveness in Politics* (New York: Oxford University Press, 1995), p. 6, cites Hannah Arendt, who identified forgiveness as one of the two capacities for genuine social change, the other being the human capacity to make new promises or covenants. In the chapter "Forgiveness in Politics in the Christian Tradition," pp. 38–45, the author examines the teachings of the Gospels on the centrality of forgiveness in building the community of the faithful in the Christian experience.

5. George F. Hourani, "Ẓulm al-nafs in the Qur'an, in the Light of Aristotle," in *Recherches d'Islamologie*, ed. S. van Riet (Paris: Bibliothèque Philosophique de Louvain, 1978), pp. 147–148.

6. Quṭb, *Fī ẓilāl al-qur'ān*, vol. 5, pp. 3058–3059.

7. The Koran uses two terms for the act of forgiveness: *al-ʿafw* and *al-ghufrān*. Although in meaning they are synonymous, *al-ʿafw* (to wipe off and to pardon) and *al-ghufrān* (to forgive and to grant pardon), the former can precede or follow a punishment, whereas the latter is accompanied by no punishment at all. *Al-ghufrān* is granted without punishment. See: Muḥammad b. Aḥmad al-Qurṭūbī, *al-Jāmʿi li-aḥkām al-qur'ān* (Cairo: Dār al Kātib al-ʿArabī, 1387/1967), vol. 1, p. 339.

8. Ṭabāṭabā'ī, *al-Mīzān*, vol. 17, pp. 279–280.

9. Kumar Rupesinghe and Marcial Rubio C., eds., *The Culture of Violence* (New York: United Nations University Press, 1994), pp. 20–22.

10. I have adopted the phrase from Rupesinghe's chapter "Forms of Violence and Its Transformation," ibid., p. 25.

11. Muḥammad b. Yaʿqūb al-Kulaynī, *al-Uṣūl min al-kāfī*, 4 vols. (Tehran: Kitābfurūshī Islāmiyyah), vol. 3, pp. 421–422.

12. Douglas P. Fry and Kaj Bjorkqvist eds., *Cultural Variation in Conflict Resolution: Alternative to Violence* (Mahwah, NJ: Lawrence Erlbaum Associates, 1997), understandably avoid using the word *religion* and replace it with *culture* and *worldview* throughout this volume. Nevertheless, if one considers the multitude of definitions of *culture* provided in Rupesinghe's introduction to *The Culture of Violence*, it is important to bear in mind that since religion is grounded in the notion of a "symbolic communicative system," participants in this type of communication, which uses and manipulates symbols, do not see the disjuncture between outer behavior and inner motive that directs their social-cultural life (Salvatore, *Islam and the Political Discourse*, p. 7). Consequently, conflict, which is defined as "perceived divergence of interest or a belief that parties' current aspirations cannot be achieved simultaneously" (Fry and Bjorkqvist, *Cultural Variation*, p. 10), cannot be fully grasped without engaging in some articulation of the aspirations that dominate some conflict situations in Muslim societies. The chapter on conflict resolution in the Muslim world (pp. 115–122) could have articulated the symbolic communicative system that brought about some of the results that are sought in the religious vocabulary and historiography in the present-day Muslim world.

13. Muḥammad Mahdī al-Naraqī, *Jāmiʿ al-saʿādāt*, ed. Muḥammad Kalāntar (Najaf: Maṭbaʿat al-Ādāb, 1387/1967), vol. 2, pp. 212–214.

14. See n. 12.

15. The detailed letter is part of the famous collection of sermons and letters by Imam ʿAlī, compiled by al-Sharīf al-Raḍī under the title *Nahj al-balāgha*. This translation is rendered by William Chittick in *A Shīʿite Anthology* (London: Muhammadi Trust of Great Britain and Northern Ireland, 1980), p. 69.

16. Ibid.

17. Ṭabāṭabā'ī, *al-Mīzān*, vol. 17, p. 102; Ibn Kathīr, *Tafsīr*, vol. 5, pp. 622–623; Quṭb, *Fī ẓilāl al-qur'ān*, vol. 5, p. 2970.

18. *A Shī'ite Anthology*, p. 69.

19. In his short article, Khaled Abou el Fadl, "Arrogance and Apology," *Minaret*, July 1998, p. 41, takes up the search for an ethics of forgiveness in Islam and the requirement to take violated human rights seriously in the process of the ethical restoration of an offender.

20. Quṭb, *Fī ẓilāl al-qur'ān*, vol. 1, pp. 164–165; Ṭabāṭabā'ī, *al-Mīzān*, vol. 2, pp. 432–433.

21. John Kelsay, *Islam and War: The Gulf War and Beyond* (Louisville, KY: Westminster/John Knox Press, 1993), discusses the problems connected with the interpretations and contemporary discussions of *jihād* in chapters 2 and 3.

22. Abdulaziz Sachedina, "The Development of *Jihād* in Islamic Revelation and History," in *Cross, Crescent, and Sword: The Justification and Limitation of War in Western and Islamic Tradition*, ed. James T. Johnson and John Kelsay (New York: Greenwood Press, 1990), pp. 35–50.

23. See the section "Freedom of Conscience and Religion in the Qur'an in Sachedina, Little, and Kelsay, *Human Rights*, pp. 76–85, for the justifications for and restrictions for the use of force. See my chapter "Justifications for Violence in Islam" in *War and Its Discontents*, pp. 122–160, where I further elaborate the moral restrictions on the use of physical force that are in place in the Koran.

24. The term *fitna* has been understood in different ways in the Koran and the *ḥadīth* literature. Four senses of the term have been identified, depending on the context: (1) as a punishment; (2) as a trial; (3) as a preparatory test; and (4) as the result of punishment. *Fitna* presents itself as an inevitable and all-pervasive force of human moral life. See: Abdulkader Tayob, "Fitnah: The Ideology of Conservative Islam," *Journal of Theology for Southern Africa*, December 1989.

25. Ṭabārī, *Jāmi' al-bayān*, takes the word *fiṭna* (dissension) to mean 'shirk,' that is, a form of disbelief in which a person would ascribe divinity to things not worthy of such ascription. Other Koranic exegetes agree with Ṭabarī on this point. See, for instance, al-Bayḍawī, *Anwār al-tanzīl*, p. 41. Quṭb, *Fī ẓilāl al-qur'ān*, vol. 1, pp. 189–190, regards *fitna* when related to religion as signifying aggression committed against that which is held sacred in human life. It is in that sense that it is worse than slaughter. This kind of *fitna* corrupts people, drives them away from the path of God, and embellishes for them their disbelief in and opposition to God. Quṭb points out that the best example of this situation is the communist system of government, which prohibits the teaching of religion and condones heresy and other social vices like adultery, wine drinking, and so on. The freedom of religion that Islam advocates is based on opposing such corrupt and antinomian social behavior.

26. See the article "Djihād," *Encyclopedia of Islam*, vol. 2, p. 538, for the opinions of Muslim jurists. The basic assumption of the article is that there is essentially only one kind of *jihād* in Islamic doctrine, as well as in its historical practice, namely, "mili-

tary action with the object of the expansion of Islam and, if need be, of its defense." As I have shown elsewhere, the Koranic *jihād* needs to be distinctly separated from the historical *jihād* in which Muslim powers engaged to conquer the surrounding regions for territorial expansion.

27. Discussion in this and the following section is based on my earlier research reported in "The Development of *Jihad*," pp. 35–50.

28. This territory is sometimes identified as *dar al-sulh*. As a spatial-religious concept, it conveys the essence of Muslim cognition of their emigration in non-Muslim countries. It provides a Muslim minority with the legal and ethical sources for furthering the ways that are necessary to relate themselves as members of a family and a community in a predominantly non-Muslim environment. Closely related to this concept is the notion of *dār al-ḥijra* (the sphere of emigration), which not only suggests that every corner of the earth is open to such emigration to seek God's universal bounty, but also considers any part of the earth unrestrictedly and potentially capable of providing humanity with all necessary conditions to direct it toward obedience to God. See my article "Islam and Muslims in Diaspora," *Bulletin of the Institute of Middle Eastern Studies* 7 (March 1993), pp. 109–146.

29. Kelsay, *Islam and War*, p. 2.

30. The tradition occurs in varying forms, with clear permission to enjoin the oppressor. See: al-Nawawī, *Riyāḍ al-ṣāliḥīn* (Beirut: Dār al-Ḥadīth, 1974), p. 109.

31. Abou El Fadl, "*Aḥkām Al-Bughāt*, p. 162, cites all the relevant juridical sources on the issue.

32. Anwar Sadat's assassins relied on the righteousness of the duty of *jihād* to validate their questionable method of irregular warfare against the Egyptian state. See: Johannes J. G. Jansen, *The Neglected Duty: The Creed of Sadat's Assassins and Islamic Resurgence in the Middle East* (New York: MacMillan, 1986), pp. 25–29.

33. *Ṣaḥīḥ al-Bukhārī*, *Kitāb al-fitan*, *ḥadīth* 206.

34. Information in this section is derived from several articles that deal with Islamic criminal law in M. Cherif Bassiouni, ed., *The Islamic Criminal Justice System* (New York: Oceana Publications, 1982).

35. N. J. Coulson, *A History of Islamic Law* (Edinburgh: University Press, 1964), and Joseph Schacht, *An Introduction to Islamic Law* (Oxford: Clarendon Press, 1979), provide the most adequate definitions of the terminology and their discussion in the context of Muslim penal law.

Chapter 5

1. Several volumes of the annual proceedings of the conference on civil society and democratic changes in Arab nations have appeared in this decade. Of particular significance are debates between Muslim Brotherhood members and academicians. See, for instance, *al-Mujtamaʿ al-madanī wa al-taḥawwul al-dimuqraṭī fī al-waṭan al-ʿarabī* (Beirut: Markaz Dirāsāt al-Waḥdat al-ʿArabiyya, 1992), pp. 319–337. In Iran also, debate on issues related to secularism and its implications for the development of

a new political culture that respects the basic freedoms has been led by ʿAbd al-Karīm Soroush on the academic side and Ayatollah Miṣbāḥ Yazdī and his colleagues in Qumm from traditional centers of Islamic learning.

2. These debates appear in several volumes of *Kiyān* and *Kitāb-i naqd*, to mention only two journals, both published in Tehran: the former is the mouthpiece for Soroush's academic ideas, whereas the latter carries meticulous criticism of these academic articles and provides a progressive view, solidly based on traditional sources, authored by prominent religious scholars in Qumm.

3. In the majority of these publications, whether from the Arab world or Iran, the tendency is to engage in polemics. It is for this reason that the necessary conversation between Muslim scholars representing the two centers of higher education, namely, universities and seminaries, has yet to take proper root.

4. To cite an example, in a recently published volume on religious pluralism in *Kitāb- naqd: pluralizm-i dīnī va takaththurgarāʾī* 4 (1998), in which prominent Shīʿite philosopher-jurists like Ayatollah Miṣbāḥ Yazdī and mystical-jurists like Ayatollah Jawādī Āmulī, among others, have responded to Soroush's articles on religious pluralism in *Kiyān* and have severely criticized John Hecks's version of religious pluralism, the authors have clearly conceded Koranic pluralism as a principle of coexistence among peoples of the Book.

Bibliography

Abī Yaʿqūb, Aḥmad b. *Ta'rīkh al-yaʿqūbī*. Ed. Muḥammad Ṣādiq Baḥr al-ʿUlūm. Najaf: al-Maktaba al-Ḥaydariyya, 1394/1974.

Abou El Fadl, Khalid. "*Aḥkām Al-Bughāt*: Irregular Warfare and the Law of Rebellion in Islam." *Cross, Crescent, and Sword: The Justification and Limitation of War in Western and Islamic Tradition*. Ed. James Turner Johnson and John Kelsay. New York: Greenwood Press, 1990.

———. "Arrogance and Apology." *Minaret*. July 1998.

ʿAli b. Abī Ṭālib *Nahj al-Balāghā*. Ed. Muḥammad ʿAbduh. 4 vols. Beirut: Dār al-Maʿrifa, n.d.

ʿAmāra, Muḥammad. *Al-ʿalmāniyya wa nahḍat al-ḥadīth*. Cairo: Dār al-Shurūq, 1986.

'Ashmāwī, Muḥammad Saʿīd, al-. *Al-Islām al-siyāsī*. Cairo: Sīnā li al-Nashr, 1987.

———. *Al-Sharīʿa al-islāmiyya wa al-qānūn al-maṣrī*. Cairo: Maktaba Madbūlī, 1988.

———. *Uṣūl al-sharīʿa*. Cairo: Dār al-Kitāb al-Maṣrī, 1979.

The Assissi Declarations: Messages on Man and Nature from Buddhism, Christianity, Hinduism, Islam, and Judaism. Gland, Switzerland: WWF International, 1986.

Avruch, K., P. W. Black, and J. A. Scimecca, eds. *Conflict Resolution: Cross Cultural Perspectives*. Westport, CT: Greenwood Press, 1991.

ʿAwda, al-Qāḍī al-Shahīd ʿAbd al-Qādir. *Al-Aʿmāl al-Kāmila*. Cairo: al-Mukhtār al-Islāmī, 1994.

ʿAwwā, Muḥammad Salīm al-. *Fī niẓām al-siyāsī li al-dawlat al-islāmiyya*. Cairo: Maktab al-Maṣrī al-Ḥadīth, 1983.
Ayoub, Mahmoud M. *The Qur'an and Its Interpreters*. Vol. 1. Albany: State University of New York Press, 1984.
Balādhurī, Aḥmad b. Yaḥya, al-. *Futūḥ al-buldān*. Ed. M. J. de Goeje. Leiden: E. J. Brill, 1866.
Ball, T., J. Farr, and R. L. Hanson, eds. *Political Innovation and Conceptual Change*. Cambridge: Cambridge University Press, 1989.
Barr, James. *Biblical Faith and Natural Theology*. Oxford: Clarendon Press, 1993.
Bassiouni, M. Cerif, ed. *The Islamic Criminal Justice System*. New York: Oceana Publications, 1982.
Bellah, Robert. "Islamic Tradition and the Problems of Modernization." *Beyond Belief: Essays on Religion in the Post-Traditional World*. New York: Harper and Row, 1970.
Bouamrane, Chikh. *Le problème de la liberté humane dans la pensée musulmane*. Paris: Librairie Philosophique J. Vrin, 1978.
Broad, C. D. "Conscience and Conscientious Action." *Conscience*. Ed. J. Donelly and L. Lyons. New York: Alba House, 1973.
Braude, Benjamin, and Bernard Lewis, eds. *Christians and Jews in the Ottoman Empire: The Functioning of a Plural Society*. New York: Holmes and Meier, 1982.
Burton, John. "Introductory Essay: 'The Meaning of Naskh.'" Abū ʿUbaid al-Qāsim b. Sallām's *K. al-nāsikh wa-l-mansūkh*. Ed. with a commentary by John Burton. E. J. W. Gibb Memorial Series, New Series, XXX. Suffolk: St. Edmundsbury Press, 1987.
Chittick, William. *A Shiʿite Anthology*. London: Muhammadi Trust of Great Britain and Northern Ireland, 1980.
Cohen, Mark R. *Under Crescent and Cross: The Jews in the Middle Ages*. Princeton: Princeton University Press, 1997.
Coulson, N. J. *A History of Islamic Law*. Edinburgh: University Press, 1964.
Courbage, Youssef, and Philippe Fargues. *Christians and Jews under Islam*. Trans. Judy Mabro. London: I. B. Tauris Publishers, 1997.
Dickey, Walter J. "Forgiveness and Crime: The Possibilities of Restorative Justice." *Exploring Forgiveness*. Ed. Robert D. Enright and Joanna North. Madison: University of Wisconsin Press, 1998.
Dunn, John. *Western Political Theory in the Face of the Future*. Cambridge: Cambridge University Press, 1993.
Elton, G. R. "Introduction," *Studies in Church History*. Vol. 21: *Persecution and Toleration*. Ed. W. J. Shields. Oxford: Basil Blackwell, 1984.
Enayat, Hamed. *Modern Islamic Political Thought*. Austin: University of Texas Press, 1991.
Esposito, John L. *The Islamic Threat: Myth or a Reality*? New York: Oxford University Press, 1992.
Farīd, Fatḥī. *Min asrār al-maghfira wa al-istighfār fī al-qur'ān al-karīm*. Cairo: Maktaba al-Nahḍa al-Maṣriyya, 1993.

Fry, Douglas P., and Kaj Bjorkqvist, eds. *Cultural Variation in Conflict Resolution: Alternative to Violence*. Mahwah, NJ: Lawrence Erlbaum Associates, 1997.

Ghazālī, Muḥammad b. Muḥammad al-. *Al-Mustaṣfā min ʿilm al-uṣūl*. 2 vols. Cairo: Būlāq, 1322/1904.

Giddens, A. *The Consequences of Modernity*. Stanford: Stanford University Press, 1990.

Haykal, Khalīl. *Mawqif al-dastūrī al-taqlīdī wa al-fiqh al-islāmī min bināʾ wa tanẓīm al-dawla*. Cairo: Dār Nahḍa al-ʿArabiyya, 1989.

Heyd, David, ed. *Toleration: An Elusive Virtue*. Princeton: Princeton University Press, 1996.

Hodgson, Marshall G. S. *The Venture of Islam: Conscience and History in a World Civilization*. 3 vols. Chicago: University of Chicago Press, 1977.

Horton, John, and Harriet Crabtree, eds. *Toleration and Integrity in a Multi-faith Society*. London: The Interfaith Network, 1992.

Hourani, George F. *Islamic Rationalism: The Ethics of ʿAbd al-Jabbār*. Oxford: Clarendon, 1971.

———. "Ẓulm al-nafs in the Qurʾan, in the Light of Aristotle." *Recherches d'Islamologie*. Ed. S. van Riet. Paris: Bibliothèque Philosophique de Louvain, 1978.

Hunter, Shireen T. *The Future of Islam and the West: Clash of Civilizations or Peaceful Coexistence?* Westport, CT: Praeger, 1998.

Huntington, Samuel P. *The Clash of Civilizations and the Remaking of World Order*. New York: Simon and Schuster, 1996.

Huwaydī, Fahmī. *Al-Islām wa al-dimuqrāṭiyya*. Cairo: Muʿassasa al-Ahrām, 1993.

Ibn Kathīr, ʿImād al-Dīn Ismāʿīl. *Tafsīr al-qurʾān al-ʿaẓīm*. 7 vols. Beirut: Dār al-Fikr, 1389/1970.

Ibn Saʿd. *Al-Ṭabaqāt al-kubrā*. 8 vols. Beirut: Dār Ṣādir, 1380/1960.

Islam and Democracy: Religion, Politics, and Power in the Middle East. Washington, DC: U.S. Institute of Peace Press, 1992.

Jābir, Ḥusayn b. Muḥammad b. ʿAlī. *Al-Ṭarīq ilā jamāʿat al-muslimīn*. Cairo: Dār al-Wafāʾ, 1987.

Jansen, Johannes J. G. *The Neglected Duty: The Creed of Sadat's Assassins and Islamic Resurgence in the Middle East*. New York: MacMillan, 1986.

Jones, D. G. and R. E. Richey, eds. *American Civil Religion*. New York: Harper and Row, 1974.

Kelsay, John. *Islam and War: The Gulf War and Beyond*. Louisville, KY: Westminster/John Knox Press, 1993.

Khalaf Allāh, Muḥammad Aḥmad. *Mafāhīm qurʾāniyya*. Kuwait: ʿĀlam al-Maʿrifa, 1984.

Khūʾī, Al-Sayyid Abū al-Qāsim al-Mūsawī al-. *The Prolegomena to the Qurʾan*. Trans. with an introduction by Abdulaziz A. Sachedina. New York: Oxford University Press, 1998.

Kitāb-i naqd: pluralizm-i dīnī va takaththurgarāʾī. Vol. 4. Tehran: Andīshah-i Muʿāṣir, 1998.

Kulaynī, Muḥammad b. Ya'qūb al-. *Al-Uṣūl min al-kāfī*. 4 vols. Tehran: Kitābfurūshī Islāmiyyah, 1392/1972.
Küng, Hans. *Global Responsibility: In Search of a New World Ethic*. New York: Crossroads, 1991.
Küng, Hans, and Karl-Josef Kuschel, eds. *A Global Ethic: The Declaration of the Parliament of the World's Religions*. London: SCM Press, 1993.
Kuschel, Karl-Josef. *Abraham: Sign of Hope for Jews, Christians, and Muslims*. New York: Continuum, 1995.
Lambton, Ann K. S. *State and Government in Medieval Islam*. Oxford: Oxford University Press, 1981.
Lawrence, Bruce. *Defenders of God: The Fundamentalist Revolt Against the Modern Age*. New York: Harper and Row, 1989.
Lewis, Bernard. *Cultures in Conflict: Christians, Muslims, and Jews in the Age of Discovery*. New York: Oxford University Press, 1995.
———. *Islam: From the Prophet Muḥammad to the Capture of Constantinople*. Vol. 2: *Religion and Society*. New York: Oxford University Press, 1987.
Little, David. "Duties of Station vs. Duties of Conscience: Are There Two Moralities?" *Private and Public Ethics: Tensions Between Conscience and Institutional Responsibility*. Ed. Donald G. Jones. New York: Edwin Mellen Press, 1978.
———. "The Nature and Basis of Human Rights." *Prospects for a Common Morality*. Ed. Gene Outka and John P. Reeder, Jr. Princeton: Princeton University Press, 1993.
Lubbe, Gerrie. "The Role of Religion in the Process of Nation-building: From Plurality to Pluralism." *Religion and Theology* 2 (1995), pp. 159–170.
Luckmann, T. *The Invisible Religion: The Problem of Religion in Modern Society*. New York: Macmillan, 1967.
Maṣrī, Ḥusnī Amīn. *Al-'afw fī al-qur'ān wa al-sunna*. Cairo: Dār al-Manār, 1986.
McAuliffe, Jane D. *Qur'anic Christians: An Analysis of Classical and Modern Exegesis*. Cambridge: Cambridge University Press, 1991.
Mujtama' al-madanī wa al-taḥawwul al-dimuqraṭī fī al-waṭan al-'arabī, al-. Beirut: Markaz Dirāsāt al-Waḥdat al-'Arabiyya, 1992.
Nafīsī, 'Abd Allāh Fahd al-, ed., *al-Ḥarakat al-islāmiyya: ru'ya mustaqbala awrāq fī naqd al-dhātī, al-*. Cairo: Maktabat al-Madbūlī, 1989.
Na'im, Abdullahi Ahmed An-. *Toward an Islamic Reformation: Civil Liberties, Human Rights, and International Law*. Syracuse: Syracuse University Press, 1990.
Naraqī, Muḥammad Mahdī al-. *Jāmi' al-sa'ādāt*. Ed. Muḥammad Kalāntar. Najaf: Maṭba'at al-Ādāb, 1387/1967.
Parsons, Gerald, ed. *The Growth of Religious Diversity: Britain from 1945*. Vol. 1: *Traditions*. London: Routledge, 1993.
Qurṭūbī, Muḥammad b. Aḥmad al-. *Al-Jām'i li-aḥkām al-qur'ān*. 18 vols. Cairo: Dār al-Kātib al-'Arabī, 1387/1967.
Quṭb, Sayyid. *Fī ẓilāl al-qur'ān*. 8 vols. Beirut: Dār al-Shurūq, 1973.
Rahman, Fazlur. *Islam and Modernity: Transformation of an Intellectual Tradition*. Chicago: University of Chicago Press, 1984.

Rawls, John. *Political Liberalism*. New York: Columbia University Press, 1993.

———. "The Priority of Right and Ideas of the Good." *Philosophy and Public Affairs* 17, 4, pp. 251–276.

Rāzī, Fakhr al-Dīn al-. *Al-Tafsīr al-kabīr*. 32 vols. Cairo: al-Matbaʿa al-Bahiya, n.d.

Reichley, A. James. "Religion and American Democracy." *Morality and Religion in Liberal Democratic Societies*. Ed. Gordon L. Anderson and Morton A. Kaplan. New York: Paragon House, 1992.

Riḍā, Rashīd. *Tafsīr al-qurʾān al-ḥakīm al-shahīr bi-tafsīr al-manār*. Beirut: Dār al-Maʿrifa, 1970.

Rupesinghe, Kumar and Rubio C. Marcial, eds. *The Culture of Violence*. New York: United Nations University Press, 1994.

Sachedina, Abdulaziz. "The Development of *Jihād* in Islamic Revelation and History." *Cross, Crescent, and Sword: The Justification and Limitation of War in Western and Islamic Tradition*. Ed. James T. Johnson and John Kelsay. New York: Greenwood Press, 1990.

———. "Is Islam an Abrogation of Judeo-Christian Revelation?" *Concilium International Review of Theology: Islam: A Challenge for Christianity*. Ed. Hans Küng and Jürgen Moltmann. London: SCM Press, 1994, pp. 94–102.

———. "Islam and Muslims in Diaspora." *Bulletin of the Institute of Middle Eastern Studies* 7 (1993), pp. 109–146.

———. "Jews, Christians, and Muslims According to the Qurʾan." *Greek Orthodox Theological Review* 31 (1986), 1–2, pp. 105–120.

———. "Justifications for Violence in Islam." *War and Its Discontents: Pacifism and Quietism in the Abrahamic Traditions*. Ed. J. Patout Burns. Washington, DC: Georgetown University Press, 1996.

Sachedina, Abdulaziz, David Little, and John Kelsay. *Human Rights and the Conflict of Cultures: Western and Islamic Perspectives on Religious Liberty*. Columbia: University of South Carolina Press, 1988.

Sadowski, Yahya. "The New Orientalism and Democracy." *Political Islam: Essays from Middle East Report*. Ed. Joel Beinin and Joe Stork. Berkeley: University of California Press, 1997.

Salvatore, Armando. *Islam and the Political Discourse of Modernity*. London: Ithaca Press, 1997.

Saqqā, Shaykh Aḥmad Ḥijāzī, al-. *Al-ʿInayat al-ilāhiyya bayn al-muslimīn wa ahl al-kitāb*. Cairo: Maktaba al-Īmān, 1991.

Schacht, Joseph. *An Introduction to Islamic Law*. Oxford: Clarendon Press, 1979.

Seligman, Adam B. *The Idea of Civil Society*. New York: Free Press, 1992.

Shāfiʿī, Muḥammad b. Idrīs al-. *Kitāb al-umm*. 7 vols. Cairo: Dār al-Shaʿb, 1321/1903.

Shriver, Donald W., Jr. *An Ethic for Enemies: Forgiveness in Politics*. New York: Oxford University Press, 1995.

Simon, Marcel. *Versus Israel: A Study of the Relations Between Christians and Jews in the Roman Empire* (*AD 135–425*). New York: Oxford University Press, 1986.

Smith, Wilfred Cantwell. *Islam in Modern History*. Princeton: Princeton University Press, 1977.

Sponsel, L. E., and T. Gregor, eds. *The Anthropology of Peace and Nonviolence.* Boulder, CO: Lynne Reinner, 1994.

Stodard, Philip H., ed. *Change in the Muslim World.* Syracuse: Syracuse University Press, 1981.

Ṭabarī, Muḥammad b. Jarīr al-. *Jāmiʿ al-bayān ʿan taʿwīl āy al-qurʾān.* 16 vols. Cairo: Dār al-Maʿārif, 1332/1954.

Ṭabāṭabāʾī, Sayyid Muḥammad Ḥusayn al-. *Al-Mīzān fī tafsīr al-qurʾān.* 20 vols. Beirut: Muʿassasa al-Aʿlamī, 1392/1972.

Tayob, Abdulkader. "Fitnah: The Ideology of Conservative Islam." *Journal of Theology for Southern Africa.* December 1989. Pp. 65–71.

Turābī, Ḥasan ʿAbd Allāh al-. "Al-shūrā wa al-dīmuqraṭiyya: ishkālāt al-muṣtalaḥ wa al-mafhūm." *Al-Mustaqbal al-ʿArabī wa al-qaḍiyat al-filastiniyya baʿda azmat al-khalīj.* Ed. Ibrāhīm Saʿduddīn. Cairo: Markaz Ittiḥād al-Muhāmīn al-ʿArab, 1991.

Ṭurṭūshī, Muḥammad b. al-Walīd al-. *Sirāj al-mulūk.* Cairo: al-Dār al-Miṣriyya al-Lubnāniyya, 1994.

Wāfī, ʿAbd al-Wāḥid. *Al-Ḥuriyya fī al-islām.* Cairo: Dār al-Maʿārif, 1968.

Wensinck, A. J. *The Muslim Creed: Its Genesis and Historical Development.* London: Frank Cass, 1965.

Westbrook, David A. "Islamic International Law and Public International Law: Separate Expressions of World Order." *Virginia Journal of International Law* 33 (1993), pp. 819–897.

Ye'or, Bat. *The Decline of Eastern Christianity under Islam: From Jihad to Dhimmitude.* Trans. M. Kochan and D. Littman. Madison, NJ: Fairleigh Dickinson University Press, 1996.

Zakariyya, Fu'ād. *Al-Ṣaḥwat al-islāmiyya fī mīzān al-ʿaql.* Cairo: Dār al-Fikr, 1989.

Zamakhsharī, Maḥmūd b. ʿUmar al-. *Al-Kashshāf ʿan haqāʾiq al-tanzīl wa ʿuyūn al-aqāwil fī wujūh al-taʾwīl.* 4 vols. Cairo, Musṭafā al-Bābī al-Ḥalabī, 1966.

Index

ʿAbbasid caliphate, 80
ʿAbduh, Muḥammad, 33, 59, 92–94
Abraham, 33, 68
Abrahamic religions
  ecumenical spirit, 33
  ethical orientation, 73
  exclusivist tendencies in, 108
  forgiveness in, 106
  pluralism within, 27–28, 35
  See also Christianity, Judaism
abrogation (*naskh*), 29–30, 31, 40, 147n.15, 147n.19
Abū Ḥanīfa, 133
Adam, 135
Afghanistan, 75
ahl al dhimma ("protected" minorities). *See* minority (*dhimmī*)
ahl al-kitāb. *See* Peoples of the Book
Algeria, 75
ʿAlī b. Abī Ṭālib, 110, 111, 137
  on human dignity, 110–11
  instructions to Mālik, 110
  on Koran, 20
altruism (*īthār*), 112
analogical deduction (*al-qiyās*), 58
anti-Westernism, 60, 61
apostasy, 75, 98–101, 118, 127
  al-murtaddūn, 90, 100
  irtidād, 97, 99–100
  ridda, 100–101
arrogance (*istikbār*), 75, 107–109
Ash ʿarite theology, 87
  independent reasoning in, 21
  Koran in, 19–20
Ashtar, Mālik, al-, 110
Augustine, 117, 148n.35
authoritarianism, 41
autonomy, 18, 84, 96
awareness, 73
ʿAwf, Sālim b., 90

Ba ʿthist ideology, 53
blood money, 105
Bosnia, 9
Buddhism, 104
Bukhārī on *dhimma*, 66
Byzantine empire, 64, 79, 80

Caliphal policy
'Abbasid, 65
Umayyad, 65
call (*al-da'wa*), 117
capacity (*istiṭā 'a*), 72
capital offense, 100
capital punishment, 126
cases in law (*far'iyyāt*), 71
chastisement (*ta'zīr*), 101, 126
Children of Israel, 116
Christianity, 4, 25, 28, 31, 66, 68, 83
apostasy in, 100
conscience in, 92
Injīl, 48
Jewish relations with, 148n.22
Muslim relations with, 47, 48, 67, 74, 147n.17
Najran, 64
polltax (*jizya*), 67
revelation in, 37
salvation in, 29, 34
supercession in, 32
churches, 65, 74
church-state, 5, 78. *See also* disestablishment
circumstantial aspects (of rulings) (*mawḍū'āt*), 49
citizenship, 80–81, 110
civil religion, 83–84, 154n.45
Classical age, 60
Communitarianism, 97
compassion (*raḥma*), 112
conscience, 25, 74, 77, 79, 85, 87, 145n.6
fiṭra, 91–96
Koran on, 83–91
moral cognition, 43
consensus (of scholars) (*ijmā'*), 30
cultural relativism, 54

Damascus, 65
dār al-ḥarb (sphere of war), 5, 47, 48, 116, 135 148n.34
dār al-īmān (sphere of belief), 116, 135
dār al-islām (sphere of submission), 5, 25, 50, 54, 112, 116, 135, 148n.34
dār al-kufr (sphere of disbelief), 43, 116, 135, 148n.34, 150n.6
Day of Judgment/Last day, 28, 33, 91, 92, 123–124, 139
democratic governance, 11
democratization, 41
dīn (religion, God), 38–39, 71, 74
directing of conscience (*al-dalāla*), 93
disestablishment, 3, 141n.1
divine nature (*fiṭrat allāh*), 14, 89

effective causes (*'ilal*), 49, 68, 71
egocentric corruption (*istikbār*). *See* arrogance (*istikbār*)
Egypt, 110
elders (*salaf*), 81
epistemology, 57–58, 59, 60, 61, 71
general principles in (*uṣūl al-awwaliyya*), 71
equity (*istiḥsān*), 45
exclusivity, 4

faith, 43–44, 50, 71, 83, 91, 107, 148n.34, 155n.54
history and, 47
natural faith (*al-īmān al-fiṭrī*), 89
power and, 47
See also dār al-īmān
family, 76
Fertile Crescent, 64
fiṭra. See human nature
forgiveness, 105–106, 108, 109–110, 112, 157n.4, 158n.7
al-'afw (pardon), 158n.7
ghufrān (forgive), 107
free choice, 91
freedom, religious, 63–70, 96–97, 101, 103
fundamentalism, 12, 45, 57–58, 60, 132, 133–134, 142n.7, 143n.18, 146n.8
American Protestant, 51
Bonyādgarā in Iran, 52

murtaji'īn, 52
pluralism, 51–57
Return to the Koran, 52
ṭabaqa-yi murtaji' (reactionaries), 52
uṣūliyyūn in Arab world, 51
furū' al-dīn (religious practices), 24

generalizations in law (*aḥkām 'āmma*), 71
Genesis, 135
Ghannūshī, Rashīd al-, 57, 59
Ghazālī, Muḥammad al-, 57, 80
girdle (*zunnār*), 67
God-human relationships (*'ibādāt*), 98, 137
Governance of the jurist (*wilāyat al-faqīh*), 61
guidance
ethical, 85–89
religious, 94
universal, 92–93
Gulf War (1990–1991), 53, 55, 57, 60, 75

ḥadīth (traditions), 18, 27, 30, 66, 150n.4
harming oneself (*ẓulm al-nafs*), 106
heart (*qalb*), seat of conscience, 87, 91–92, 94, 155n.50
heresy (*ilḥād*), 97
hermeneutics, intra-textual, 19, 40
prerequisites for, 20
Hinduism, 104
Ḥizb al-Taḥrīr, 54
honor (*karam*), 71
Hudhayfa's *ḥadīth*, 124
human nature, 34–35, 129
autonomy in orientation, 71
endowed with free will, 33
fiṭra (innate, primordial nature), 26, 28, 42, 43, 70, 71, 74, 76, 81–82, 83–91, 91–96, 111, 112, 114, 127, 128, 134, 148n.35, 152n.26, 152n.27, 143n.42, 155n.48
individually responsible, 71
natural disposition (*khilqa*), 89
original nature (*fiṭrat allāh*), 71. *See also* divine nature (*fiṭrat allāh*)
Quṭb, Sayyid on, 71, 152n.26, 152n.27
rational, 21
responsibile, 21, 33
taqwā (moral awareness), 73, 82, 86, 87, 88, 89, 113, 155n.49
upright (*ḥanīfa*), 71
human rights, 9, 10, 15
Hussein, Saddam, 53

'ibādāt (service to God), 25
Ibn Kathīr (Sunnī exegete) 32, 39
identity
communal, 24
political, 41
idol worshippers (*ahl al-awthān*), 49
tribute paid by, 49
ijtihād (independent reasoning), 54, 58, 133
imām
Shī'ite leader, 119–120
Sunnī political leader, 48–49
tribute decisions by, 48–49, 67
imperialism, 132–133
insurrection (*khurūj*), 121
intercourse, 99
interhuman relationships (*mu'āmalāt*), 98, 137
Iran, 132
Iranian Revolution, 58, 60
Iraq-Iran War, 75
iṣlāḥ (putting things in order), 126
Islam (religion)
defined, 15
islām (submission to God's will), 32–33, 38–39, 43, 54, 64, 86, 89–90, 94, 155n.54
aslama (he submitted), 39
muslim (one who submitted), 68, 69
Islamic Awakening, 57
istiṣḥāb (juristic practice of 'linking'), 58

Jabal, Muʿādh b., 64
jealousy (*ḥasad*), 107–109
Jerusalem, 65
Jesus, 68
jihād, 5, 43, 63, 75, 142n.4, 149n.99, 156n.67, 160n.26
  abrogating tolerance, 90
  against non-believers 47–48
  against one's ego, 82
  as martyrdom, 127–128
  holy war, 103
  ideological tool, 130, 134, 138
  just war, 119–121
  offensive, 89
  theology of, 112–124
Judaism, 28, 31, 64, 68, 105
  Christian relations with, 148n.22
  revelation in, 37
  salvation in, 29, 34
  supersession in, 32, 74
  Tawrāt (The Torah), 48
judgments (*fatāwā*), 71
jurists (ulema, *faqīh*), 56
  wilāyat al-muṭlaqa (absolute juristic authority), 61
justice as virtue, 110

kalām (theology), 60
Khomeini, Ayatollah, 61
kitāb al-jihād (classical rulings on warfare), 54
known paradigms (*al-maʿrūf*), 72, 73
  unknown (*al-maṭlūb*), 73
Koran, the, 45, 79, 80–18, 82
  application of, 14
  Christian/Jewish relations in, 31, 69, 74
  chronology (Medinan/Mekkan), 26, 114–115, 145n.8
  commentaries on, 19, 31–32
  conflict resolution in, 55
  ethics in, 70, 72, 134, 136
  exegesis of, 15–20, 29
  fundamentals of, 52, 60, 61
  human experience in, 17, 43, 84, 103
  jihād in, 112–121, 127
  mutawatir (continuously transmitted) of, 46
  pluralism verses of, 13–14, 16, 23, 25, 26–27, 31, 36, 38, 50, 71, 95–96, 138–139, 146n.8
  restorative justice in, 126–127
  retributive justice in, 104–107
  society in, 128–131, 137
  surrender in, 39

legal principles and rules (*uṣūl al fiqh*), 19, 71

madrasa (seminary), 44
Mālik (Sunnī jurist), 133
  on tribute, 48
Margalit, Avishai, 35
martyrdom, 127–128
al-maʿrūf (well-known), 88
mercy, 108, 109–110
messiah (*mahdī*), 78
millet system, 96–97
minority (*dhimmī*), 64–67, 74–75, 97, 142n.4, 150n.5
misdemeanor (*jināyāt*), 99
monotheism, monotheists (*muwaḥḥidūn*), 27–28, 31, 35–36, 48, 68, 74–75, 115–116, 137
morality
  common, 70–73, 152n.24
  moral good (*al-khayr*, *al-maʿrūf*), 70, 82
Moses, 68
Muslim Brotherhood, 53, 56, 160n.1
  Quṭb, Sayyid, 19
Mutawakkil, al-, 74
Muʿtazilism, 20–21, 33, 87
  Koran in, 19, 20

Nabahānī, Shaykh Taqiyuddīn, al-, 54
natural law, 83
natural theology, 43

Neo-orientalism, 5, 141n.3
"no compulsion," 90–91

Old Testament, 104

Pact (*ʿahd*) of ʿUmar, 65–67
Pakistan, 75, 105
Palestine, 53, 55, 74, 105
paradise, 127
path (*ṭarīqa*), 78
patronymics (*kunya*), 67
peace, 44
 through *aṣlaḥa* (restoration), 55
People of divine religions, 33
Peoples of the Book (*ahl al-kitāb*)
 acceptance of, 91
 coexistence with, 26
 defined, 146n.9
 dispute with, 68–69
 endowed with divine religions, 33
 inclusive theology with, 28
 salvation in Koran, 38
 sword verse (9:29) against, 48
 tension with, 35, 103
 treatment of, 150n.9
 unbelief of, 115
persecution (*fitna*), 114
Persian monarchy, 80
piety, 102–103
pluralism, 13, 14, 70–71, 83–84
 in Abrahamic family, 27–28
 anti-pluralism in religions, 36–40, 132
 communal identity and, 22–23
 democratic, 73–75
 divinely ordained, 49–51
 Koran on, 26–27, 31, 34, 69, 94
 religious, 11, 18, 24, 34, 35, 36, 41, 132–133, 161n.4
 salvation and, 28–35
 Sharīʿa and, 25
political theory, 3–4
pride (*kibr*), 108
private claim (*ḥaqq ādamī*), 99, 126
private/public, 23–25, 78, 82
Prophet, 42, 48, 68, 69, 78, 83, 91, 94–95, 96, 105, 112, 113, 115, 119, 135, 139
 in Koran, 16, 18
 minorities and belief in, 66, 67
 salvation dependent on, 29, 34
prophets, 37
prosperity (*falāḥiyya*), 87
public interest (*maṣlaḥa*), 45
punishment (*ḥadd*), 99

Qaraḍāwī, Yūsuf, al-, 56, 58
 "Islam is the solution," 60
Quṭb, Sayyid, 39–40, 71, 90, 106, 112
 Fī ẓilāl al-qurʾān, 19–21

Ramadan, 74
Rāzī, al- (Sunnī exegete), 89, 90–91
reason (*taʿwīl*), 121
reasoning (*ʿaql*), 30, 33
rebellion (*al-baghy*), 121
reconciliation (*shifāʾ al-ṣudūr*), 111
religion
 fundamental principles of (*uṣūl al-dīn*), 24
 general religion, 5–6
 global context of, 6
religiosity, 14, 34, 129
religious-moral duties (*takālīf al-sharʿiyya*), 24
repentance (*tawba*), 106, 111
responsibility, 45–46, 73, 74, 82–83, 86, 87–88, 91, 103, 111–112, 139
restorative justice, 123, 124–127, 157n.3
restrictive ordinances (*ḥudūd*), 126
retribution, 103
 qiṣāṣ, 126
 retributive justice, 104–107, 112
revelation (*asbāb al-nuzūl*), 16, 32, 33, 61
 declarative (*khabariyya*), 36–37
 imperative (*ʾamr*), 36–37
 Koran, 46, 57
 religious pluralism, 38

Riḍā, Muḥammad Rashīd, 33, 34, 59
rights
of God qua God (*ḥaqq allāh*), 111
of human qua human (*ḥaqq al-ʿibād*), 111

Ṣādiq, Imām Jaʿfar, al-, 108
Safavid dynasty, 75
safe conduct (*amān*), 66, 67
salvation, 25, 28–35, 36, 57, 84
Sassanian empire, 79
Satan, 110–111
Scriptures, 74, 78, 134
secularism, 3, 9, 77, 82
secularity, 5, 9, 77, 82, 137–138, 142n.5
self-defense, 125
self-determination, 121–124
Shāfīʿi, 68, 133
on "The Pact," 66
on tribute, 49, 67
shahāda (declaration of faith), 31
Sharīʿa:
antipluralist rulings in, 69
apostasy in, 99–101
divine will, 43–44
ethical imperative of, 81
implementation of, 68–69
Islamic state under, 13, 56, 68
Jihād in, 103ff.
just order under, 118
justice in, 130
methodology, 59
minorities in, 97–98
moral/spiritual distinction in, 137
rebellion under, 123ff.
religious-moral duties in, 24
religious/temporal in, 5
Shīʿite, 20, 80, 103, 105, 119, 132, 150n.9
fundamentalism, 60–61
Iranian, 52–58
Salvation, 29
social transactions (*umūr ḥisbiyya*), 24
South Africa, 9
Sunna (tradition), 6, 13, 17, 52, 80–81, 103, 124, 146n.10
fundamentalism based on, 60, 61, 104, 116
Sunnī, 20, 29, 59, 61, 66, 75, 80, 103, 105, 119, 132
fundamentalism, 57
support in rebellion (*shawka*), 122

Ṭabarī, Muḥammad b. Jarīr al-, 32, 47, 48, 91
Jāmiʿ al-bayān (exegesis), 90
Ṭabāṭabāʾī, ʿAllāma, 34, 71, 90, 112
al-Mīzān (Shīʿite exegesis), 19, 20, 21
Tawḥīd (affirmation of divine unity), 30
technology, 22
Tehran, 61
theistic subjectivism, ethics of, 21
tolerance, 7, 8–9, 10, 35, 76–77
as acceptance, 12
transactions (social) (*muʿāmalāt*), 25
tribute (*jizya*), 48–49
polltax, 64, 67, 90
Turābī, Ḥasan, al-, 57, 58, 59
Twelver Shiʿite School, 20

ʿUmar b. al-Khaṭṭāb, 65, 66
instructions to his successor, 66
message to Christians, 65
the Pact of, 66–67
Umayyad, 79, 80, 124, 150n.9
Umma (community), 17, 24, 42, 53, 78, 79, 100, 135–138, 139, 144n.1, 145n.2
ideal (*khayr ummatin*), 38
median (*umma wasaṭa*), 38
unbelievers (*kuffār*), 64, 113
unitarian (*muwaḥḥid*),
Abraham, 33
See also monotheism, monotheists (*muwaḥḥidūn*)
unity (*tawḥīd*), 77, 89

vicegerent (*khalīfa*), 135
violence, 103–104, 108, 119–121, 158n.12

West Bank, 105
will power (*irāda*), 72
world order, 42
  international relations, 49

Zamakhsharī, al- (Muʿtazilite exegete), 89, 90, 91
Zoroastrians, 48